Fresh Ways with Hors-d'Oeuvre

COVER
Dressed with an orange and yogurt sauce, strips of chicken and asparagus (recipe, page 115) nestle in a delicate phyllo flower. This crisp, low-calorie container, made by draping squares of pastry round a mould (page 50), can be used for any moist filling.

MYSTERIES OF THE UNKNOWN
TIME-LIFE HISTORY OF THE WORLD
FITNESS, HEALTH & NUTRITION
HEALTHY HOME COOKING
UNDERSTANDING COMPUTERS
THE ENCHANTED WORLD
LIBRARY OF NATIONS
HOME REPAIR AND IMPROVEMENT
CLASSICS OF EXPLORATION
PLANET EARTH
PEOPLES OF THE WILD
THE EPIC OF FLIGHT
THE SEAFARERS
WORLD WAR II
THE GOOD COOK
THE TIME-LIFE ENCYCLOPAEDIA OF GARDENING
THE GREAT CITIES
THE OLD WEST
THE WORLD'S WILD PLACES
THE EMERGENCE OF MAN
LIFE LIBRARY OF PHOTOGRAPHY
TIME-LIFE LIBRARY OF ART
GREAT AGES OF MAN
LIFE SCIENCE LIBRARY
LIFE NATURE LIBRARY
THE TIME-LIFE BOOK OF BOATING
TECHNIQUES OF PHOTOGRAPHY
LIFE AT WAR
LIFE GOES TO THE MOVIES
BEST OF LIFE
LIFE IN SPACE

First European English language printing.

ISBN 0 7054 1560 0

THE CONTRIBUTORS

PAT ALBUREY is a home economist with a wide experience of preparing foods for photography, teaching cookery and creating recipes. She has written a number of cookery books and was the studio consultant for the Time-Life series *The Good Cook.*

CAROLE HANDSLIP is a cookery writer and broadcaster with a particular interest in healthy eating; the books she has written include *Wholefood Cookery* and *Vegetarian Cookery.* She has taught at the Cordon Bleu Cookery School in London.

NORMA MACMILLAN has written several cookery books and edited many others. She has worked on various cookery publications, including *Grand Diplôme* and *Supercook.*

NIGEL SLATER learnt cooking in Paris and in English hotels and restaurants. He is a regular contributor to food magazines.

HILARY WALDEN is a food technologist. She has written numerous books and articles on all aspects of cookery.

The following also contributed recipes to this volume: Joanna Blythman, Maddalena Bonino, Jo Chalmers, Carole Clements, Sylvija Davidson, Graeme Gore-Rowe, Antony Kwok, Cecilia Norman, Lynn Rutherford, Lorna Walker.

THE COOKS

The recipes in this book were cooked for photography by Pat Alburey, Jacki Baxter, Allyson Birch, Jill Eggleton, Carole Handslip, Antony Kwok, Dolly Meers, Lynn Rutherford, Nigel Slater. *Studio assistant* Rita Walters.

NUTRITION CONSULTANT

PATRICIA JUDD trained as a dietician and worked in hospital practice before returning to university to obtain her MSc and PhD degrees. For the last 10 years she has lectured in Nutrition and Dietetics at London University.

Nutritional analyses for *Fresh Ways with Hors-d'Oeuvre* were derived from McCance and Widdowson's *The Composition of Food* by A.A. Paul and D.A.T. Southgate, and other current data.

This volume is one of a series of illustrated cookery books that emphasize the preparation of healthy dishes for today's weight-conscious, nutrition-minded eaters.

HEALTHY HOME COOKING

Fresh Ways with Hors-d'Oeuvre

BY

THE EDITORS OF TIME-LIFE BOOKS

TIME-LIFE BOOKS/AMSTERDAM

Contents

Pickled Peppers with Mussels

Minted Broccoli and Cauliflower

Okra Stuffed with Indian Spices

almon-Filled Choux Buns

Scorzonera with Walnuts and Chervil

Warm Skate Salad with Red Pepper Vinaigrette

Auspicious Beginnings

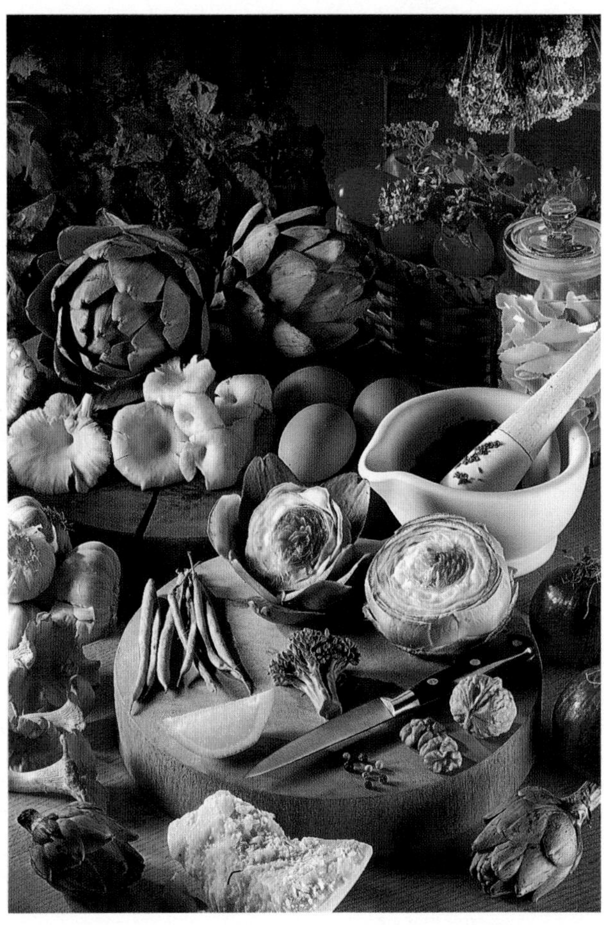

To the first course in a menu falls the happy task of enticement. Like a musical overture, an hors-d'oeuvre heightens expectations and sets the stage for what is to follow. Whatever tempting form an hors-d'oeuvre takes — barbecued seafood, savoury tartlets or a layered terrine of many hues — it gives pleasure in itself, yet stimulates the appetite instead of sating it.

Such delights need not be restricted to dinner parties or grand occasions. For an ordinary family meal, a plate of raw vegetables encircling a creamy dip, or a piping-hot portion of pasta, makes a welcome start and, what is more, a healthy one. For the good news is that none of the 123 hors-d'oeuvre in this book, from the simplest to the most elaborate, is unworthy of a place in a healthy diet.

The recipes in this volume were developed in the Healthy Home Cooking test kitchens in accordance with established nutritional guidelines. It is acknowledged that foods that are high in saturated fats, if consumed in excess, may trigger an increase in blood cholesterol, implicated in the development of heart disease. The effects of salt on health are still a matter of debate, but the sodium in salt is thought to contribute to high blood pressure in susceptible people. A certain amount of salt is essential, but most people, especially those who consume a high proportion of processed foods, take in far more salt than their bodies need.

In most of the recipes that follow, one serving of average size contains no more than 250 calories, 6 to 9 g of fat — of which only 3 g or less are saturated fat — 75 mg of cholesterol, and 400 mg of sodium. A few of the hors-d'oeuvre, appropriate for special occasions that merit a little self-indulgence, exceed these limits. The majority fall well below, thus leaving plenty of scope for planning the remaining courses.

Hors-d'oeuvre, literally, means "outside the work" — an extra dish peripheral to the main business of the meal. In 18th-century aristocratic France, the term described something eaten away from the dining table, or consumed as a diversion from the extravagant assemblages set before the guests. In modern usage, an hors-d'oeuvre is defined as a small dish served at the beginning of a meal to whet the appetite. Greater precision is impossible, for these so-called small dishes embrace the entire culinary universe. Indeed, the making of hors-d'oeuvre is cookery in microcosm. Every cooking method is called upon and every class of ingredient, from the humblest root vegetables to the choicest seafoods to the most exotic spices, has its part to play.

The recipes here indicate the breadth of the subject. Divided into three chapters, covering cold, hot and microwaved hors-d'oeuvre, and grouped within these sections according to their principal ingredients, they demonstrate a remarkable variety of possible first courses: simple and elaborate salads; a dozen different stuffed vegetables, ranging from artichokes to okra; moulded aspics, aromatic stews, roulades, fresh fish and shellfish prepared in over 30 ways; crêpes, croustades and pastry cases concealing all manner of delicacies; cold meats with robust dressings; purées heady with fresh herbs and garlic; kebabs, quenelles, timbales and spicy meatballs; pasta and pulses; rice and other grains in many guises.

A new style of cooking

But one common approach underlies this diversity. All these recipes express a new philosophy of cooking, based on the conviction that it is possible to eat well and still eat wisely. The emphasis is on fresh foods, chosen from those richest in nutritional benefits, and cooked in ways that preserve their goodness without undue reliance on saturated fats, cholesterol and salt.

Flavours are clean and vibrant. Natural piquancy or intrinsic sweetness is heightened by marination in lively mixtures of fruit juices, vinegars, aromatic vegetables, wines and spices, and by the liberal addition of the fresh herbs now available in ever-wider varieties. Basil, for example, was once largely restricted to those lucky enough to live in sunny climates; now several different types, from the tiny peppery leaves of bush basil to the large, decorative opal basil, perfume the air of delicatessen shops and specialist greengrocers. Mint, dill, sorrel and a host of others are available even in supermarkets, and are no longer the exclusive preserve of green-fingered rural and suburban gardeners.

When sauces are used, they are based on vegetable or fruit purées, or on cooking juices thickened by reduction rather than by pastes of fats and flour. Creaminess is achieved by the addition of the low-fat soft cheese known as *fromage frais* or of yogurt — either plain low-fat yogurt, or the thick Greek yogurt, often made from goat's or ewe's milk, which contains only half the fat of single cream, and does not separate during cooking.

Dressings for salads are light: fine oils of distinctive flavour, such as virgin olive oil or those derived from hazelnuts or walnuts, need be used only sparingly. They are partnered with vinegars of quality, varied provenance and distinctive aromas: wine, cider, raspberry, and the uniquely sour-sweet balsamic vinegar, aged in casks of chestnut, juniper or mulberry wood.

An emphasis on vegetables and seafood

More than three quarters of the recipes feature vegetables, fish or shellfish. The visual appeal of these ingredients, and their wonderful range of flavours, would be reason enough to choose them as inviting hors-d'oeuvre. But they are also among the most nutritious foods that Nature bestows upon us.

Vegetables are abundantly endowed with vitamins and minerals. Sweet peppers, for instance, are a prime source of the all-important vitamin C, essential for body maintenance and tissue repair; spinach is a generous supplier of iron, carrots a good source of vitamin A. But — with the notable exception of avocados — vegetables possess almost no fat. They are low in calories, generally low in sodium and virtually cholesterol free.

Fish and shellfish are rich in concentrated protein; an average 125 g (4 oz) portion of seafood provides up to half the protein an adult needs in a day. Lean fish, such as cod and sole, are remarkably low in cholesterol and calories; fatty varieties, such as tuna, salmon or mackerel, are still far lower in calories and saturated fat than an equivalent helping of steak. Indeed, current research suggests that the types of fat contained in oily-fleshed fish help prevent the development of certain illnesses, and that many shellfish, especially molluscs such as the mussel, may actually reduce the amount of cholesterol the body absorbs.

Yet healthy hors-d'oeuvre need not be limited to the offerings of the garden or the sea. Meat and poultry confer generous helpings of protein and other nutrients. They warrant a place in your hors-d'oeuvre repertoire as long as you choose lean cuts, scrupulously trim all visible fat, and remove the fat-laden skin of chicken, duck and other birds. For a first course, a small quantity of meat, poultry or game is all that is necessary to provide a stuffing for vegetable cases or pastries, thin slices for a salad, or a forcemeat for meatballs or quenelles. Meat or poultry first courses are particularly suitable for menus with main dishes that are not particularly rich in protein, such as rice pilaffs, certain pasta preparations or vegetable stews.

Hors-d'oeuvre that might have been dismissed, regretfully, as forbidden fruit are redeemed by a few inventive adjustments. Airy, egg-enriched choux dough, for example, which lends itself as well to savoury treatments as it does to patisserie and desserts, is made here with polyunsaturated margarine instead of butter, and less egg yolk than normally required to produce the same amount of dough. The result possesses only half the fat of conventional versions, a considerable reduction in cholesterol, and a texture that is markedly lighter than ordinary choux, but still strong enough to support a filling. Soufflés, normally laden with egg yolks and based on white sauces made with whole milk and butter, rely instead on the support of well-aerated egg whites, low-fat cheeses such as *fromage frais* and vegetable purées. Crêpes are produced with a skimmed-milk batter.

Crisp pastries, to avoid a heavy load of fat, are made of phyllo dough, a Middle-Eastern product now widely available in supermarkets and delicatessens. Its thin, fragile sheets contain no fat, and will dry out and break unless covered with a damp cloth until the moment they are filled, shaped and baked. Although phyllo is traditionally brushed liberally with butter before cooking, here it is baked with little or no lubrication, and still yields light, crackling envelopes for spinach, cheese and shellfish.

Similarly, the sculpted bread cases known as croustades are usually saturated in melted butter before they are crisped in the oven and filled. Yet a light coating of oil gives the same crunchy results with only a fraction of the fat.

Food without frontiers

As well as being healthy, the new cooking is also eclectic. The hors-d'oeuvre recipes in this volume reflect a rich and varied heritage. From Spain come *tapas*, little dishes of sauced or marinated meats and seafood. The *mezze* or first course of the Middle East yields, besides the phyllo-pastry parcels, vegetable purées and spiced chicken wings. The groaning hors-d'oeuvre tables of northern Europe — Scandinavian *smorgasbord* and the *zakuski* of Russia — contribute fish in robust marinades and sauces, as well as blinis, the delicate pancakes that are caviare's time-honoured accompaniment. The delicacies that the Chinese call *dim sum* inspire savoury dumplings.

Although drawing from many ethnic cuisines, the recipes never follow tradition for its own sake. Unorthodox partnerships of flavour abound, the techniques of East and West are juxtaposed. Exotic ingredients are used creatively, to yield scores of truly original and memorable hors-d'oeuvre.

The Key to Better Eating

This book, like others in the Healthy Home Cooking series, presents an analysis of nutrients contained in a single serving of each dish, listed beside the recipe itself, as on the right. Approximate counts for calories, protein, cholesterol, total fat, saturated fat (the kind that increases the body's blood cholesterol) and sodium are given.

Healthy Home Cooking addresses the concerns of today's weight-conscious and health-minded cooks by providing recipes that take into account guidelines set by nutritionists. The secret of eating well has to do with maintaining a balance of foods in the diet; most of us consume too much sugar and salt, too much fat, too many calories, and even more protein than we need. In planning a meal, the cook using the recipes in this book should take into account what the rest of the meal is likely to contribute nutritionally. The cook should also bear in mind that moderation, as in all things, is a good policy when seeking to prepare a balanced meal.

Interpreting the chart

The chart below gives dietary guidelines for healthy men, women and children. Recommended figures vary from country to country, but the principles are the same everywhere. Here, the average daily amounts of calories and protein are from a report by the U.K. Department of Health and Social Security; the maximum advisable daily intake of fat is based on guidelines given by the National Advisory Committee on Nutrition Education (NACNE); those for cholesterol and sodium are based on upper limits suggested by the World Health Organization.

The volumes in the Healthy Home Cooking series do not purport to be diet books, nor do they focus on health foods. Rather, they express a commonsense approach to cooking that uses salt, sugar, cream, butter and oil in moderation while employing other ingredients — herbs, spices, fruits, aromatic vegetables, wines and vinegars — to provide additional flavour and satisfaction.

Calories **180**
Protein **6g**
Cholesterol **70mg**
Total fat **8g**
Saturated fat **2g**
Sodium **70mg**

The recipes make few unusual demands. Naturally they call for fresh ingredients, offering substitutes when these are unavailable. (The substitute is not calculated in the nutrient analysis, however.) Most of the recipe ingredients can be found in any well-stocked supermarket; the occasional exception can be bought in speciality or ethnic shops.

In Healthy Home Cooking's test kitchens, heavy-bottomed pots and pans are used to guard against foods burning and sticking whenever a small amount of oil is used; non-stick pans are utilized as well. Both safflower oil and virgin olive oil are favoured for sautéing. Safflower oil was chosen because it is the most highly polyunsaturated vegetable fat available in supermarkets, and polyunsaturated fats reduce blood cholesterol; if unobtainable, use sunflower oil, which is also high in polyunsaturated fats. Virgin olive oil is used because it has a fine fruity flavour lacking in the lesser grade known as "pure". In addition, it is — like all olive oil — high in monounsaturated fats, which are thought not to increase blood cholesterol. Virgin and safflower oils can be combined, with olive oil contributing its fruitiness to the safflower oil. When virgin olive oil is unavailable, "pure" may be substituted.

About cooking times

To help the cook plan ahead effectively, Healthy Home Cooking takes time into account in all its recipes. While recognizing that everyone cooks at a different speed, and that stoves and ovens differ in temperatures, the series provides approximate "working" and "total" times for every dish. Working time stands for the minutes actively spent on preparation; total time includes unattended cooking time, as well as any other time devoted to marinating, steeping or soaking ingredients. Since the recipes emphasize fresh foods, they may take a bit longer to prepare than quick and easy dishes that call for canned or packaged products, but the payoff in flavour and often in nutrition should compensate for the little extra time involved.

Recommended Dietary Guidelines

		Average Daily Intake		**Maximum Daily Intake**			
		CALORIES	PROTEIN *grams*	CHOLESTEROL *milligrams*	TOTAL FAT *grams*	SATURATED FAT *grams*	SODIUM *milligrams*
Females	7-8	1900	47	300	80	32	2000*
	9-11	2050	51	300	77	35	2000
	12-17	2150	53	300	81	36	2000
	18-54	2150	54	300	81	36	2000
	54-74	1900	47	300	72	32	2000
Males	7-8	1980	49	300	80	33	2000
	9-11	2280	57	300	77	38	2000
	12-14	2640	66	300	99	44	2000
	15-17	2880	72	300	108	48	2000
	18-34	2900	72	300	109	48	2000
	35-64	2750	69	300	104	35	2000
	65-74	2400	60	300	91	40	2000

* *(or 5g salt)*

Fish Stock

Makes about 2 litres (3½ pints)
Working time: about 15 minutes
Total time: about 40 minutes

1 kg	*lean fish bones, fins and tails discarded, the bones rinsed thoroughly and chopped into large pieces*	*2 lb*
2	*onions, thinly sliced*	*2*
2	*sticks celery, chopped*	*2*
1	*carrot, peeled and thinly sliced*	*1*
½ litre	*dry white wine*	*16 fl oz*
2 tbsp	*fresh lemon juice*	*2 tbsp*
1	*leek (optional), trimmed, split, washed thoroughly to remove all grit, and sliced*	*1*
3	*garlic cloves (optional), crushed*	*3*
10	*parsley stems*	*10*
3	*fresh thyme sprigs, or 1 tsp dried thyme*	*3*
1	*bay leaf*	*1*
5	*black peppercorns, cracked*	*5*

Put the fish bones, onions, celery, carrot, wine, lemon juice, 2 litres (3½ pints) of water, and the leek and garlic, if you are using them, in a large non-reactive stockpot. Bring the liquid to the boil, then reduce the heat to medium to maintain a strong simmer. Skim off all the scum that rises to the surface.

Add the parsley, thyme, bay leaf and peppercorns. Reduce the heat to medium low and simmer the stock for 20 minutes.

Strain the stock through a fine sieve lined with muslin. Allow the stock to cool before refrigerating or freezing it. The fish stock will keep for three days in the refrigerator or, if it is stored in small, well-sealed freezer containers, it may be kept frozen for as long as two months.

EDITOR'S NOTE: *Because the bones from oilier fish produce a strong flavour, be sure to use only the bones from lean fish. Sole, plaice, turbot and other flat fish are best. Do not include the fish skin; it could discolour the stock.*

The shells from shrimps, prawns and crabs may be added to the stock to give it a pronounced shellfish flavour.

Chicken Stock

Makes 2 to 3 litres (3½ to 5¼ pints)
Working time: about 20 minutes
Total time: about 3 hours

2 to 2.5 kg	*uncooked chicken trimmings and bones (preferably wings, necks and backs), the bones cracked with a heavy knife*	*4 to 5 lb*
2	*carrots, cut into 1 cm (½ inch) rounds*	*2*
2	*sticks celery, cut into 2.5 cm (1 inch) pieces*	*2*
2	*large onions, cut in half, one half stuck with 2 cloves*	*2*
2	*sprigs fresh thyme, or ½ tsp dried thyme*	*2*
1 or 2	*bay leaves*	*1 or 2*
10 to 15	*parsley stems*	*10 to 15*
5	*black peppercorns*	*5*

Put the trimmings and bones in a heavy stockpot with enough water to cover them by 5 cm (2 inches). Bring the liquid to the boil, skimming off the scum that rises to the surface. Simmer for 10 minutes, skimming and adding a little cold water to help precipitate the scum. Add the vegetables, herbs and peppercorns, and submerge them in the liquid. If necessary, add enough additional water to cover the vegetables or bones. Return to the boil, then lower the heat and simmer for 2 to 3 hours, skimming once more.

Strain the stock and allow it to stand until tepid, then refrigerate it overnight or freeze it long enough for the fat to congeal. Spoon off and discard the layer of fat.

Tightly covered, the stock may safely be kept for three to four days in the refrigerator. Stored in small, well-covered freezer containers, the stock may be kept frozen for up to six months.

EDITOR'S NOTE: *The chicken gizzard and heart may be added to the stock, along with the bird's uncooked skin. Wings and necks — rich in natural gelatine — produce a particularly gelatinous stock, ideal for sauces and jellied dishes.*

Preparations for Colour and Flavour

The vibrant hues and piquant characters of aromatic vegetables and herbs give many hors-d'oeuvre their visual and gustatory appeal. The tomato is probably the most versatile and frequently used vegetable, adding both colour and bite to numerous dishes. For the best results choose firm-fleshed, preferably sun-ripened tomatoes; before cooking, skin, seed and chop them *(below)*. To release the fragrant oil of sweet peppers, roast or grill them and remove the peel *(opposite page, above)*.

Garlic, sliced, chopped or puréed — as here *(opposite page, below)* — adds spark to many dishes in this book. To peel a garlic clove, place the clove beneath the blade of a broad heavy knife and give the blade a thump to split the skin.

Many herbs — oregano, thyme, marjoram and savory, for example — are useful in a dried form, but most are at their best when fresh. They should be chopped with a clean sharp knife, just before using, and should have only minimal cooking. To keep herbs fresh for several days, simply roll them in a dampened cloth or paper towel and store them in the salad compartment of the refrigerator.

Chopping Parsley

1 *COARSE CHOPPING. Wash the parsley and pat it dry with a tea towel so that the leaves will not stick together. Grip the stems of the parsley, curling your fingertips back to protect them from the knife's blade, and slice through the leaves to cut them into thin shreds.*

2 *FINE CHOPPING. Gather the chopped parsley into a mound. Steady the tip of the knife with one hand while raising and lowering the knife handle with the other, moving the blade from side to side in an arc. Continue until the parsley is the desired size.*

Skinning and Seeding Tomatoes

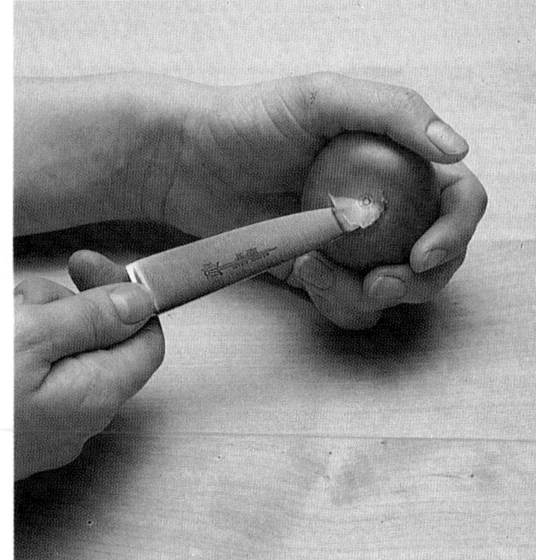

1 *LOOSENING THE SKIN. With a small, sharp knife held at an angle, loosen a small column of flesh round the core at the stem end of the tomato and lift it out. Cut a small cross in the skin on the bottom of the tomato and plunge it into boiling water for 10 to 12 seconds.*

2 *PEELING. When the tomato is cool enough to handle, catch the skin between your thumb and the knife blade and strip it off in sections. Start at the cross cut in the base and work towards the stem end where the skin adheres more firmly.*

3 *SEEDING. Divide the tomato horizontally to expose the seed pockets. Gently squeeze a ripe tomato with your hand to force out the seeds. Alternatively, for a firm tomato, scrape out the seeds with a teaspoon (above), taking care not to damage the seed pockets.*

Peeling and Purêeing Peppers

1 *PEELING THE PEPPERS. Roast whole peppers under a medium grill or in a hot oven, turning them occasionally, until their skins blister and blacken. Place them under a damp tea towel; the towel will trap the steam and loosen the skins. When the peppers are cool enough to handle, peel off the skins, working over a plate (above).*

2 *REMOVING THE SEEDS. Cut or tear open each pepper. Pull off the stem and the cluster of seeds attached to it. Use a teaspoon to pick out the remaining seeds. Discard the skin, stem and seeds, but reserve the pepper juices that have collected on the plate.*

3 *PURÉEING THE PEPPERS. Set a sturdy metal sieve over a bowl. Push the peppers through the sieve with a pestle. A pepper purée produced by sieving has more body and a more uniform consistency than one made by any other method. Add the pepper juice if desired, or reserve it for another purpose.*

Puréeing Garlic

CRUSHING THE CLOVES. Place a few peeled garlic cloves in a mortar. Add about ¼ teaspoon of salt and pound together firmly with a pestle until the garlic is thoroughly pulverized with an almost liquid consistency.

1 Cooked ahead of time to allow its flavours to mingle, this fragrant melange of vegetables contains only 3g of fat per serving (recipe, page 25).

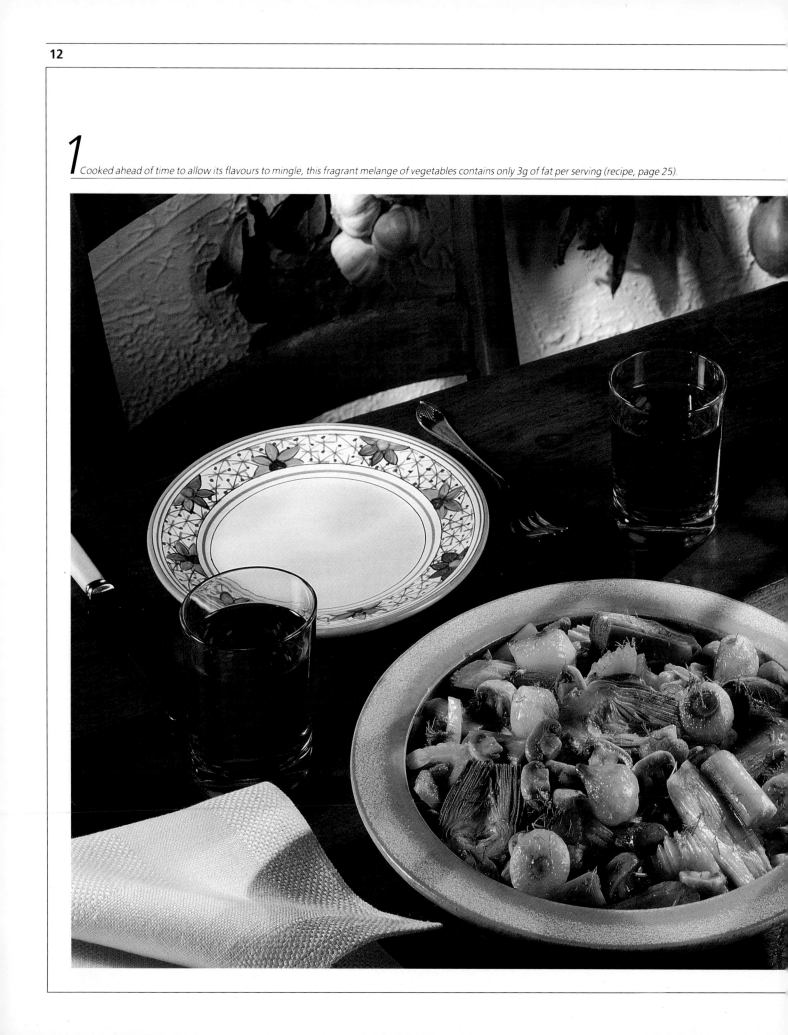

Cold Starters for All Seasons

A cold hors-d'oeuvre may be as simple as a mound of grated raw carrot lightly tossed in a lemony dressing *(page 16)*, or as elaborate as a multicoloured, layered terrine of salmon, sweet peppers and rice, which amply repays the time and effort spent on its preparation *(page 32)*. But whether they are destined to begin a family meal or launch a dinner party, the 50 dishes in this chapter have two things in common: all have been devised with a view to healthy eating, and most are easy to put together in advance, needing — at most — a few finishing touches at serving time.

The recipes that follow need not be treated as rigid formulae, but as starting points for experimentation with the best ingredients that the season has to offer. The large tossed salad on page 19, for instance, could be made with virtually any selection of fresh leaves and other raw or cooked ingredients. Success lies in knowing which of its elements will profit from marinating in vinaigrette dressing, and which should be added at the last minute. Cooked meat, poultry and fish, raw onions and most cooked vegetables (except for French beans and mange-tout) benefit from up to half an hour's steeping; salad leaves, fresh herbs and hard-boiled eggs are best incorporated at the moment the salad is tossed and served.

Throughout the chapter, familiar dishes appear in lighter guises. Sweet-and-sour herring, for example, is divested of its high-fat coating of soured cream and instead is bound with *fromage frais (page 45)*. Aubergines in tomato sauce, a Middle Eastern classic, usually consists of vegetables that have been sautéed in a large amount of oil; here the dish is rendered far more delicate, but equally delicious, by eliminating the frying stage *(page 30)*.

New ideas abound. Cold chicken, instead of being sauced as it so often is with cholesterol-laden mayonnaise, is dressed with a low-fat fruit vinaigrette *(page 54)*. Moulded cheese hearts, more commonly served as the rich dessert known as *coeurs à la crème*, appear on page 39 as a savoury hors-d'oeuvre based on a low-fat cheese mixture liberally seasoned with herbs and orange rind. Drawn from many different culinary traditions, yet reflecting a contemporary awareness of the need for a healthy, well-balanced diet, these and other recipes will expand any cook's repertoire of easily prepared first courses to fit all seasons, moods and menus.

Crudités

Raw vegetables, known by the French term crudités, make the simplest and healthiest of hors-d'oeuvre. They are free of fat and cholesterol, amply endowed with vitamins and minerals, and high in fibre.

Let the season and the market guide your choice. Small vegetables such as cherry tomatoes, button mushrooms, spring onions and young French beans can be left whole; others such as broccoli, cauliflower, carrots, cucumber, sweet pepper, chicory, cos lettuce, celery, fennel, kohlrabi and Chinese cabbage should be cut into manageable pieces. To serve, arrange the vegetables on a platter or in a basket, accompanied by oil and vinegar or one of the purées on the right.

For an equally quick and nutritious first course, raw or blanched vegetables may be sliced or grated and tossed in a light dressing *(pages 16 and 17)*.

Haricot Bean Purée

GARLICKY PURÉES, LIBERALLY SEASONED WITH LEMON JUICE AND OLIVE OIL, ARE FOUND IN THE COOKERY OF VIRTUALLY ALL THE LANDS OF THE EASTERN MEDITERRANEAN. IN THIS RECIPE, THE ADDITION OF QUARK LIGHTENS THE PURÉE. THE QUARK'S HIGH PROTEIN CONTENT MAKES THIS PURÉE AN IDEAL FIRST COURSE FOR A VEGETARIAN MEAL.

Serves 16
Working time: about 45 minutes
Total time: about 15 hours
(includes soaking and chilling)

250 g	*dried haricot beans, soaked overnight in enough water to cover them*	*8 oz*
1	*onion, quartered*	*1*
4	*large garlic cloves, peeled*	*4*
2 tbsp	*virgin olive oil*	*2 tbsp*
2 tbsp	*white wine vinegar*	*2 tbsp*
½ tsp	*salt*	*½ tsp*
	freshly ground black pepper	
60 g	*quark*	*2 oz*
½ tsp	*Dijon mustard*	*½ tsp*
2 tbsp	*fresh lemon juice*	*2 tbsp*
1	*sweet red pepper, skinned and seeded (page 11)*	*1*
2 tbsp	*finely chopped parsley*	*2 tbsp*
1 tsp	*chopped fresh rosemary, or ½ tsp dried rosemary*	*1 tsp*

Calories **65**
Protein **4g**
Cholesterol **0mg**
Total fat **2g**
Saturated fat **0g**
Sodium **55mg**

Drain the beans in a colander and transfer them to a saucepan. Add the onion and garlic, cover the beans with cold water and bring them to the boil. Boil the beans vigorously for 15 minutes, then reduce the heat to low and simmer them until they are very tender — about 1½ hours. Drain the beans in a colander and let them cool for a few minutes.

Place the bean mixture, the oil and the vinegar in a food processor and blend the mixture to a purée. To give the purée a smooth texture, rub it through a fine sieve. Season with the salt and some pepper.

When the bean purée has cooled, mix in the quark, mustard and lemon juice. Dice the red pepper and fold it into the bean mixture with the parsley and rosemary. Turn the purée into a serving bowl and cover it. Refrigerate it for at least 4 hours to allow the flavours to blend. Remove the purée from the refrigerator about an hour before serving, to bring it up to room temperature.

SUGGESTED ACCOMPANIMENTS: *crudités (opposite); toast fingers or strips of warm pitta bread.*

Skordalia

SKORDALIA IS A RICH GREEK SAUCE CONTAINING GARLIC, OLIVE OIL AND BREAD, WITH A CONSISTENCY RESEMBLING THAT OF MAYONNAISE. IT IS TRADITIONALLY SERVED WITH RAW VEGETABLES, SEAFOOD OR HARD-BOILED EGGS. IN THIS LIGHTER VERSION, THE CREAMY TEXTURE IS RETAINED BUT THE FAT CONTENT IS REDUCED BY REPLACING SOME OF THE OLIVE OIL WITH *FROMAGE FRAIS*. NEVERTHELESS, A LITTLE GOES A LONG WAY.

Serves 18
Working (and total) time: about 15 minutes

5	*cloves garlic, crushed*	*5*
125 g	*white bread, crusts removed*	*4 oz*
2	*parsley sprigs*	*2*
2 tbsp	*white wine vinegar*	*2 tbsp*
½ tsp	*salt*	*½ tsp*
12.5 cl	*virgin olive oil*	*4 fl oz*
175 g	*fromage frais*	*6 oz*

Calories **90**
Protein **1g**
Cholesterol **0mg**
Total fat **8g**
Saturated fat **2g**
Sodium **80mg**

Place the garlic, bread and parsley sprigs in a food processor and blend until the mixture forms crumbs. Add the vinegar, salt and 3 tablespoons of water, and process until the mixture is thoroughly blended.

With the motor still running, begin adding the oil a teaspoon at a time, so that the sauce will not separate. When the sauce begins to thicken, pour in the rest of the oil in a thin stream, then add the *fromage frais*. Turn the skordalia into a shallow dish to serve.

SUGGESTED ACCOMPANIMENTS: *crudités (opposite); toast fingers or strips of warm pitta bread.*

Aubergine and Sesame Purée

Serves 14
Working time: about 20 minutes
Total time: about 5 hours (includes chilling)

2	*aubergines (about 600g/1 ¼ lb)*	*2*
1	*large garlic clove, crushed*	*1*
2 tbsp	*virgin olive oil*	*2 tbsp*
4 tbsp	*fresh lemon juice*	*4 tbsp*
2 tbsp	*light tahini*	*2 tbsp*
½ tsp	*salt*	*½ tsp*
	freshly ground black pepper	
3 tbsp	*chopped fresh mint*	*3 tbsp*

Calories **40**
Protein **1g**
Cholesterol **0mg**
Total fat **3g**
Saturated fat **1g**
Sodium **60mg**

Preheat the oven to 180°C (350°F or Mark 4). Prick the aubergines all over with a fork, place them on a baking sheet and bake them until they are soft and their skins are shrivelled — 45 minutes to 1 hour. Set them aside to cool.

When the aubergines are cool enough to handle, cut them in half lengthwise, scoop out the pulp, and transfer it to a food processor. Add the garlic and process the mixture to a fairly smooth purée.

Continue processing the purée while you pour in the oil, a little at a time. When all the oil has been incorporated, add the lemon juice, tahini, salt and some black pepper, and process the purée again until it is smooth and thoroughly blended. Turn the mixture into a bowl and fold in the chopped mint. Cover the bowl with plastic film and refrigerate the purée for at least 4 hours to allow its flavours to develop.

When you are ready to serve stir the mixture again and turn the chilled purée into a serving dish.

SUGGESTED ACCOMPANIMENTS: *crudités (opposite); toast fingers or strips of warm pitta bread.*

EDITOR'S NOTE: *If fresh mint is not available, flat-leaf parsley may be used instead.*

Celeriac in a Creamy Mustard Dressing

SIMPLE SALADS OF CELERIAC TOSSED IN A CREAMY SAUCE APPEAR THROUGHOUT FRANCE AS STARTERS FOR FAMILY MEALS AND ON RESTAURANT MENUS.

Serves 4
Working (and total) time: about 15 minutes

2 tsp	*golden mustard seeds*	*2 tsp*
½ tsp	*Dijon mustard*	*½ tsp*
½ tbsp	*balsamic vinegar*	*½ tbsp*
90 g	*fromage frais*	*3 oz*
1	*celeriac (about 500 g/1 lb), peeled and cut into thin julienne*	*1*

Calories **45**
Protein **3**
Cholesterol **0mg**
Total fat **2g**
Saturated fat **1g**
Sodium **30mg**

In a small, heavy frying pan, heat the mustard seeds for a few seconds, until they begin to pop. Transfer the mustard seeds to a small bowl; mix in the Dijon mustard, balsamic vinegar and *fromage frais* to make a creamy dressing.

Place the celeriac strips in a serving bowl and toss them with the mustard dressing until they are thoroughly coated. Either serve the salad immediately or place it in the refrigerator until serving time, stirring it well just before you serve it.

Grated Carrot Salad

A SALAD OF GRATED RAW CARROTS MAKES A CRISP, REFRESHING HORS-D'OEUVRE, RICH IN VITAMIN A. IT IS PARTICULARLY WELCOME IN WINTER, WHEN MANY FRESH SALAD INGREDIENTS ARE HARD TO COME BY.

Serves 4
Working (and total) time: about 10 minutes

60 g	*fromage frais*	*2 oz*
1 tbsp	*fresh lemon juice*	*1 tbsp*
½ tsp	*grainy mustard*	*½ tsp*
2 tsp	*tarragon leaves, chopped*	*2 tsp*
250 g	*carrots, grated in a mouli julienne or in a food processor*	*8 oz*

Calories **30**
Protein **2g**
Cholesterol **0mg**
Total fat **2g**
Saturated fat **1g**
Sodium **15mg**

In a small bowl, whisk together the *fromage frais,* lemon juice, mustard and tarragon leaves. Arrange the grated carrots in a large dish, spoon the dressing over them and serve the salad immediately.

French Beans with Anchovies and Lemon

Serves 4
Working (and total) time: about 25 minutes

250 g	*French beans, topped and tailed*	*8 oz*
3	*anchovy fillets, soaked in a little milk for 15 minutes to reduce their saltiness*	*3*
2 tbsp	*virgin olive oil*	*2 tbsp*
1 tbsp	*fresh lemon juice*	*1 tbsp*
½	*lemon, roughly chopped, rind only*	*½*
	freshly ground black pepper	
½	*garlic clove*	*½*
1 tbsp	*finely cut chives*	*1 tbsp*

Calories **95**
Protein **3g**
Cholesterol **0mg**
Total fat **8g**
Saturated fat **1g**
Sodium **100mg**

Fill a saucepan with water and parboil the French beans for 2 minutes. Drain the beans in a colander, refresh them under cold running water and drain them a second time. Remove the anchovies from the milk, drain them and pat them dry with kitchen paper. With a sharp knife, cut the fillets lengthwise into thin strips, then cut the strips horizontally to make 2.5 cm (1 inch) pieces.

To make the dressing, whisk together the oil and lemon juice in a small bowl. Stir in the lemon rind and some pepper. Rub a serving bowl with the garlic. Place the beans, anchovies, and chopped chives in the bowl and toss the beans with the dressing until they are well coated.

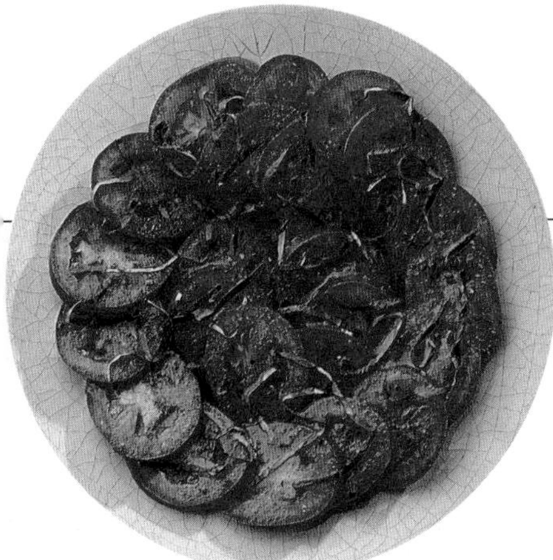

Tomatoes with Basil

A SIMPLE TOMATO SALAD MAKES A WONDERFUL HORS-D'OEUVRE IN HIGH SUMMER, WHEN FRESH TOMATOES ARE AT THEIR PEAK OF COLOUR AND FLAVOUR.

Serves 4
Working (and total) time: about 10 minutes

4	*ripe tomatoes*	4
6	*basil leaves, cut into chiffonade*	6
¼ tsp	*salt*	¼ tsp
1 tbsp	*white wine vinegar*	1 tbsp
2 tbsp	*virgin olive oil*	2 tbsp
	freshly ground black pepper	

Calories **80**
Protein **1g**
Cholesterol **0mg**
Total fat **8g**
Saturated fat **1g**
Sodium **100mg**

With a sharp knife, cut the four tomatoes into thin slices. Arrange the slices on a serving plate, slightly overlapping, and sprinkle the shredded basil leaves over them.

In a small bowl, stir the salt and vinegar together until the salt dissolves. Whisk in the olive oil, beating until the oil and vinegar are thoroughly blended. Dress the tomato slices with the vinaigrette, add plenty of black pepper and serve the salad immediately.

Baby Courgettes Vinaigrette

Serves 4
Working (and total) time: about 15 minutes

500 g	*baby courgettes*	1 lb
1	*garlic clove, finely chopped*	1
¼ tsp	*salt*	¼ tsp
1 tsp	*grainy mustard*	1 tsp
½ tsp	*Dijon mustard*	½ tsp
	freshly ground black pepper	
1 tbsp	*white wine vinegar*	1 tbsp
2 tbsp	*virgin olive oil*	2 tbsp
7	*purple basil leaves, torn*	7

Calories **90**
Protein **1g**
Cholesterol **0mg**
Total fat **8g**
Saturated fat **1g**
Sodium **200mg**

With a sharp knife, slice the courgettes diagonally into 2.5 cm (1 inch) pieces and plunge them into a saucepan filled with boiling water. Boil the courgettes until they are just tender — about 5 minutes.

While the courgettes cook, prepare the dressing. Place the garlic and the salt in a mortar and pound them with a pestle until the garlic has broken down into a purée. Mix in the two mustards, the pepper and the vinegar, then whisk in the olive oil.

Remove the courgettes from the heat, drain them in a colander, and refresh them quickly under cold running water to arrest their cooking. Drain them thoroughly again.

Transfer the drained courgettes on to a shallow serving dish. Toss them with the mustard dressing and the basil leaves, and serve the salad immediately.

EDITOR'S NOTE: *If purple basil is unavailable, use ordinary fresh basil leaves instead.*

Fennel Salad

Serves 4
Working (and total) time: about 10 minutes

½ tsp	*salt*	½ tsp
1 tbsp	*white wine vinegar*	1 tbsp
2 tbsp	*virgin olive oil*	2 tbsp
3 tbsp	*finely chopped parsley*	3 tbsp
	white pepper	
2	*fennel bulbs, sliced*	2

Calories **75**
Protein **1g**
Cholesterol **0mg**
Total fat **8g**
Saturated fat **1g**
Sodium **265mg**

In a small bowl, stir the salt and vinegar together until the salt dissolves. Add the olive oil, parsley and some white pepper, whisking until the dressing is well blended.

Place the fennel slices in a serving bowl. Toss them with the vinaigrette dressing just before serving.

Salad of Leaves and Flowers

EDIBLE FLOWERS, SUCH AS VIOLETS, ROSE PETALS AND NASTURTIUM LEAVES, ADD COLOUR AND PIQUANCY TO SIMPLE TOSSED SALADS. SOME GREENGROCERS AND SUPERMARKETS NOW STOCK A VARIETY OF EDIBLE BLOOMS. IF YOU ARE USING GARDEN FLOWERS, AVOID ANY THAT HAVE BEEN SPRAYED WITH CHEMICALS AND INSECTICIDES. FLOWERS SOLD BY FLORISTS SHOULD NOT BE USED FOR CULINARY PURPOSES.

Serves 6
Working (and total) time: about 10 minutes

Calories **75**
Protein **1g**
Cholesterol **0mg**
Total fat **8g**
Saturated fat **1g**
Sodium **5mg**

1	*lettuce heart, separated into leaves, washed and dried*	*1*
5	*oak leaf lettuce leaves, washed and dried*	*5*
30 g	*curly endive, washed and dried*	*1 oz*
8	*nasturtium leaves*	*8*
2 tsp	*lavender florets*	*2 tsp*
1 tsp	*borage flowers*	*1 tsp*
2 tsp	*thyme flowers*	*2 tsp*
8	*rose petals*	*8*
6	*violets or pansies*	*6*
6	*chervil sprigs*	*6*
	Tarragon vinaigrette	
3 tbsp	*safflower oil*	*3 tbsp*
1½ tbsp	*white wine vinegar*	*1½ tbsp*
1 tsp	*crushed coriander seeds*	*1 tsp*
	freshly ground black pepper	
½ tsp	*fresh tarragon leaves*	*½ tsp*

In a small bowl, whisk together the oil and the vinegar for the dressing. Stir in the coriander seeds, some pepper and the tarragon, and mix well.

Lay the lettuce, the endive and the nasturtium leaves loosely in a deep bowl. Sprinkle the lavender, borage and thyme flowers, the rose petals, the violets or pansies and the chervil over the top. Add the dressing, toss the salad and serve it immediately.

EDITOR'S NOTE: *Any selection of mild and bitter salad leaves and edible flowers can be used. Aim for a combination that offers vivid contrasts of colour, flavour and texture. Perfect freshness of all ingredients is the sole requirement.*

Tossed Salad with Eggs and French Beans

Serves 6
Working time: about 15 minutes
Total time: about 40 minutes (includes marinating)

Calories **115**
Protein **3g**
Cholesterol **75mg**
Total fat **10g**
Saturated fat **2g**
Sodium **100mg**

½	*small red onion, cut thinly into rings*	*½*
1	*small red lollo lettuce, washed and dried, leaves torn*	*1*
30 g	*rocket, washed and dried*	*1 oz*
90 g	*French beans, topped and blanched for 3 minutes in boiling water*	*3 oz*
2	*eggs, hard-boiled, each cut into six wedges*	*2*
6	*black olives*	*6*
3	*red basil sprigs*	*3*
3	*green basil sprigs*	*3*
	Vinaigrette dressing	
1	*garlic clove, crushed*	*1*
¼ tsp	*salt*	*¼ tsp*
	freshly ground black pepper	
1 tbsp	*red wine vinegar*	*1 tbsp*
3 tbsp	*virgin olive oil*	*3 tbsp*

First prepare the vinaigrette. Place the garlic, salt and some pepper in a large salad bowl. Using a wooden pestle, pound the ingredients until they break down into a paste. Add the vinegar and stir until the salt dissolves. Pour in the olive oil and mix thoroughly.

With your hands or the pestle, stir the onion slices into the vinaigrette to coat them well. Set them aside to marinate for 30 minutes.

Cross a pair of salad servers over the bottom of the bowl, to keep the dressing separate from the leaves that will be added before the salad is tossed. Lay a few of the largest lettuce leaves on the servers, then fill the bowl with the remaining lettuce and the rocket.

Top the leaves with the French beans, hard-boiled eggs, olives and basil. Draw out the servers from the bed of lettuce and rocket and toss the salad with the servers, or by hand, until all its ingredients are lightly coated with the dressing.

Artichoke and Potato Bowl

Serves 4
Working time: about 20 minutes
Total time: about 1 hour and 20 minutes (includes chilling)

Calories **150**
Protein **2 g**
Cholesterol **0 mg**
Total fat **10 g**
Saturated fat **2 g**
Sodium **35 mg**

2 tbsp	*fresh lemon juice or vinegar*	*2 tbsp*
350 g	*baby artichokes, stems cut off flush with base, tough outer leaves removed and discarded (page 26, Step 1)*	*12 oz*
250 g	*small new potatoes, scrubbed*	*8 oz*
1	*small head radicchio, washed and dried*	*1*
1	*small head lettuce, washed and dried*	*1*
2 tbsp	*finely cut chives*	*2 tbsp*
	Balsamic vinaigrette	
1 tbsp	*balsamic vinegar*	*1 tbsp*
¼ tsp	*dry mustard*	*¼ tsp*
½	*garlic clove, finely chopped*	*½*
	freshly ground black pepper	
2½ tbsp	*virgin olive oil*	*2½ tbsp*

Add the lemon juice or vinegar to a large saucepan of boiling water and drop in the artichokes. Submerge the artichokes by weighting them down with a heavy plate or the lid from a smaller saucepan, and cook them until tender — 20 to 25 minutes. Drain the artichokes in a colander and set them aside to cool. Meanwhile, cut the potatoes in half and cook them in a covered pan of boiling water until tender — about 12 minutes.

To make the vinaigrette, place the balsamic vinegar in a small jar with a lid and add the mustard, garlic and some pepper. Shake or stir the ingredients to combine them, then add the oil. Cover the jar and shake it to mix everything well.

When the potatoes are cooked, transfer them to a large bowl. Shake the jar of dressing again and add some of the dressing while the potatoes are hot. Toss the potatoes to coat them well.

Cut off the top 2.5 cm (1 inch) of the cooked artichokes and gently remove any outer leaves that are still fibrous. Cut the artichokes in half lengthwise and remove the fuzzy choke if there is one. Add the artichoke halves to the potatoes. Shake the jar of dressing again and add the remaining dressing to the salad. Toss the vegetables carefully to combine them. Cover the salad with plastic film and chill it in the refrigerator for about 30 minutes.

Line a large salad bowl with the radicchio and lettuce, scatter the salad over the lettuces and sprinkle it with chopped chives before serving.

EDITOR'S NOTE: *The dressing for the salad may also be made with a good quality wine vinegar, although the resulting vinaigrette will be less aromatic than with balsamic vinegar.*

Caesar Salad

PREREQUISITES FOR THE CLASSIC CAESAR SALAD INCLUDE DEEP-FRIED CROÛTONS AND A RAW EGG IN THE DRESSING. IN THIS LIGHTER VERSION THE FRIED CROÛTONS ARE REPLACED BY CUBES OF TOASTED WHOLEMEAL BREAD.

Serves 4
Working (and total) time: about 30 minutes

Calories **120**
Protein **6g**
Cholesterol **35mg**
Total fat **8g**
Saturated fat **2g**
Sodium **400mg**

30g	*radicchio, washed and dried*	*1 oz*
90g	*Batavian endive, washed and dried*	*3 oz*
90g	*cos lettuce, washed and dried*	*3 oz*
2	*thin slices wholemeal bread*	*2*
30g	*anchovy fillets*	*1 oz*
15g	*freshly grated Parmesan cheese*	*½ oz*
	Egg and lemon dressing	
½	*beaten small egg*	*½*
1 tbsp	*virgin olive oil*	*1 tbsp*
1 tbsp	*fresh lemon juice*	*1 tbsp*
1 tbsp	*finely grated lemon rind*	*1 tbsp*
1	*small garlic clove, crushed*	*1*

Tear the salad leaves and put them into a large salad bowl. Cover the bowl with plastic film and place in the refrigerator for 20 to 30 minutes to crisp the leaves.

Meanwhile, toast the slices of wholemeal bread until they are golden-brown. Remove the crusts and cut the toast into small dice. Drain the anchovy fillets thoroughly on absorbent kitchen paper, then chop them roughly.

Just before serving, put the dressing ingredients into a bowl and whisk them until they are thoroughly blended. Remove the salad leaves from the refrigerator, and sprinkle them with the diced toast, chopped anchovy fillets and grated Parmesan cheese. Pour the dressing over the salad, toss it gently and serve immediately.

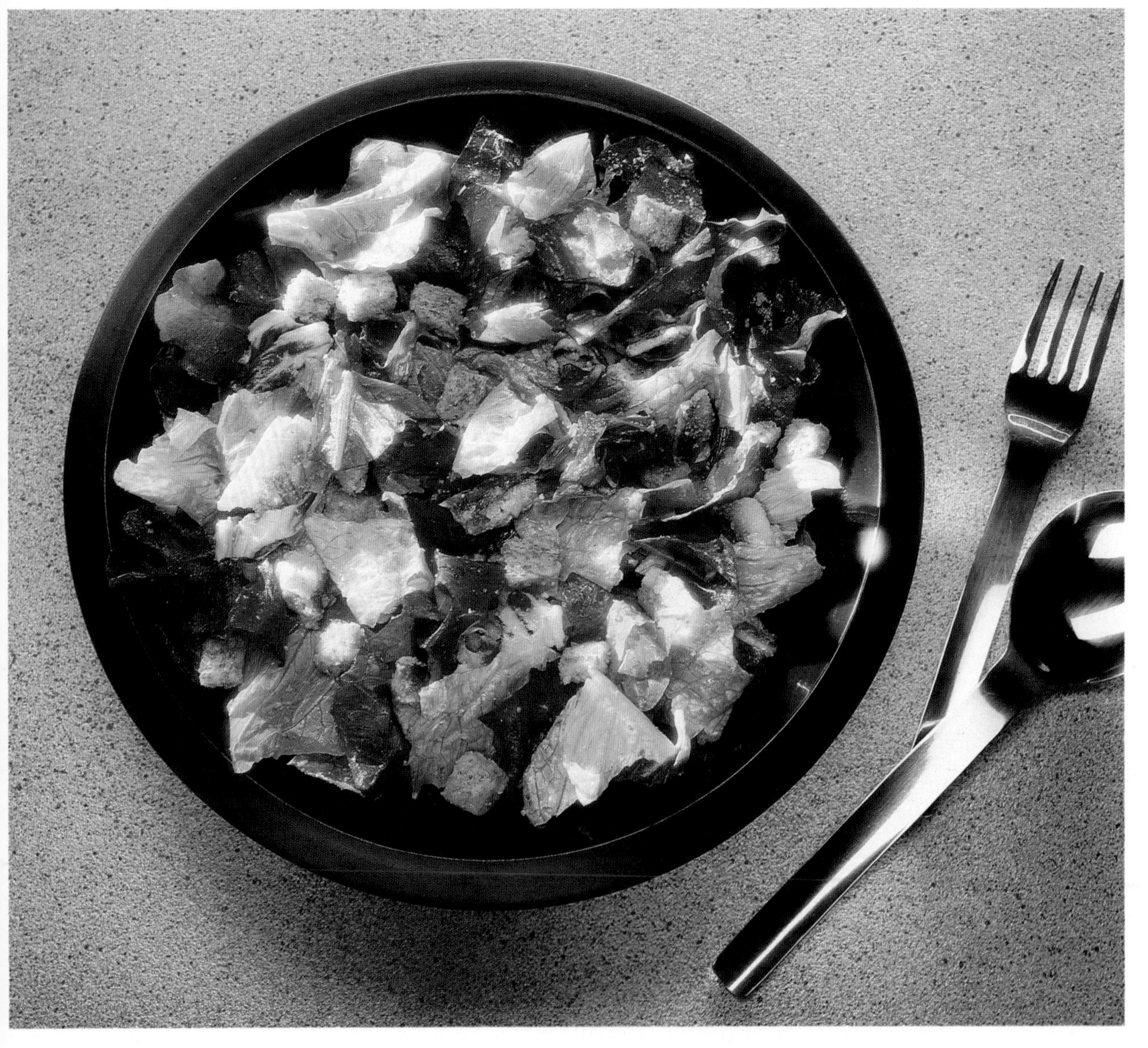

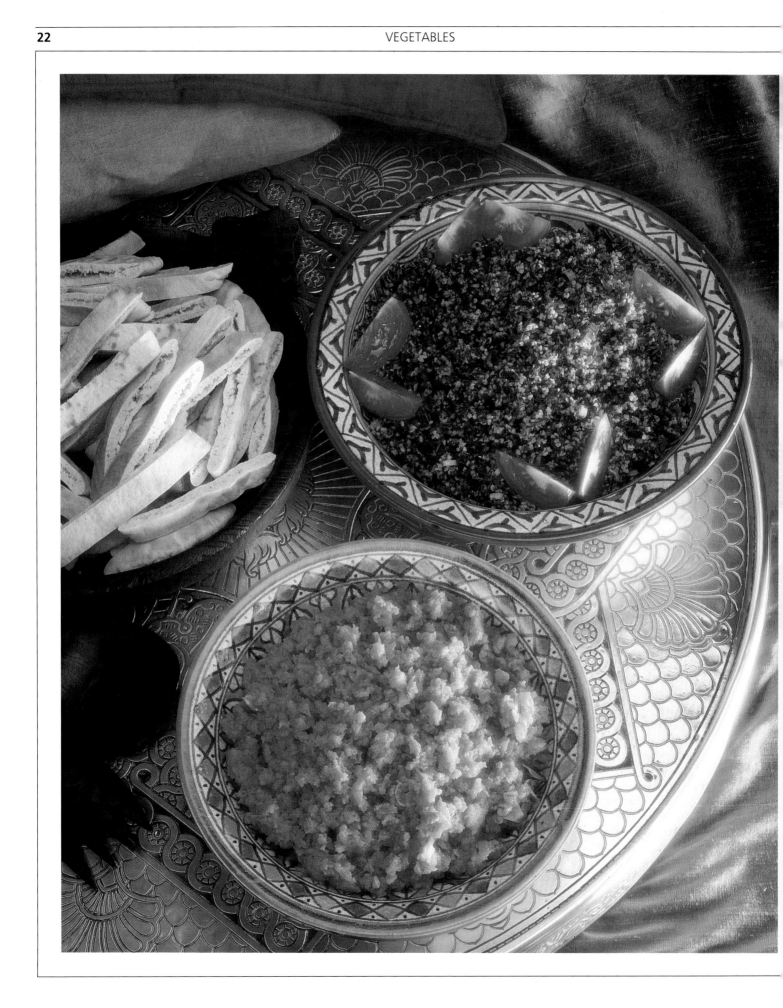

Parsley and Burghul Salad

IN THIS MIDDLE-EASTERN PARSLEY SALAD, THE BURGHUL — CRACKED WHEAT — NEEDS ONLY BRIEF SOAKING AND NO COOKING.

Serves 6
Working time: about 10 minutes
Total time: about 1 hour (includes soaking and cooling)

Calories **155**
Protein **4g**
Cholesterol **0mg**
Total fat **8g**
Saturated fat **1g**
Sodium **75mg**

125 g	*burghul*	*4 oz*
125 g	*parsley leaves, chopped*	*4 oz*
60 g	*fresh mint leaves, chopped*	*2 oz*
4	*spring onions, chopped*	*4*
4 tbsp	*fresh lemon juice*	*4 tbsp*
3 tbsp	*virgin olive oil*	*3 tbsp*
¼ tsp	*salt*	*¼ tsp*
	freshly ground black pepper	
1	*tomato, cut into thin wedges*	*1*

Place the burghul in a bowl, cover it with 60 cl (1 pint) of boiling water, and leave it to soak for 30 minutes. Drain the soaked burghul through a colander lined with muslin and squeeze it dry, a handful at a time, extracting as much water as possible.

Place the burghul in a mixing bowl. Add the parsley, mint, spring onions, lemon juice, oil, salt and some pepper. Mix the ingredients thoroughly, and leave the salad in a cool place for 15 to 20 minutes to allow its flavours to blend.

Turn the salad out on to a shallow dish or platter and serve it garnished with the tomato wedges.

Middle-Eastern Spiced Carrot Salad

Serves 6
Working time: about 10 minutes
Total time: about 1 hour (includes cooling)

Calories **75**
Protein **1g**
Cholesterol **0mg**
Total fat **5g**
Saturated fat **1g**
Sodium **190mg**

1 kg	*carrots, peeled and sliced into thick rounds*	*2 lb*
2	*garlic cloves, sliced*	*2*
2 tbsp	*virgin olive oil*	*2 tbsp*
¼ tsp	*cayenne pepper*	*¼ tsp*
2 tsp	*ground cumin*	*2 tsp*
2 tsp	*fresh lemon juice*	*2 tsp*
¼ tsp	*salt*	*¼ tsp*

Put the carrots and garlic in a saucepan. Cover them with hot water and boil them until they are soft — about 15 minutes. Drain the vegetables and mash them thoroughly.

In a small frying pan, heat the olive oil and fry the cayenne pepper and ground cumin for 1 minute. Stir the spice mixture into the carrot purée, mix in the lemon juice and the salt, and set the purée aside to cool at room temperature.

SUGGESTED ACCOMPANIMENT: *strips of warm pitta bread.*

Creamed Tahini Spread

THIS HORS-D'OEUVRE, BASED ON A MIDDLE EASTERN DISH, SHOULD BE SERVED WITH THIN SLICES OF WHOLEMEAL TOAST OR WARM PITTA BREAD.

Serves 12
Working (and total) time: 10 minutes

Calories **110**
Protein **5g**
Cholesterol **0mg**
Total fat **7g**
Saturated fat **1g**
Sodium **55mg**

15 g	*parsley, stems removed*	*½ oz*
1	*small garlic clove, sliced*	*1*
2	*slices wholemeal bread, crusts removed and discarded, cut into cubes*	*2*
15 cl	*tahini*	*¼ pt*
4 tbsp	*fresh lemon juice*	*4 tbsp*
350 g	*fromage frais*	*12 oz*
¼ tsp	*salt*	*¼ tsp*
¼ tsp	*freshly ground black pepper*	*¼ tsp*

Place the parsley, garlic and bread in a food processor or blender, and process the mixture until it breaks down into coarse crumbs. Add the tahini, lemon juice, *fromage frais*, salt and some pepper, and blend until they form a thick paste. Taste the spread and adjust the seasoning, adding more lemon juice or pepper as desired. Turn the mixture into a small serving bowl.

Three-Mushroom Marinade

Serves 8
Working time: about 30 minutes
Total time: about 5 hours (includes marinating)

Calories **60**
Protein **2g**
Cholesterol **0mg**
Total fat **4g**
Saturated fat **1g**
Sodium **60mg**

15 cl	*dry white wine*	*¼ pint*
1	*lemon, juice only*	*1*
1	*garlic clove, crushed*	*1*
250 g	*oyster mushrooms, trimmed, wiped and sliced*	*8 oz*
250 g	*button mushrooms, trimmed and wiped*	*8 oz*
175 g	*fresh shiitake mushrooms, trimmed, wiped, and halved if large*	*6 oz*
2 tbsp	*virgin olive oil*	*2 tbsp*
2 tbsp	*chopped parsley*	*2 tbsp*
¼ tsp	*salt*	*¼ tsp*
	freshly ground black pepper	
	oakleaf or other lettuce leaves, washed and dried	

In a large saucepan, combine the wine, lemon juice and garlic and bring the mixture to the boil. Add the prepared mushrooms, reduce the heat, cover the pan and cook gently until the mushrooms are tender but not overcooked — 6 to 8 minutes.

Place a colander over a bowl and drain the mushrooms, reserving the liquid. Return the mushroom juices to the saucepan, bring to the boil and reduce to 15 cl (¼ pint). Remove the pan from the heat and whisk in the oil, parsley, salt and some pepper. Pour this mixture into a bowl and add the drained mushrooms. Let the mushrooms cool in the marinade, then cover the bowl with plastic film and refrigerate for at least 4 hours, or overnight.

Arrange the lettuce leaves on eight plates. Using a slotted spoon, lift the mushrooms from the marinade and transfer them to the plates. Spoon a little of the marinade over them and serve them immediately.

SUGGESTED ACCOMPANIMENT: *Melba toast.*

EDITOR'S NOTE: *Any combination of cultivated or edible wild mushrooms can be used in this marinade.*

Mediterranean Vegetable Stew

TO PREPARE BABY ARTICHOKES, SIMPLY REMOVE ANY TOUGH OUTER LEAVES AND TRIM THE TOPS.

Serves 6
Working time: about 35 minutes
Total time: about 2 hours and 45 minutes (includes cooling)

:alories **45**
rotein **2g**
:holesterol **0mg**
otal fat **3g**
aturated fat **1g**
odium **175mg**

2	*large tomatoes, skinned, seeded (page 10) and chopped*	*2*
6	*baby artichokes (about 350g/12 oz), trimmed and halved*	*6*
2 tbsp	*fresh lemon juice*	*2 tbsp*
4	*sticks celery, sliced*	*4*
1	*fennel bulb, thinly sliced*	*1*
3	*thin leeks, trimmed and sliced into 1 cm (½ inch) rings*	*3*
1	*bay leaf*	*1*
12	*small onions*	*12*
1 tbsp	*virgin olive oil*	*1 tbsp*
300 g	*chestnut or button mushrooms, wiped clean, stalks trimmed, cut in half*	*10 oz*
½ tsp	*salt*	*½ tsp*
	freshly ground black pepper	
1 tbsp	*chopped fennel leaves*	*1 tbsp*

In a large, heavy-bottomed saucepan, heat the tomatoes, artichokes and lemon juice, stirring frequently until the mixture comes to the boil. Continue to cook the vegetables over high heat, stirring occasionally, for another 10 minutes.

Add the celery, fennel, leeks and bay leaf to the tomatoes and artichokes, and simmer uncovered, stirring occasionally, until the vegetables are almost tender — about 20 minutes.

Meanwhile, in a small, heavy-bottomed saucepan, sauté the onions in the oil until they are soft and well browned — about 20 minutes. Shake the saucepan frequently to prevent the onions from sticking to the bottom or burning.

When the vegetables in the large pan are nearly cooked, add the mushrooms and simmer for another 10 minutes. Remove the pan from the heat and mix in the salt, some pepper and the onions. Leave the mixture to cool for about 2 hours.

Remove the bay leaf and discard it. Before serving, transfer the stew to a large serving dish and sprinkle the fennel leaves over the top.

EDITOR'S NOTE: *If baby artichokes are unavailable, substitute three artichoke bottoms (page 27) cut into quarters.*

Preparing an Artichoke for Cooking

1 *TRIMMING THE LEAVES. Cut off the stem and small outer leaves from the base of the artichoke with a stainless steel knife. Rub the cut surfaces with freshly cut lemon to keep them from turning brown. Cut off the top third of the artichoke. Then snip off the sharp tips of the outer leaves with kitchen scissors.*

2 *REMOVING THE CHOKE. With a teaspoon, scoop out the tiny inner leaves and the hairy choke from the centre of the artichoke to reveal the smooth, green heart. The artichoke is now ready for cooking. (On large, mature artichokes, the choke may be difficult to remove until after the artichoke has been cooked.)*

Artichokes with an Egg and Herb Vinaigrette

Serves 6
Working time: about 20 minutes
Total time: about 1 hour

Calories **100**
Protein **2g**
Cholesterol **35mg**
Total fat **8g**
Saturated fat **1g**
Sodium **20mg**

6	*artichokes, trimmed, chokes removed (above)*	*6*
1	*egg, hard-boiled*	*1*
1 tbsp	*white wine vinegar*	*1 tbsp*
½ tsp	*fresh lemon juice*	*½ tsp*
3 tbsp	*virgin olive oil*	*3 tbsp*
¼ tsp	*salt*	*¼ tsp*
	freshly ground black pepper	
1 tbsp	*chopped parsley*	*1 tbsp*
1 tsp	*chopped lemon balm*	*1 tsp*
1 tsp	*finely cut chives*	*1 tsp*
1 tsp	*torn summer savory leaves*	*1 tsp*

In a large, non-reactive saucepan, bring 5 litres (8½ pints) of water to the boil. Add the artichokes and 1 tablespoon of salt, and boil the artichokes until they are tender — about 40 minutes. Place a colander over a bowl and drain the artichokes, reserving 2 tablespoons of their cooking water.

While the artichokes are cooling, shell the hard-boiled egg and chop it coarsely. In a small bowl, whisk together the vinegar, lemon juice, reserved cooking water from the artichokes, olive oil, the ¼ teaspoon of salt and some black pepper. When the dressing is thoroughly combined, stir in the chopped egg, parsley, lemon balm, chives and summer savory.

Place the cooled artichokes on individual serving plates. Divide the herb dressing among the hollowed-out centres, and serve the artichokes.

EDITOR'S NOTE: *The easiest way to eat artichokes presented in this manner is to break off the outer leaves first and use them to scoop out the dressing. When the leaves are finished, use a knife and fork to eat the tender artichoke bottoms, with the remaining herb vinaigrette. Each diner should be supplied with a finger bowl.*

Artichoke Bottoms Filled with Vegetables Vinaigrette

Serves 4
Working time: about 20 minutes
Total time: about 45 minutes

Calories **110g**
Protein **2g**
Cholesterol **0mg**
Total fat **10g**
Saturated fat **1g**
Sodium **110mg**

½	*lemon, juice only*	½
4	*artichoke bottoms (box, right)*	4
30 g	*baby carrots, cut into 1 cm (½ inch) diagonal slices*	1 oz
30 g	*trimmed broccoli florets*	1 oz
30 g	*French beans, topped, tailed and cut into 2.5 cm (1 inch) pieces*	1 oz
30 g	*baby courgettes, sliced into thin rounds*	1 oz
	Walnut dressing	
1 tbsp	*white wine vinegar*	1 tbsp
¼ tsp	*salt*	¼ tsp
2 tbsp	*walnut oil*	2 tbsp
	white pepper	
1 tbsp	*coarsely chopped walnuts*	1 tbsp

In a large non-reactive saucepan, bring 1 litre (1¾ pints) of water to the boil. Add the lemon juice to the water, drop in the artichoke bottoms and simmer them until they are tender — about 25 minutes.

While the artichokes are cooking, parboil the other vegetables separately in boiling water — the carrots and broccoli for about 2 minutes each, the French beans and courgettes for about 1 minute each. Drain each of the vegetables in a colander, refresh them under cold running water, drain them thoroughly again and set them aside.

When the artichoke bottoms are cooked, lift them from the water with a slotted spoon and set them upside down on a tea towel to drain.

To prepare the walnut dressing, mix the vinegar and the salt in a small bowl, stirring well until the salt dissolves. Whisk in the walnut oil, add some pepper and stir in the walnuts. Toss the broccoli, carrots, French beans and courgettes in the dressing, spoon them into the artichoke bottoms, and serve.

EDITOR'S NOTE: *Any colourful combination of fresh vegetables may be used in the filling for the artichokes. Alternative possibilities to those above include sautéed mushrooms, cooked green peas, diced and parboiled baby turnips, or slivers of blanched mange-tout.*

Turning an Artichoke Bottom

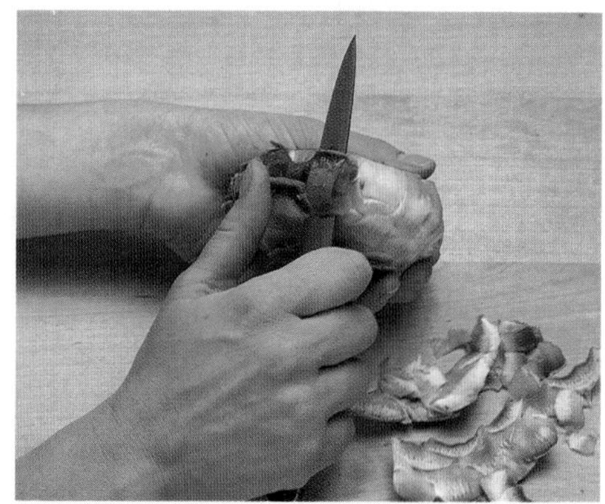

PREPARING THE BOTTOM. Cut off the stem using a stainless steel knife. Bend back each outer leaf, snapping the tough upper part from the fleshy base, until you reach the tender, pale inner leaves. Rub the cut surfaces with lemon as you work. Cut off the top two thirds of the artichoke. Pare away the tough, dark green bases of the leaves (above). Scrape out the choke (Step 2, opposite).

Minted Broccoli and Cauliflower

Serves 6
Working time: about 15 minutes
Total time: about 3 hours and 15 minutes (includes marinating)

Calories **60**
Protein **3g**
Cholesterol **0mg**
Total fat **5g**
Saturated fat **1g**
Sodium **10mg**

350 g	*trimmed cauliflower florets*	*12 oz*
250 g	*trimmed broccoli florets*	*8 oz*
6	*sprigs fresh mint*	*6*
1 tbsp	*white wine vinegar*	*1 tbsp*
2	*garlic cloves, crushed*	*2*
½ tsp	*salt*	*½ tsp*
1 tbsp	*roughly cut chives*	*1 tbsp*
1 tbsp	*chopped fresh marjoram*	*1 tbsp*
1 tsp	*Dijon mustard*	*1 tsp*
2 tbsp	*virgin olive oil*	*2 tbsp*
	freshly ground black pepper	

Pour enough water into a large saucepan to fill it about 2.5 cm (1 inch) deep. Set a vegetable steamer in the pan and bring the water to the boil. Add the cauliflower and broccoli florets with four of the mint sprigs, and steam them, covered, until they are just tender — about 5 minutes. Pour the florets into a colander, refresh them under cold running water and drain them thoroughly. Discard the mint sprigs.

Put the vinegar, garlic, salt, chives, marjoram, mustard, olive oil and some black pepper in a large bowl and mix them well. Add the cauliflower and broccoli to the marinade, turning the florets gently until they are well coated. Cover the bowl with plastic film and allow the vegetables to marinate, in the refrigerator, for at least 3 hours.

Just before serving, garnish the vegetables with the leaves from the remaining mint sprigs.

Spinach Roulade

Serves 6
Working time: about 1 hour
Total time: about 2 hours (includes cooling)

Calories **165**
Protein **10g**
Cholesterol **75mg**
Total fat **8g**
Saturated fat **2g**
Sodium **280mg**

350 g	*fresh spinach, stemmed, washed but not dried*	*12 oz*
45 g	*plain flour*	*1½ oz*
30 cl	*skimmed milk*	*½ pint*
½ tsp	*dry mustard*	*½ tsp*
1 tsp	*salt*	*1 tsp*
	freshly ground black pepper	
2	*egg yolks*	*2*
4	*egg whites*	*4*
1 tbsp	*fresh Parmesan cheese, finely grated*	*1 tbsp*
	Mushroom and pepper filling	
125 g	*chestnut or button mushrooms, finely diced*	*4 oz*
½	*sweet red pepper, cored, seeded and finely diced*	*½*
½	*sweet yellow pepper, cored, seeded and finely diced*	*½*
3	*spring onions, thinly sliced*	*3*
1 tbsp	*virgin olive oil*	*1 tbsp*
100 g	*fromage frais*	*3½ oz*

Put the spinach in a large saucepan, cover the pan and cook the spinach over high heat in the water clinging to its leaves until it begins to wilt. Remove the lid and continue cooking the spinach over medium heat, turning frequently, until the spinach has wilted completely — 5 to 7 minutes. Drain the spinach in a colander, pressing out all excess water with a saucer or a wooden spoon. Transfer the spinach to a food processor, blend it to a smooth purée, and set it aside. Preheat the oven to 170°C (325°F or Mark 3).

In a bowl, mix the flour to a paste with a little of the milk. Put the remaining milk in a small saucepan and heat it until bubbles appear round the edge. Add the hot milk to the flour paste and whisk until the sauce is perfectly smooth. (If any lumps of flour remain, rub the mixture through a fine sieve.) Pour the sauce into the saucepan and cook it over medium heat, stirring briskly, until it thickens and comes to the boil. Reduce the heat and simmer the sauce for 5 minutes, stirring constantly.

Cool the sauce slightly, then add it to the spinach purée in the food processor, along with the mustard, the salt and some pepper. Blend the ingredients thoroughly. Add the egg yolks and blend again briefly. Turn the mixture into a bowl.

In another bowl, beat the egg whites until they are stiff. Fold the beaten whites into the spinach sauce with a metal spoon. Line a 30 by 20 cm (12 by 8 inch) Swiss roll tin with greaseproof paper and oil the paper. Spread out the spinach mixture evenly in the tin and bake it until it is risen and just set — 35 to 40 minutes.

While it bakes, prepare the filling. Heat the oil in a non-stick frying pan. Cook the mushrooms, red and yellow peppers and spring onions over medium heat, stirring frequently, until they are tender but still firm — 4 to 5 minutes. Remove the vegetables from the heat, transfer them to a colander to drain off their liquid, and leave them to cool.

Place a sheet of greaseproof paper, slightly larger than the Swiss roll tin, on a flat surface and sprinkle it evenly with the grated Parmesan cheese. When the spinach roulade mixture is cooked, turn it out on to the cheese-coated paper. Peel off the lining paper very carefully and trim away any crusty edges from the spinach base. Then roll up the spinach base together with the cheese-coated paper, and set the roll aside to cool.

When the vegetables are cold, mix them with the *fromage frais.* Unroll the spinach base, remove the paper and spread the filling over the spinach. Roll up the roulade again, and place it seam side down on a serving dish.

Cut the roulade into slices and serve immediately.

Aubergines in Tomato Sauce

THIS IS A VARIATION ON THE CLASSIC TURKISH DISH *IMAM BAYILDI*, WHICH TRANSLATES LITERALLY AS "THE HOLY MAN FAINTED". TRADITIONALLY, THE AUBERGINE IS FRIED IN A LARGE AMOUNT OF OIL; HERE IT IS SIMMERED IN A TOMATO SAUCE.

Serves 6
Working time: about 20 minutes
Total time: about 2 hours

Calories **100**
Protein **3g**
Cholesterol **0mg**
Total fat **6g**
Saturated fat **1g**
Sodium **75mg**

500 g	*aubergines, sliced*	*1 lb*
1¼ tsp	*salt*	*1¼ tsp*
2 tbsp	*virgin olive oil*	*2 tbsp*
1	*onion, sliced*	*1*
2	*garlic cloves, chopped*	*2*
750 g	*ripe tomatoes, skinned, seeded (page 10) and chopped, or 400 g (14 oz) canned tomatoes, drained and coarsely chopped*	*1½ lb*
1 tsp	*tomato paste*	*1 tsp*
1	*bay leaf*	*1*
	freshly ground black pepper	
15 g	*pine-nuts, tossed in a heavy frying pan over medium heat until golden-brown*	*½ oz*
1 tbsp	*chopped parsley*	*1 tbsp*

Sprinkle the aubergine slices with 1 teaspoon of the salt and let them drain in a colander for 30 minutes to draw out their bitter juices. Meanwhile, heat the oil in a large, heavy-bottomed saucepan, and fry the sliced onion and the garlic until they are softened. Add the chopped tomatoes, tomato paste, bay leaf, the remaining salt and some pepper, then cover the pan and simmer the sauce for 10 minutes.

Rinse the aubergines in cold water and pat them dry with kitchen paper. Add the aubergines to the pan,

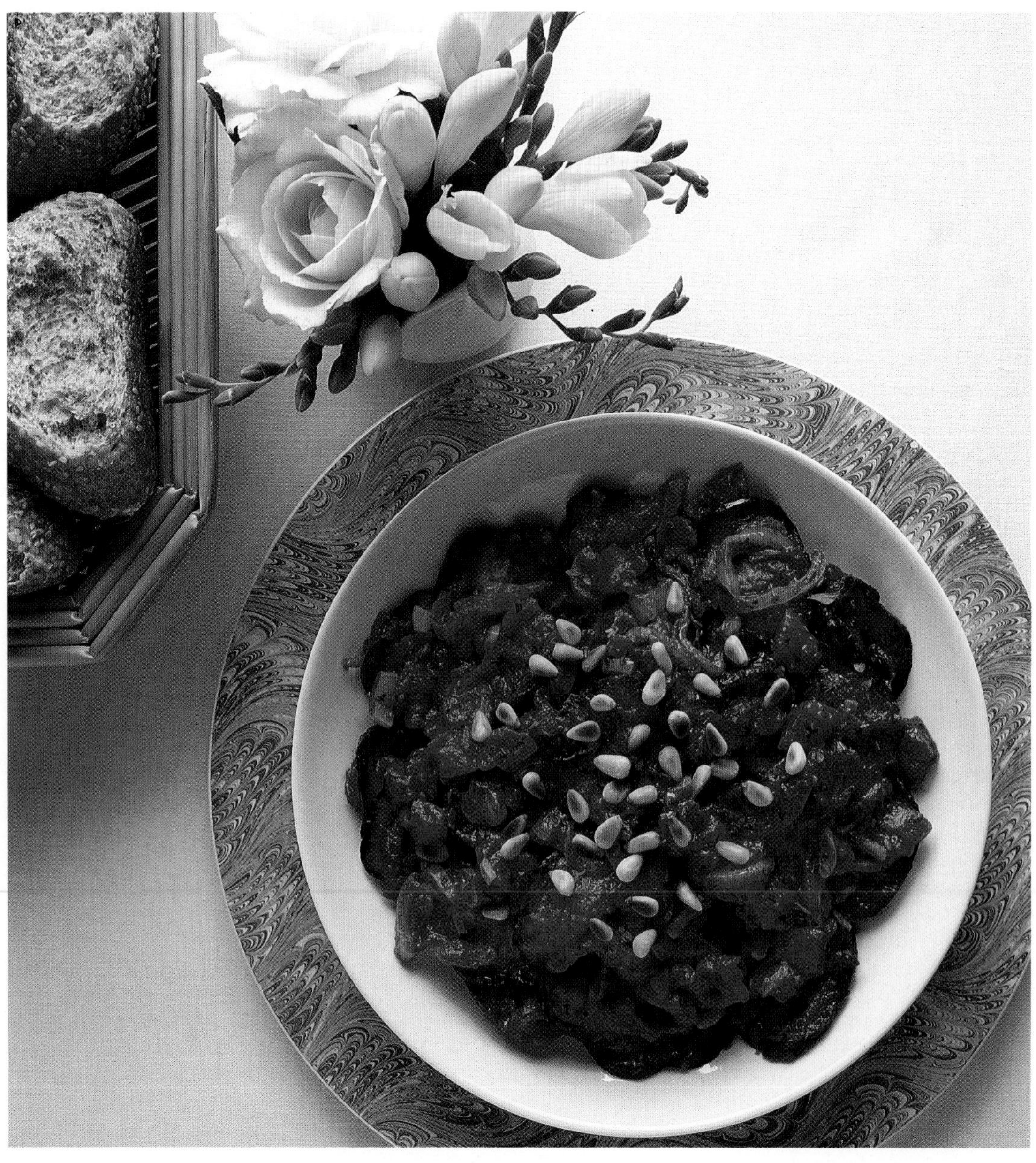

coat them well with the sauce, then cover the saucepan and simmer the mixture gently for a further 30 minutes. Remove the bay leaf.

Let the sauced aubergines cool in the pan. Turn them out on to a shallow dish, sprinkle them with the pine-nuts and parsley, and serve at room temperature.

Baby Beetroot and Blackcurrant Moulds

Serves 6
Working time: about 55 minutes
Total time: about 1 hour and 45 minutes
(includes setting and chilling)

Calories **65**
Protein **4g**
Cholesterol **5mg**
Total fat **2g**
Saturated fat **1g**
Sodium **35mg**

10	*baby beetroots, washed but not peeled, tops trimmed off (about 500 g/1 lb)*	*10*
60 cl	*blackcurrant juice*	*1 pint*
15 g	*powdered gelatine*	*½ oz*
	Lime-yogurt sauce	
250 g	*thick Greek yogurt*	*8 oz*
2	*limes, juice and finely grated rind*	*2*
	freshly ground black pepper	

In a saucepan, cook the beetroots in enough boiling water to cover them until they are tender — about 25 minutes. Drain them in a colander, leave them until they are cool enough to handle, then peel them while they are still warm. Reserve five of the beetroots, and use a sharp knife to slice the remainder thinly. Divide the slices between six 12.5 cl (4 fl oz) jelly moulds.

In a non-reactive saucepan, bring the blackcurrant juice to the boil. Remove it from the heat and sprinkle the powdered gelatine over the hot liquid. When the gelatine has dissolved completely, pour the blackcurrant mixture into the moulds. Refrigerate the beetroot until the jelly has set — about 1 hour.

Meanwhile, prepare the lime-yogurt sauce. Place the Greek yogurt in a bowl. Add the lime rind and juice, and beat them into the yogurt with a small whisk. Chill the sauce in the refrigerator.

To unmould the jellies, dip the base of each mould into a pan of boiling water for a couple of seconds and then turn it out on to a serving plate. Slice the reserved beetroots, arrange them round each mould, and serve immediately, accompanied by the lime-yogurt sauce.

EDITOR'S NOTE: *The blackcurrant juice renders the jelly fairly tart. For a less tart jelly, apple juice can be substituted for half of the blackcurrant juice.*

Tricolour Terrine

Serves 8
Working time: about 1 hour and 30 minutes
Total time: about 13 hours (includes marinating)

Calories **275**
Protein **12g**
Cholesterol **35mg**
Total fat **12g**
Saturated fat **2g**
Sodium **55mg**

2	*fresh salmon fillets, skinned and trimmed (about 400 g/14 oz)*	2
½ tsp	*caster sugar*	½ tsp
2 tsp	*chopped fresh dill*	2 tsp
250 g	*sushi rice*	8 oz
1 tbsp	*rice or white wine vinegar*	1 tbsp
3	*sheets nori seaweed*	3
1	*sweet yellow pepper, skinned, seeded (page 11) and deribbed, cut into 1 cm (½ inch) wide strips and patted dry*	1
1	*cos lettuce, ribs removed, leaves blanched, refreshed in cold water and drained thoroughly*	1
4	*dill sprigs, leaves only*	4
1	*sweet red pepper, skinned, seeded (page 11) and deribbed, cut into 1 cm (½ inch) wide strips and patted dry*	1
12	*salad leaves, such as oakleaf lettuce and curly endive, washed and dried*	12
	Horseradish vinaigrette	
½ tbsp	*rice or white wine vinegar*	½ tbsp
3 tbsp	*grapeseed oil or safflower oil*	3 tbsp
¼ tsp	*wasabi powder (Japanese horseradish)*	¼ tsp

Place the salmon on a wooden board or work surface. Combine the sugar and the chopped dill in a small bowl and rub this dry marinade all over the fish.

Sandwich the salmon fillets between two flat plates, wrap plastic film round the plates, and stand weights — such as kitchen weights or unopened tins — on top. Place the fish in the refrigerator to marinate for 12 to 24 hours. To make sure the fish becomes thoroughly permeated by the marinade, remove the plates from the refrigerator once or twice during this period, unwrap the fillets and turn them over in the marinade, then refrigerate them, well wrapped, once again.

When the fish has been marinating long enough, rinse the rice in cold water and drain it in a sieve. Put the rice in a saucepan with ¼ litre (8 fl oz) of water, bring it to the boil, cover the pan with a lid, and simmer the rice over very low heat for 20 minutes. Turn off the heat and leave the rice to steam for a further 10 minutes with the lid on. Remove the lid, mix in the rice vinegar and set the rice aside until it is cool — 20 to 30 minutes.

Remove the salmon from the refrigerator, pour off the liquid that has collected in the dish, and use a knife to scrape off the dry marinade. Dry the fish with paper towels, and cut it across the grain into strips about 1 cm (½ inch) wide.

Rub the base and sides of a ¾ litre (1¼ pint) terrine with wet paper towels to moisten them, and line the terrine with the nori, draping about 2 cm (¾ inch) of the seaweed sheets over the sides of the dish.

Divide the rice into four equal portions. Place one quarter of the rice in the terrine, pressing it down with your fingertips to make an even base. Top the rice with the yellow pepper and follow with another layer of rice, pressing both layers.

Place half the lettuce and a sprinkling of dill on the second layer of rice. Top the leaves with the salmon strips, followed by the remaining lettuce and the dill. Pressing each layer down as you go along, cover the lettuce with the third portion of rice, top the rice with the red pepper strips and finish with a final rice layer. Place a sheet of nori on top of the terrine, and tuck down its edges over the rice.

Cover the terrine with a sheet of plastic film. Set a piece of cardboard on the plastic film and place a weight on top of the cardboard. Put the weighted terrine in the refrigerator to set for 30 minutes. Meanwhile, combine the vinaigrette ingredients in a small bowl and mix them thoroughly with a fork.

Remove the terrine from the refrigerator and unmould it by inverting it over a platter. To serve the terrine, slice it carefully with a knife that has been dipped in water to prevent the rice from sticking. Accompany each slice with a selection of the lettuce leaves and some of the vinaigrette in a small bowl.

EDITOR'S NOTE: *Because the salmon in this recipe is not cooked, only the freshest fish should be used. Nori, sushi rice and wasabi powder can be purchased from Oriental grocers or health food shops. If sushi rice is unobtainable, another glutinous rice such as pudding rice may be substituted.*

Rolled Vine Leaves

Serves 8
Working time: about 45 minutes
Total time: about 2 hours and 30 minutes

Calories **110**
Protein **4g**
Cholesterol **20mg**
Total fat **5g**
Saturated fat **2g**
Sodium **65mg**

125 g	*lean minced lamb*	*4 oz*
1	*onion, chopped*	*1*
2	*garlic cloves, chopped*	*2*
90 g	*brown rice*	*3 oz*
2 tbsp	*chopped fresh mint*	*2 tbsp*
2 tbsp	*chopped parsley*	*2 tbsp*
1 tbsp	*tomato paste*	*1 tbsp*
2	*tomatoes, skinned, seeded (page 10) and chopped*	*2*
	freshly ground black pepper	
125 g	*fresh vine leaves, blanched for 1 minute in boiling water, rinsed and drained well*	*4 oz*
1 tbsp	*virgin olive oil*	*1 tbsp*
1	*lemon, juice only*	*1*
	lemon wedges, for garnish	

In a non-stick or heavy cast-iron frying pan, cook the minced lamb over low heat until the meat begins to release its juices. Increase the heat to medium and continue to fry the lamb until it has browned. Place a colander over a bowl and transfer the lamb and its juices to the colander to drain. Return 1 tablespoon of the meat juices to the pan and sauté the onion and the garlic in these juices over low heat, until soft — about 10 minutes. Discard the remaining meat juices.

Return the drained lamb to the frying pan and stir in the brown rice, mint, parsley, tomato paste, tomatoes and some pepper. Add 20 cl (7 fl oz) of water, and bring the mixture to the boil. Cover the pan and cook the stuffing for 10 minutes, then set it aside for a few minutes to cool slightly.

Preheat the oven to 180°C (350°F or Mark 4).

Lay the vine leaves out flat on the work surface. Place a spoonful of stuffing on the centre of each leaf. Fold the stem end up over the stuffing, fold both sides towards the middle, then roll into a small parcel. Take care not to wrap the parcels too tightly: the rice needs room to expand as it cooks.

Lay any spare or damaged vine leaves in the base of a heavy casserole. Set the stuffed parcels in the casserole, packing them in tightly to keep them from unrolling. Pour the oil, lemon juice and 45 cl (¾ pint) of water over the rolls.

Cover the casserole and cook the vine leaves in the oven for about 1¼ hours, adding extra water if the liquid in the casserole evaporates. Leave the parcels to cool in the casserole. Serve them cold, garnished with lemon wedges.

EDITOR'S NOTE: *Preserved vine leaves may be used if fresh leaves are not available. Wash them in cold water to rid them of excess salt, then drain them thoroughly on a folded tea towel. They do not require blanching.*

Chicken-Stuffed Peppers

Serves 6
Working time: about 45 minutes
Total time: about 7 hours (includes chilling)

Calories **140**
Protein **9g**
Cholesterol **20mg**
Total fat **4g**
Saturated fat **1g**
Sodium **75mg**

3	*small sweet red peppers, tops cut off and reserved, seeds and ribs removed*	*3*
3	*small sweet yellow peppers, tops cut off and reserved, seeds and ribs removed*	*3*
15 cl	*unsalted chicken stock (recipe, page 9)*	*¼ pint*
1 tbsp	*virgin olive oil*	*1 tbsp*
	Spiced chicken stuffing	
½ tbsp	*virgin olive oil*	*½ tbsp*
1	*onion, finely chopped*	*1*
125 g	*long-grain rice*	*4 oz*
2	*garlic cloves, crushed*	*2*
½ tsp	*ground cardamom*	*½ tsp*
½ tsp	*ground cumin*	*½ tsp*
250 g	*boned chicken breast, skinned and cut into tiny cubes*	*8 oz*
30 cl	*unsalted chicken stock (recipe, page 9)*	*½ pint*
¼ tsp	*salt*	*¼ tsp*
	freshly ground black pepper	

First prepare the stuffing. In a large saucepan, heat the oil, then add the onion and cook gently until the onion has softened but not browned — 5 to 6 minutes. Stir in the rice, garlic, cardamom and cumin. Cook for 1 to 2 minutes, then stir in the chicken pieces, stock, salt and some pepper. Bring the mixture to the boil, reduce the heat, cover the pan with a tightly fitting lid and cook very gently until the rice is tender and all of the stock has been absorbed — 25 to 30 minutes.

Preheat the oven to 180°C (350°F or Mark 4).

Cook the peppers and their lids in boiling water until they soften slightly — 4 to 5 minutes. Place the peppers in a large colander, refresh them under cold running water and drain them well.

Fill the peppers with the rice and chicken mixture and cover them with their lids. Stand the peppers in a deep ovenproof dish, add the chicken stock and cover the dish with a lid or with foil. Bake the peppers in the oven until they are very tender — about 1½ hours.

Using a slotted spoon, carefully transfer the cooked peppers to a serving dish. Pour the juices left in the baking dish into a saucepan, bring them to the boil and boil rapidly until they are reduced by half, then whisk in the olive oil. Pour this liquid over the peppers, and set them aside to cool. When the peppers have cooled, cover them with plastic film and place them in the refrigerator until they are well chilled — 3 to 4 hours, or overnight — before serving.

Melon, Bacon and Mint Melange

Serves 4
Working (and total) time: about 20 minutes

Calories **130**
Protein **5g**
Cholesterol **15mg**
Total fat **10g**
Saturated fat **3g**
Sodium **290mg**

½	*Gallia or other green melon*	½
1	*small cantaloupe or Charentais melon*	1
125 g	*cucumber*	4 oz
2	*lean rashers bacon (about 60 g/2 oz)*	2
2 tbsp	*fresh lemon juice*	2 tbsp
1 tbsp	*safflower oil*	1 tbsp
	freshly ground black pepper	
40	*young mint leaves*	40

Peel the melons with a sharp knife. Discard their seeds, and cut the flesh into 2.5 cm (1 inch) cubes. Using a vegetable peeler, remove thin strips of peel lengthwise from the cucumber to produce a striped effect. Slice the cucumber into paper-thin rounds.

Cut off and discard the bacon rind and fat, then cook the rashers in a heavy, ungreased frying pan until they are crisp. Remove the bacon from the pan and lay it on paper towels to drain.

Cut the bacon into short strips and place them in a mixing bowl with the melon cubes and cucumber slices. Toss the bacon and fruit gently together, and transfer the salad to individual serving plates.

Add the lemon juice and oil to the frying pan and cook the mixture for a few minutes over gentle heat, stirring and scraping loose the meaty residues on the bottom of the pan.

Stir the mint leaves into the hot lemon juice and oil mixture and spoon the dressing over the salad. Serve the salad immediately.

Summer Fruits with Hazelnut Dressing

A SAVOURY FRUIT SALAD MAKES A REFRESHING OPENING TO A HOT-WEATHER MEAL, ESPECIALLY IF THE SERVING PLATES ARE CHILLED FOR AN HOUR IN ADVANCE.

Serves 6
Working time: about 15 minutes
Total time: about 1 hour

Calories **145**
Protein **2g**
Cholesterol **0mg**
Total fat **7g**
Saturated fat **1g**
Sodium **10mg**

4	*ripe peaches, peeled and sliced*	*4*
1 tbsp	*fresh lemon juice*	*1 tbsp*
1	*mango, peeled and sliced*	*1*
250 g	*blueberries*	*8 oz*
250 g	*strawberries, halved*	*8 oz*
2 tbsp	*hazelnut oil*	*2 tbsp*
6	*basil leaves*	*6*

Place six serving plates in the refrigerator until well chilled — about 1 hour. Rub the peach slices with a little of the lemon juice to prevent discoloration. Arrange the peaches, mango slices, blueberries and strawberry halves on the chilled serving plates.

In a small jug, stir the hazelnut oil and the remaining lemon juice with a fork until thoroughly blended, and dribble this dressing over the fruit. Garnish each plate with a basil leaf, and serve the salad immediately.

EDITOR'S NOTE: *Perfectly ripe persimmons (also known as sharon fruit) can be used instead of peaches.*

Figs with Goat Cheese and Walnuts

Serves 8
Working (and total) time: about 30 minutes

Calories **135**
Protein **6g**
Cholesterol **20mg**
Total fat **10g**
Saturated fat **4g**
Sodium **75mg**

8	*ripe green or purple figs*	8
8	*walnuts, shelled and chopped*	8
175 g	*soft goat cheese*	6 oz
	Herb dressing	
2 tbsp	*walnut or virgin olive oil*	2 tbsp
2 tbsp	*white wine vinegar*	2 tbsp
4 tsp	*finely chopped parsley*	4 tsp
2 tsp	*finely chopped fresh thyme*	2 tsp
½ tsp	*salt*	½ tsp
	freshly ground black pepper	

With a sharp knife, slice the tops off the figs and reserve them to be used as lids for the stuffed fruit. Hollow out the figs with a small spoon, transfer their pulp to a bowl, and mix it with the chopped walnuts. Set the mixture aside.

In a small bowl, mix together the oil and the white wine vinegar with a fork until thoroughly blended. Add the parsley, thyme, salt and some freshly ground black pepper to complete the dressing.

With the back of a fork, blend the goat cheese with the fig and walnut mixture, and spoon this filling into the figs, packing the mixture down into the hollows. Spoon the dressing over the stuffed fruit, replace the reserved tops on the figs, and serve.

Savoury Cheese Hearts

THIS IS A LOW-FAT VARIATION OF THE RICH CREAM AND CHEESE MOULDS THAT IN FRENCH CUISINE ARE CALLED *COEURS À LA CRÈME.*

Serves 4
Working time: about 15 minutes
Total time: about 12 hours (includes draining)

Calories **100**
Protein **7g**
Cholesterol **0mg**
Total fat **7g**
Saturated fat **4g**
Sodium **210mg**

350 g	*fromage frais*	*12 oz*
1 tsp	*finely chopped fresh mint*	*1 tsp*
1 tsp	*finely chopped fresh lemon verbena or parsley*	*1 tsp*
1 tsp	*finely chopped fresh basil*	*1 tsp*
1 tsp	*finely grated orange rind*	*1 tsp*
½ tsp	*whole coriander seeds*	*½ tsp*
¼ tsp	*salt*	*¼ tsp*
1	*large egg white*	*1*
	fresh herbs, such as mint, parsley and basil, for garnish	
	thin strips of orange rind for garnish	

Beat the soft cheese lightly, and combine it with the chopped mint, lemon verbena or parsley, basil, orange rind, coriander seeds and salt. In a clean, dry bowl, whisk the egg white until it is fairly stiff, then fold it gently but thoroughly into the cheese mixture.

Line four perforated heart-shaped moulds with dampened squares of muslin, smoothing out wrinkles. Gently fill each mould with the cheese mixture, set the moulds over a tray or deep platter, and leave to drain for about 12 hours, or overnight, in a cool place.

Invert the hearts on to individual serving dishes and garnish them with fresh herbs and orange rind.

EDITOR'S NOTE: *These cheese hearts are very delicate. If they break or are damaged while being unmoulded, you can repair them by dipping a rounded knife or palette knife in water and using it to pat the cheese mixture back into shape.*

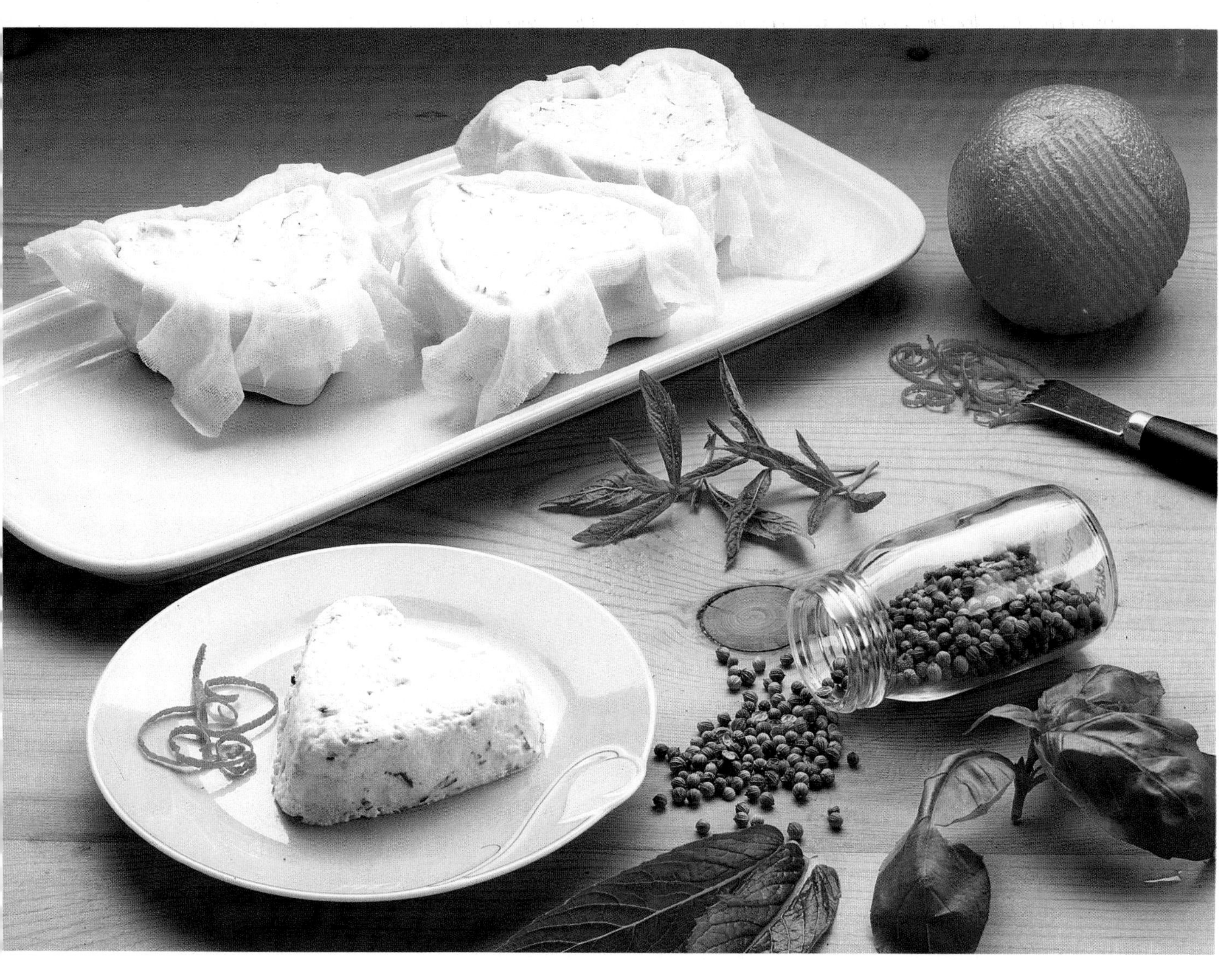

Salmon Tartare

THIS RECIPE IS INSPIRED BY THE CLASSIC HORS-D'OEUVRE OF HIGHLY SEASONED RAW BEEF KNOWN AS STEAK TARTARE.

Serves 4
Working time: about 20 minutes
Total time: about 1 hour and 20 minutes (includes chilling)

Calories **200**
Protein **12g**
Cholesterol **55mg**
Total fat **12g**
Saturated fat **5g**
Sodium **195mg**

250 g	*salmon fillet, skinned and finely chopped*	*8 oz*
½ tsp	*freshly ground black pepper*	*½ tsp*
2	*spring onions, finely sliced*	*2*
1	*lime, finely grated rind only*	*1*
6 tbsp	*soured cream*	*6 tbsp*
4	*thin slices wholemeal bread, toasted, crusts removed, cut into triangles*	*4*

In a bowl, mix the chopped fish thoroughly with the black pepper and combine it with the spring onions. Chill the salmon mixture in the refrigerator for 1 hour.

In the meantime, stir most of the grated lime rind into the soured cream. Place the soured cream mixture and four individual serving plates in the refrigerator to chill with the salmon.

At serving time, divide the salmon tartare among the four chilled plates, forming each portion into a small mound with a hollow in its centre. Spoon a quarter of the soured cream mixture into each hollow and sprinkle on the remaining lime rind. Serve the fish accompanied by the wholemeal toast.

EDITOR'S NOTE: *Because the salmon in this recipe is not cooked, only the freshest fish should be used.*

Pickled Peppers with Mussels

Serves 4
Working time: about 25 minutes
Total time: about 1 hour and 15 minutes (includes chilling)

Calories **100**
Protein **14g**
Cholesterol **10mg**
Total fat **2g**
Saturated fat **0g**
Sodium **150mg**

1	*sweet red pepper, seeded, deribbed and thinly sliced*	1
1	*sweet green pepper, seeded, deribbed and thinly sliced*	1
1	*sweet yellow pepper, seeded, deribbed and thinly sliced*	1
2	*garlic cloves, peeled and thinly sliced*	2
6 tbsp	*white wine vinegar*	6 tbsp
1 tbsp	*demerara sugar*	1 tbsp
2 tbsp	*chopped parsley*	2 tbsp
20	*large mussels (about 500 g/1 lb), scrubbed and debearded*	20

Place the sliced sweet peppers in a medium-sized saucepan with the garlic, wine vinegar and sugar. Bring the vinegar to the boil, then cover the pan and reduce the heat; simmer the peppers for 7 minutes. Stir in 1 tablespoon of the chopped parsley, and allow the peppers and their liquor to cool.

Put 3 tablespoons of water and the mussels in a large saucepan, cover the pan and bring the water to the boil. Steam the mussels until they open — 3 to 4 minutes. Drain the mussels in a colander, discarding the liquid and any mussels that remain closed. Leave the mussels to cool.

Chill the peppers and the mussels in the refrigerator for at least 30 minutes before serving. To serve, divide the peppers among four individual plates, arrange the mussels on the peppers, pour over the pepper liquor and sprinkle the remaining parsley on top.

SUGGESTED ACCOMPANIMENT: *crusty bread.*

Marinated Sardines

ONLY THE FRESHEST FISH SHOULD BE USED FOR THIS TRADITIONAL SPANISH HORS-D'OEUVRE. THE SARDINE FILLETS ARE MARINATED FOR TWO TO THREE DAYS IN AN OIL AND VINEGAR MIXTURE, WHICH TENDERIZES THE FLESH, AND THE FISH IS SERVED UNCOOKED.

Serves 6
Working time: about 45 minutes
Total time: 2 to 3 days (includes marinating)

Calories **110**
Protein **9g**
Cholesterol **40mg**
Total fat **8g**
Saturated fat **2g**
Sodium **105mg**

600 g	*fresh sardines, scaled, heads and tails removed, gutted, rinsed and patted dry*	*1¼ lb*
¾ tsp	*salt*	*¾ tsp*
2	*garlic cloves, chopped*	*2*
1 tbsp	*chopped parsley*	*1 tbsp*
1 tbsp	*virgin olive oil*	*1 tbsp*
12.5 cl	*wine vinegar*	*4 fl oz*

Remove the backbone from each sardine and separate the two fillets lengthwise, leaving the skin intact.

Sprinkle the fish with the salt and place a layer of the fillets, skin side uppermost, in a shallow, non-reactive dish. Top the sardines with the garlic and parsley. If the dish is not large enough to accommodate all the sardines in a single layer, add a second layer on top of the first.

Pour the oil and the vinegar over the fish, until the mixture covers the sardines. Cover the dish with plastic film and place it in the refrigerator to marinate for two to three days before serving.

SUGGESTED ACCOMPANIMENT: *crusty bread.*

EDITOR'S NOTE: *Fresh anchovies or small sprats, no longer than 12 cm (5 inches), can be used instead of sardines.*

Soused Trout with Apple

Serves 4
Working time: about 45 minutes
Total time: about 2 hours and 30 minutes
(includes chilling)

Calories **120**
Protein **15g**
Cholesterol **30mg**
Total fat **3g**
Saturated fat **1g**
Sodium **100mg**

2	*trout, cleaned and scaled*	*2*
30 g	*fresh wholemeal breadcrumbs*	*1 oz*
½	*lemon, grated rind and juice*	*½*
2 tsp	*chopped fresh dill*	*2 tsp*
	freshly ground black pepper	
1	*small onion, thinly sliced*	*1*
1	*bay leaf*	*1*
3	*cloves*	*3*
1	*small blade mace*	*1*
4	*black peppercorns*	*4*
6 tbsp	*cider vinegar*	*6 tbsp*
1	*red dessert apple*	*1*
1	*green dessert apple*	*1*

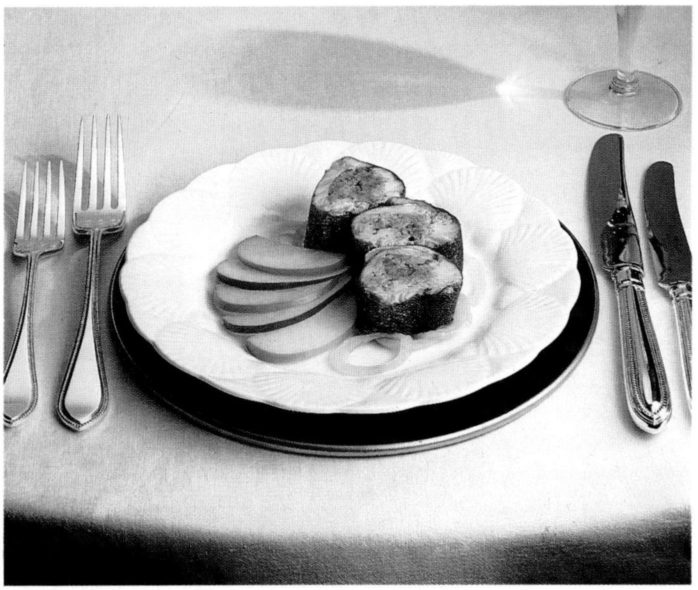

Preheat the oven to 190°C (375°F or Mark 5). Fillet the trout, following the directions below.

In a small bowl, combine the fresh breadcrumbs, the grated lemon rind and all but 1 teaspoon of the juice, the chopped dill, and some black pepper. Lay the trout fillets flat on the work surface, skin side down. Spoon a little of the breadcrumb mixture on each of the trout pieces and roll up the fish, starting from the tail end, to enclose the bread filling. Secure the stuffed rolls with cocktail sticks.

Arrange the onion slices in the base of an ovenproof dish. Add the bay leaf, cloves, mace and peppercorns, and arrange the trout in one layer on top of the onions and spices. Mix the cider vinegar with 6 tablespoons of water and pour this liquid over the fish. Cover the baking dish with foil and bake for 30 minutes. Remove the dish from the oven, let the fish rolls cool to room temperature, then refrigerate them in their cooking liquid for at least 1 hour before serving.

To serve the soused trout, remove the cocktail sticks and cut the fish rolls into 2.5 cm (1 inch) slices with a sharp knife. Core, halve and thinly slice the apples. Toss the slices in the remaining lemon juice to prevent discoloration. Serve the fish with the spiced onion from the baking dish and the apple slices.

EDITOR'S NOTE: *Fresh herring can be used instead of trout in this recipe, filleted in the same way.*

Gutting and Boning a Round Fish

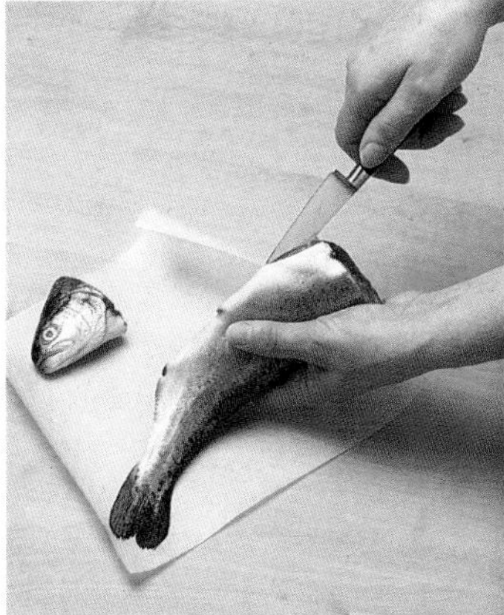

1 *GUTTING THE FISH. With a knife, cut off the head behind the last gill opening, then slit the belly open as far as the vent. Pull out and discard the viscera. Rinse out the cavity under cold running water.*

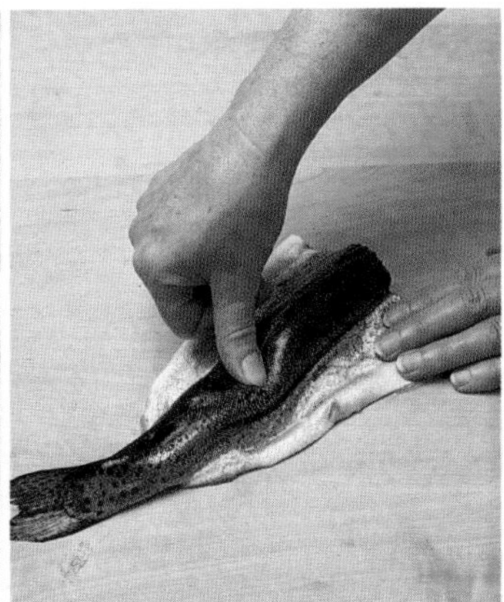

2 *RELEASING THE BACKBONE. On a work surface, place the fish belly down, spreading the rib cavity apart slightly. Run your thumb firmly along the backbone from head to tail to loosen it from the flesh.*

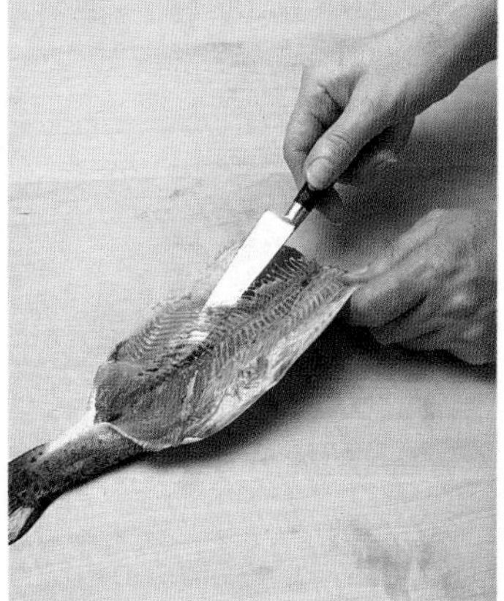

3 *FREEING THE RIB BONES. Turn the fish over and open it out: take care not to break the skin. Holding the fish at the head end, slide the knife blade between the ribs and flesh and ease the bones free.*

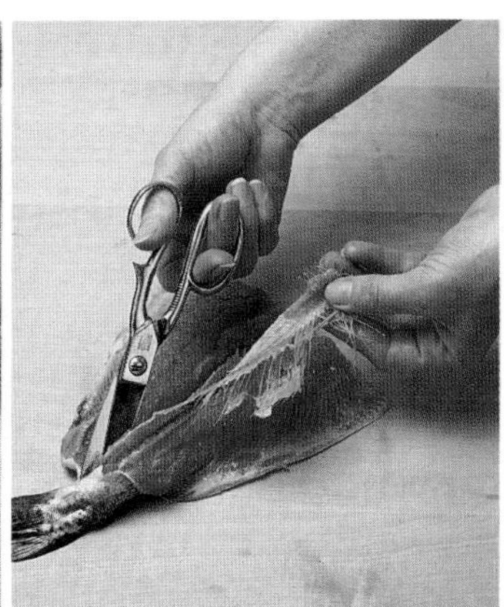

4 *REMOVING THE BACKBONE. Lift the backbone away from the flesh — the entire backbone with the ribs still attached should come easily. With scissors, snip off the backbone as close to the tail as possible.*

Macerated Mackerel

THE RICH, OILY FLESH OF MACKEREL IS ENHANCED BY PARTNERSHIP WITH TART FRUITS. HERE, THE JUICES OF APPLES AND LEMON OR LIME PROVIDE A PIQUANT MARINADE. BECAUSE THE MACKEREL IS NOT COOKED, ONLY THE FRESHEST FISH SHOULD BE USED.

Serves 6
Working time: about 20 minutes
Total time: 1 to 2 days (includes marinating)

Calories **210**
Protein **16g**
Cholesterol **40mg**
Total fat **7g**
Saturated fat **3g**
Sodium **370mg**

2	*mackerel (about 750 g/1½ lb), cleaned, skinned and filleted (page 43)*	*2*
1 tsp	*salt*	*1 tsp*
½ tsp	*caster sugar*	*½ tsp*
1 tsp	*coriander seeds, finely crushed*	*1 tsp*
2 tsp	*fresh lime or lemon juice*	*2 tsp*
4 tbsp	*apple juice*	*4 tbsp*
1	*red apple*	*1*
4	*red lollo lettuce leaves, washed, dried*	*4*
4	*small radicchio leaves, washed, dried*	*4*
2 tbsp	*coriander leaves*	*2 tbsp*
1 tbsp	*salad burnet (optional)*	*1 tbsp*
2 tsp	*sesame seeds*	*2 tsp*

Apple dressing		
3 tbsp	*apple juice*	*3 tbsp*
1 tsp	*virgin olive oil*	*1 tsp*
½ tsp	*fresh lime or lemon juice*	*½ tsp*
	white pepper	

Place two of the mackerel fillets in a shallow glass or ceramic dish. In a mortar, pound the salt, sugar and coriander seeds together. Spread half of this mixture over the fillets in the dish. Mix the lime juice or lemon juice with the apple juice and sprinkle 3 tablespoons of the blended juices over the fish.

Lay the two remaining fillets on top of the spice-coated mackerel. Spread on the rest of the salt, sugar and spice mixture, and spoon the remaining blended juices over the top. Cover the dish with plastic film, set a weighted board on top of the film, and put the fish in a cool place (not the refrigerator) to marinate for one to two days.

About an hour before serving, place six plates in the refrigerator to chill. Meanwhile, using a thin, flexible, sharp knife, cut the fillets diagonally into thin slices.

To prepare the dressing, place the apple juice and oil in a small bowl, and whisk them well. Stir in the lime or lemon juice and some white pepper.

Remove the chilled plates from the refrigerator and divide the mackerel slices among them, arranging the fish in a semi-circle on each plate. Core and thinly slice the apple. Tear the red lollo lettuce and radicchio leaves, and toss them lightly in half of the dressing together with the apple slices, coriander leaves and salad burnet, if using. Scatter the salad on the serving plates alongside the fish. Spoon the remaining dressing over the mackerel, sprinkle the fish with the sesame seeds and serve immediately.

Sweet-and-Sour Herring

Serves 8
Working time: about 20 minutes
Total time: about 6 hours (includes marinating)

Calories **150**
Protein **12g**
Cholesterolt **25mg**
Total fat **6g**
Saturated fat **1g**
Sodium **40mg**

¼ litre	*white wine vinegar*	*8 fl oz*
2.5 cm	*piece fresh ginger root, bruised with a pestle or a heavy knife, plus ½ tsp grated fresh ginger root*	*1 inch*
2	*bay leaves*	*2*
1	*lime, rind only*	*1*
1 tbsp	*sugar*	*1 tbsp*
¼ tsp	*allspice berries*	*¼ tsp*
½ tsp	*white pepper*	*½ tsp*
5	*herrings, boned and cut into 2.5 cm (1 inch) slices*	*5*
375 g	*fromage frais*	*13 oz*
3	*spring onions, chopped*	*3*
1 tbsp	*chopped chives*	*1 tbsp*
1	*red onion, cut into rings*	*1*

In a large saucepan, bring the wine vinegar and ¼ litre (8 fl oz) of water to the boil with the piece of ginger root, the bay leaves, lime rind, sugar, allspice berries and white pepper. Simmer the mixture for 5 minutes, then set it aside to cool for a few minutes. Place the herring fillets in a shallow non-reactive bowl, cover them with the spiced vinegar mixture, and marinate them in the refrigerator for 4 to 6 hours.

Remove the fillets from the marinade and wipe them dry with paper towels. In a mixing bowl, combine the *fromage frais*, grated ginger root, spring onions and chopped chives. Toss the fish in this mixture until it is thoroughly coated. Transfer the sauced herrings to a serving dish, garnish them with the red onion rings and serve immediately.

SUGGESTED ACCOMPANIMENT: *thinly sliced dark rye bread or pumpernickel.*

EDITOR'S NOTE: *To bone herrings, follow the technique for boning trout on page 43. Because the herrings are not cooked in this recipe, only the freshest fish should be used.*

Italian Seafood Salad

Serves 8
Working time: about 1 hour
Total time: about 4 hours (includes marinating)

Calories **120**
Protein **14g**
Cholesterol **100mg**
Total fat **6g**
Saturated fat **1g**
Sodium **155mg**

1½ tbsp	*virgin olive oil*	*1½ tbsp*
1	*onion, chopped*	*1*
500 g	*squid, cleaned and rinsed thoroughly, pouches cut into rings, wings sliced into strips, tentacles left whole*	*1 lb*
1	*garlic clove, crushed*	*1*
1 tbsp	*fresh lemon juice*	*1 tbsp*
1 tbsp	*chopped parsley*	*1 tbsp*
¼ tsp	*salt*	*¼ tsp*
	freshly ground black pepper	
175 g	*peeled prawns, halved lengthwise and deveined*	*6 oz*
3	*sticks celery, thinly sliced*	*3*
250 g	*round or other lettuce, washed, dried and shredded*	*8 oz*
1	*red onion, thinly sliced*	*1*
2	*lemons, cut into wedges*	*2*

In a saucepan, heat ½ tablespoon of the oil, add the onion and cook it gently until it is softened, but not browned — 6 to 8 minutes. Add the prepared squid and the garlic, cover the saucepan and cook gently until the squid is very tender — 15 to 20 minutes. Drain the squid in a colander set over a bowl, and return the squid juices to the saucepan; boil the liquid over high heat until it is reduced by three quarters. Whisk the remaining oil, the lemon juice, parsley, salt and some freshly ground black pepper into the squid juices to make a marinade.

Put the cooked squid and the prawns into a bowl, pour the marinade over them and mix the seafood until it is well coated. Cover the mixture and place it in the refrigerator to marinate for at least 3 hours.

Just before serving, mix the sliced celery into the seafood. Serve the salad on a bed of shredded lettuce garnished with a few red onion rings, and accompanied by the lemon wedges.

EDITOR'S NOTE: *If you are using baby squid in this recipe, they will cook more rapidly. Test them for tenderness after cooking for about 5 minutes.*

Rainbow Trout with Yogurt Dressing

THIS PROTEIN-RICH SALAD MAKES A SUBSTANTIAL STARTER TO PRECEDE A LIGHT, MEATLESS MAIN COURSE SUCH AS PASTA OR A VEGETABLE STEW.

Serves 6
Working time: about 20 minutes
Total time: about 30 minutes

Calories **165**
Protein **18g**
Cholesterol **35mg**
Total fat **9g**
Saturated fat **2g**
Sodium **155mg**

3	*rainbow trout (about 750 g/1½ lb), cleaned*	*3*
4 tbsp	*white wine*	*4 tbsp*
250 g	*mixed washed and dried salad leaves, herbs and edible flowers, such as rocket, curly endive, oakleaf lettuce, chervil and borage flowers*	*8 oz*
17.5 cl	*plain low-fat yogurt*	*6 fl oz*
½	*lemon, juice only*	*½*
2 tsp	*finely chopped fresh dill*	*2 tsp*
2 tbsp	*virgin olive oil*	*2 tbsp*
⅛ tsp	*salt*	*⅛ tsp*
	freshly ground black pepper	

Preheat the oven to 200°C (400°F or Mark 6). Place the three trout on a rectangle of foil measuring approximately 35 by 30 cm (14 by 12 inches). Sprinkle the white wine over the fish, wrap them securely in the foil, and bake them in the oven for 15 minutes. Remove the trout from the foil and set them aside to cool.

Arrange the salad leaves and flowers on a large platter or on individual serving plates. To prepare the dressing, mix the yogurt, lemon juice, dill, oil, salt and some pepper in a small bowl.

When the fish is cool enough to handle, skin and fillet it, and break the flesh into bite-sized pieces.

Just before serving, dribble the yogurt dressing over the leaves and flowers and arrange the trout pieces on top of the salad.

EDITOR'S NOTE: *For the use of flowers in salads, see page 18.*

Barquettes with Three Fillings

Serves 6
Working time: about 1 hour
Total time: about 2 hours and 15 minutes (includes chilling)

Calories **260**
Protein **12g**
Cholesterol **40mg**
Total fat **15g**
Saturated fat **4g**
Sodium **490mg**

125 g	*plain flour*	*4 oz*
⅛ tsp	*salt*	*⅛ tsp*
60 g	*polyunsaturated margarine*	*2 oz*
½	*beaten egg*	*½*
	Smoked mackerel mousse	
175 g	*smoked mackerel fillet, skinned and any bones removed*	*6 oz*
15 g	*polyunsaturated margarine*	*½ oz*
¼ tsp	*salt*	*¼ tsp*
	freshly ground black pepper	
2 tsp	*fresh lemon juice*	*2 tsp*
3	*thin slices of lemon, cut into quarters*	*3*
	Asparagus cream	
175 g	*thin asparagus spears, trimmed*	*6 oz*
1 tbsp	*soured cream*	*1 tbsp*
⅛ tsp	*salt*	*⅛ tsp*
	freshly ground black pepper	
	Prawn salad	
1 tsp	*virgin olive oil*	*1 tsp*
1 tsp	*wine vinegar*	*1 tsp*
1	*garlic clove, crushed*	*1*
2 tsp	*finely chopped parsley*	*2 tsp*
	freshly ground black pepper	
90 g	*peeled prawns*	*3 oz*
2	*lettuce leaves, washed, dried and shredded*	*2*

To make the pastry, sift the flour and salt into a mixing bowl. Rub the margarine into the flour until the mixture resembles fine breadcrumbs. Mix the dry ingredients together with the beaten egg and 1 to 2 tablespoons of cold water to make a firm dough.

On a floured surface, roll the dough out very thinly. Cut it into strips long and wide enough to line eighteen 9.5 cm (3¾ inch) long barquette tins. (If you do not have that many tins, bake the pastry cases in batches.) Prick the dough all over with a fork, then place the tins on a baking sheet and refrigerate for 30 minutes. Preheat the oven to 220°C (425°F or Mark 7).

Bake the pastry cases until they are very lightly browned — 10 to 15 minutes. Carefully remove the pastry cases from the tins and transfer them to a wire rack to cool while you prepare the three fillings.

To make the smoked mackerel mousse, flake the fish and put it into a food processor or blender with the margarine, salt, some pepper and the lemon juice. Blend until the mixture is smooth and creamy. Spoon the filling into a small bowl, cover it with plastic film and place it in the refrigerator to chill.

To make the asparagus cream, boil the asparagus in 2.5 cm (1 inch) of water in a frying pan, until tender — about 3 minutes. Drain the spears and refresh them under cold running water. When cool, remove the tips from six of the spears and set them aside to use as a garnish. Finely chop the remaining asparagus and put it in a small bowl. Add the soured cream, salt and some pepper, and mix well. Cover the filling with plastic film and place it in the refrigerator.

To make the prawn salad, put the oil, vinegar, garlic and parsley into a small bowl, season with pepper and stir well. Mix the prawns with this dressing, cover with plastic film and refrigerate with the two other fillings. Chill all three fillings for at least 1 hour.

To complete the barquettes, remove the fillings from the refrigerator about 20 to 30 minutes before serving. Spoon the smoked mackerel mousse into six boats and garnish with the lemon pieces. Fill another six boats with the asparagus cream and top with the reserved asparagus tips. Fill the remaining boats with a little shredded lettuce, topped with the prawns.

Sole and Asparagus Tartlets

Serves 6
Working time: about 1 hour
Total time: about 3 hours (includes chilling)

Calories **240**
Protein **12g**
Cholesterol **50mg**
Total fat **13g**
Saturated fat **3g**
Sodium **260mg**

175 g	*skinned sole fillets*	*6 oz*
1	*egg white*	*1*
150 g	*plus 2 tbsp thick Greek yogurt*	*5 oz*
¼ tsp	*salt*	*¼ tsp*
	freshly ground black pepper	
250 g	*asparagus, trimmed, peeled and thinly sliced*	*8 oz*
45 g	*smoked salmon, cut into fine strips*	*1½ oz*
2 tsp	*finely cut chives*	*2 tsp*
	thinly sliced cucumber, for garnish	
	Tartlet shells	
125 g	*plain flour*	*4 oz*
⅛ tsp	*salt*	*⅛ tsp*
60 g	*polyunsaturated margarine*	*2 oz*
1	*egg yolk*	*1*

To prepare the filling, place the sole fillets and egg white in a food processor and process them until they form a smooth paste. Set a nylon sieve over a bowl, and work the paste through the sieve to remove any coarse fibres. Cover the bowl with plastic film and refrigerate the sole and egg mixture while you prepare the tartlet shells.

To make the pastry, sift the flour and salt into a mixing bowl. Rub the margarine into the flour until the mixture resembles fine breadcrumbs; make a well in the centre. Pour the egg yolk and 1 tablespoon of water into the well and mix the ingredients, using a table knife or your hands, until a firm dough is formed.

Knead the dough on a lightly floured surface, then roll the dough out thinly. Cut out six rounds of dough measuring about 12.5 cm (5 inches) in diameter. Line six 10 cm (4 inch) fluted tartlet tins with the dough, pressing it well into the flutes and trimming the edges. Prick the pastry lightly with a fork, and refrigerate it for 30 minutes. Meanwhile, preheat the oven to 220°C (425°F or Mark 7).

Remove the chilled sole from the refrigerator. Gradually beat in 12.5 cl (4 fl oz) of the yogurt, the salt and some pepper. Cover the fish mixture with plastic film and return it to the refrigerator.

Bring a saucepan of water to the boil and cook the sliced asparagus until it is tender — 1 to 2 minutes. Pour the asparagus into a colander, refresh it under cold running water and drain it well.

Place the chilled pastry shells on a baking sheet and bake them for 10 minutes. Remove them from the oven and reduce the oven temperature to 180°C (350°F or Mark 4). Divide the asparagus equally among the pastry cases, arranging the pieces neatly in the bottom of each one. Spoon the sole mixture on top of the asparagus, spreading it evenly. Return the tartlets to the oven and cook them until the sole mixture is very lightly set — 6 to 8 minutes.

Remove the tartlets from the oven and set them aside to cool. When they are cold enough to handle, carefully lift them from their tins, place them on a tray and cover with foil. Refrigerate the tartlets until they are well chilled — about 2 hours.

Just before serving, spread the remaining yogurt in a thin layer evenly over the top of each tartlet, arrange strips of smoked salmon around its edges, and sprinkle with the chives.

Serve the tartlets on individual plates, garnished with thinly sliced cucumber.

Phyllo Flowers with a Prawn-Tomato Filling

PAPER-THIN PHYLLO SHEETS, DRAPED OVER MOULDS WITHOUT OIL OR BUTTER, MAKE LIGHT, CRISP CASES FOR MOIST FILLINGS.

Serves 6
Working time: about 30 minutes
Total time: about 50 minutes

Calories **55**
Protein **5g**
Cholesterol **80mg**
Total fat **1g**
Saturated fat **0g**
Sodium **40mg**

3	*sheets phyllo pastry, each about 30 cm (12 inches) square*	3
60 g	*fromage frais*	2 oz
½ tsp	*tomato paste*	½ tsp
1	*garlic clove, crushed*	1
¼ tsp	*salt*	¼ tsp
	freshly ground black pepper	
2	*tomatoes, skinned, halved and seeded (page 10)*	2
125 g	*peeled cooked prawns*	4 oz
2 tsp	*finely chopped dill or fennel*	2 tsp
6	*dill or fennel sprigs, for garnish*	6

Preheat the oven to 190°C (375°F or Mark 5). Cut the phyllo sheets into 9 cm (3½ inch) squares. Stack the squares and cover them with a cloth to keep them from drying out.

Drape four squares of phyllo over a small brioche or dariole mould, giving the mould a quarter turn after you put on each square so that the points of the squares resemble a flower. Make five more flowers in the same way. Arrange them on a baking sheet and bake them in the oven until the pastry is golden-brown — 6 to 8 minutes.

In a small bowl, combine the *fromage frais* with the tomato paste, the garlic, the salt and some pepper. Set a small strainer over the bowl, place the tomato halves in the strainer and squeeze them gently so their juice falls into the *fromage frais*. Remove the tomato flesh from the sieve and cut it into strips with a sharp knife. Stir the tomato strips and the prawns into the *fromage frais* mixture.

Unmould the phyllo flowers when they have cooled, using a sharp knife to ease the baked pastry gently off the moulds. With a teaspoon, fill the phyllo flowers with the prawn and tomato mixture. Sprinkle them with the chopped dill or fennel and serve immediately, garnished with the sprigs of fennel or dill.

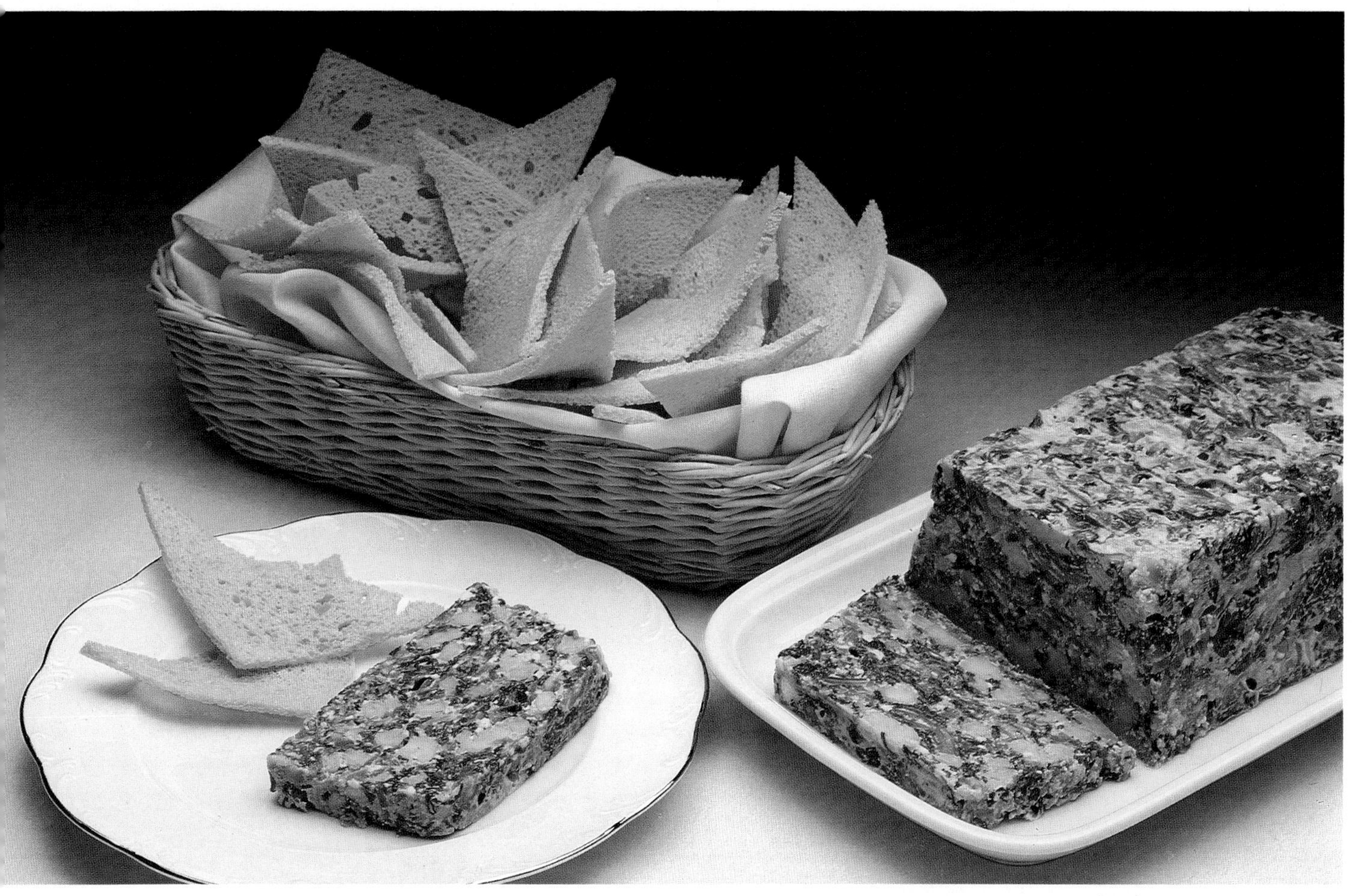

Marbled Seafood Terrine

Serves 8
Working time: about 45 minutes
Total time: about 4 hours (includes cooling)

Calories **170**
Protein **17g**
Cholesterol **70mg**
Total fat **9g**
Saturated fat **2g**
Sodium **70mg**

2 tbsp	*virgin olive oil*	*2 tbsp*
1	*large onion, finely chopped*	*1*
1	*garlic clove, finely chopped*	*1*
1 kg	*mixed Batavian endive, Chinese cabbage, lettuce and spinach leaves, washed, dried and finely shredded*	*2 lb*
250 g	*low-fat ricotta cheese*	*8 oz*
1	*egg*	*1*
2	*egg whites*	*2*
½ tsp	*ground coriander*	*½ tsp*
1 tsp	*grated lemon rind*	*1 tsp*
½ tsp	*salt*	*½ tsp*
	freshly ground black pepper	
175 g	*peeled cooked prawns*	*6 oz*
175 g	*pink trout fillets, boned (page 43), skinned and cut into 1 cm (½ inch) strips*	*6 oz*

Heat the oil in a large saucepan and cook the onion and garlic over low heat, stirring occasionally, until they are softened — about 5 minutes. Add as many of the shredded greens as the pan will hold, then cover the pan and cook the leaves for a few seconds until they begin to wilt; add the remaining greens and cook, covered, until they too are wilting. Uncover the pan and continue cooking, stirring from time to time, until the greens are tender — about 10 minutes.

Tip the vegetables into a colander and drain them thoroughly, pressing out the excess liquid with the back of a wooden spoon.

Preheat the oven to 180°C (350°F or Mark 4).

In a large bowl, mash the ricotta with a wooden spoon. Beat in the egg, egg whites, coriander, lemon rind, salt and some pepper. Add the drained greens, mix the ingredients until they are thoroughly blended, then fold in the prawns and the strips of trout.

Line the bottom of a 22 by 11 cm (9 by 4½ inch) terrine or loaf tin with a piece of dampened greaseproof paper. Spoon the seafood mixture on to the paper, spreading it evenly. Place the terrine in a roasting tin; fill the larger vessel with enough hot water to come half way up the sides of the terrine. Bake until the seafood mixture is set — about 1 hour.

Remove the terrine from the water bath and leave it in a cool place, but not in the refrigerator. When it is cold, unmould it on to a platter, peel off the paper and slice the terrine with a very sharp knife.

SUGGESTED ACCOMPANIMENT: *Melba toast.*

Fish and Watercress Terrine with Spring Onion Sauce

IT IS ESSENTIAL THAT THE INGREDIENTS BE WELL CHILLED FOR THE FISH MIXTURE TO HOLD TOGETHER. IF THE WEATHER IS WARM, CHILL THE FOOD PROCESSOR CONTAINER AND THE BLADE BEFORE USING.

Serves 8
Working time: about 30 minutes
Total time: about 4 hours (includes chilling)

Calories **165**
Protein **18g**
Cholesterol **40mg**
Total fat **6g**
Saturated fat **1g**
Sodium **230mg**

500 g	*skinned white fish fillets, such as cod, haddock, or whiting*	*1 lb*
1	*lemon, grated rind and half the juice*	*1*
4 drops	*Tabasco sauce*	*4 drops*
½ tsp	*salt*	*½ tsp*
	white pepper	
2	*egg whites*	*2*
300 g	*fromage frais*	*10 oz*
2	*bunches watercress, thick stems removed*	*2*
	lettuce leaves, for garnish	
	Spring onion sauce	
250 g	*firm tofu, drained*	*8 oz*
3 tbsp	*fresh lemon juice*	*3 tbsp*
2 tbsp	*virgin olive oil*	*2 tbsp*
3	*spring onions, coarsely chopped*	*3*
½	*small garlic clove*	*½*
¼ tsp	*salt*	*¼ tsp*
	freshly ground black pepper	

Cut the fish fillets into 2.5 cm (1 inch) cubes, put them in a food processor, and blend them briefly until they form a smooth purée. Add the lemon rind and juice, the Tabasco sauce, the salt, some pepper and one of the egg whites. Blend until the ingredients are thoroughly mixed, then add the second egg white and blend again for a few seconds. Gradually blend in 250 g (8 oz) of the *fromage frais*. When the fish mixture is smooth and well combined, turn it into a bowl. Cover the fish purée with plastic film and refrigerate it while you make the watercress purée.

Preheat the oven to 180°C (350°F or Mark 4).

Blanch the watercress in a pan of boiling water for 30 seconds. Drain it in a colander, refresh it under cold running water, then drain it again. When the watercress is cool enough to handle, squeeze it to remove all excess water.

Put the watercress in the food processor, add the remaining *fromage frais*, and blend them to a smooth purée. Add about one quarter of the fish mixture and blend again until the ingredients are well combined.

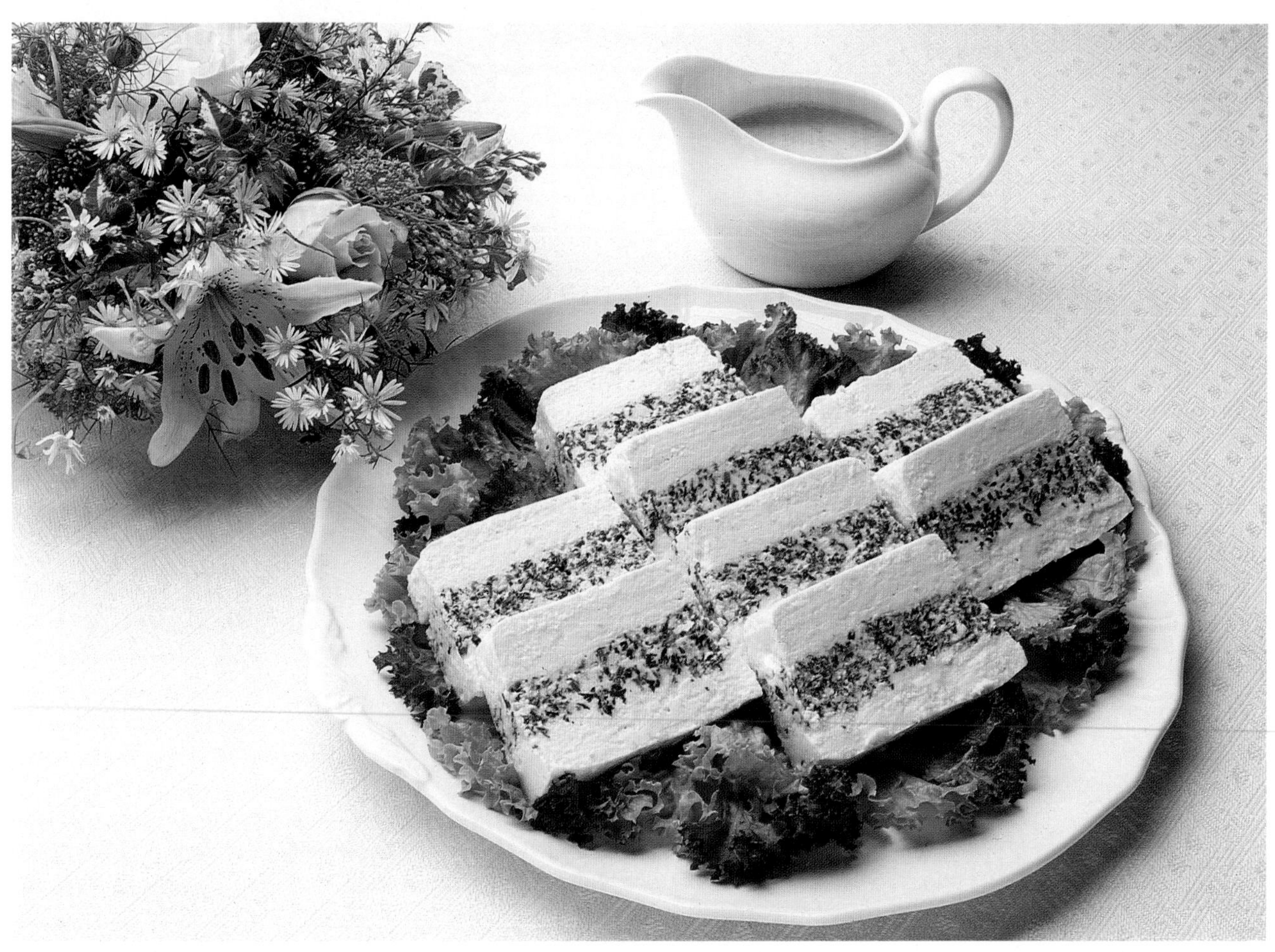

Line the bottom of a 20 by 10 by 7.5 cm (8 by 4 by 3 inch) terrine or loaf tin with a piece of dampened greaseproof paper. Put half the fish mixture into the terrine and spread it evenly. Cover with the watercress mixture, spreading it gently into an even layer. Top the watercress with the remaining fish, smoothing it down with a wooden spoon or a palette knife.

Place the terrine on a rack in a larger pan, and pour in enough hot water to come half way up the sides of the terrine. Bake the terrine uncovered until it is set — 20 to 30 minutes. The mixture inside will have drawn away slightly from the sides of the pan.

Remove the terrine from the water. Carefully pour off the liquid that has been released by the *fromage frais.* Let the terrine cool slightly, then chill it in the refrigerator until serving time.

To make the sauce, put all the ingredients in a food processor and blend them until they are smooth and well combined. Turn the sauce into a bowl, cover it with plastic film and chill it in the refrigerator.

When you are ready to serve the terrine, unmould it on to a board and cut it into slices with a sharp knife. Place the lettuce on a serving platter and arrange the sliced terrine on the bed of leaves. Stir the sauce well to mix in any liquid that has separated out during chilling, and serve the sauce with the terrine.

Jellied Salmon with Dill and Saffron

Serves 4
Working time: about 45 minutes
Total time: about 3 hours (includes chilling and setting)

Calories **125**
Protein **14g**
Cholesterol **45mg**
Total fat **8g**
Saturated fat **2g**
Sodium **70mg**

250 g	*salmon fillet, thoroughly boned*	*8 oz*
⅛ tsp	*saffron threads, soaked for 5 minutes in 1 tbsp hot water*	*⅛ tsp*
1 tbsp	*fresh lime juice*	*1 tbsp*
4	*leaves gelatine, soaked in 2 to 3 tbsp cold water for 5 minutes*	*4*
1 tbsp	*fresh dill, torn into pieces*	*1 tbsp*
1 tbsp	*parsley leaves, torn into pieces*	*1 tbsp*
½	*cucumber, peeled and sliced*	*½*
1 tsp	*red peppercorns*	*1 tsp*
	Court-bouillon	
2	*fresh thyme sprigs*	*2*
4	*parsley stems*	*4*
1	*bay leaf*	*1*
12.5 cl	*white wine*	*4 fl oz*
1	*small carrot, sliced*	*1*
½	*small onion*	*½*

For the court-bouillon, first make a bouquet garni by tying together the thyme, parsley stems and bay leaf. Put the bouquet garni in a saucepan with ¼ litre (8 fl oz) of water, the wine, carrot and onion. Bring to the boil, then simmer for about 30 minutes over low heat. Strain the court-bouillon through a sieve, discarding the bouquet garni and the vegetables.

Place the salmon in a saucepan with the strained court-bouillon. Bring the liquid to the boil and simmer it for 5 minutes. Remove the salmon from the court-bouillon with a slotted spoon, cut it into strips about 1 cm (½ inch) wide, and set it aside to cool while you prepare the aspic.

Strain the court-bouillon a second time, adding water, if necessary, to make it up to 30 cl (½ pint) of liquid. Strain the saffron water and add it to the court-bouillon together with the lime juice and the softened gelatine. Stir until the gelatine is completely dissolved.

Assemble four ramekin dishes. Place some torn herbs and two or three of the cucumber slices in the bottom of each ramekin. Add a layer of salmon pieces, more torn herbs and one or two of the red peppercorns. Top the fish with another layer of cucumber, and continue adding fish, herbs and cucumber slices, interspersed with an occasional peppercorn, until you have nearly filled the ramekins. Top each assemblage with two or three overlapping cucumber slices.

Spoon the court-bouillon gently over each dish, and float three or four peppercorns on top. Set the moulds aside for 15 minutes to let the liquid settle. If necessary, top up the ramekins with more court-bouillon; the contents should be completely covered by the liquid.

Place the dishes in the refrigerator until the aspic sets — about 2 hours. While the aspic is setting, put four small serving plates in the refrigerator to chill.

At serving time, dip the base of the ramekins into hot water for 2 seconds to loosen the aspic — no longer, lest the moulds collapse — then turn out the moulds on to the chilled plates. Serve immediately.

Chicken with a Cranberry-Walnut Vinaigrette

THIS RECIPE CAN BE MADE WITH EITHER POACHED OR ROASTED CHICKEN. THE PEPPERY FLAVOUR OF THE WATERCRESS AND CHICORY LEAVES OFFSETS THE SWEETNESS OF THE SAUCE.

Serves 4
Working (and total) time: about 20 minutes

Calories **225**
Protein **18g**
Cholesterol **45mg**
Total fat **15g**
Saturated fat **3g**
Sodium **105mg**

30 g	*cranberries*	*1 oz*
2 tsp	*clear honey*	*2 tsp*
1 tbsp	*wine vinegar*	*1 tbsp*
1 tsp	*Dijon mustard*	*1 tsp*
⅛ tsp	*salt*	*⅛ tsp*
	freshly ground black pepper	
3 tbsp	*walnut oil*	*3 tbsp*
8	*radicchio leaves, washed and dried, torn into small pieces*	*8*
1	*head of chicory, sliced diagonally into 1 cm (1/2 inch) slices*	*1*
15 g	*shelled walnuts, roughly chopped*	*½ oz*
½	*bunch watercress, washed, dried, divided into sprigs, thick stems discarded*	*½*
12	*slices cooked chicken breast meat (about 250 g/8 oz)*	*12*

Place the cranberries, the honey and 2 teaspoons of water in a small saucepan and cook them gently for 3 to 4 minutes. Cool the fruit mixture slightly and pass it through a sieve set over a bowl.

In a small bowl, combine the vinegar, mustard, salt and some freshly ground black pepper. Stir in the walnut oil until the ingredients are thoroughly blended. Set half of this dressing aside and mix the rest with the cranberry purée.

In a bowl, toss the radicchio leaves, chicory slices, chopped walnuts and watercress with the reserved walnut-oil dressing. Transfer the dressed salad to four individual serving plates.

Arrange the sliced chicken on each bed of salad. Pour the cranberry-walnut vinaigrette over the chicken slices just before serving.

Cold Beef Salad

POACHING BEEF WITH AROMATIC HERBS AND VEGETABLES PRODUCES MOIST, TENDER AND FLAVOURFUL MEAT, AND THE RESULTING BEEF BROTH MAKES A DELICIOUS STOCK.

Serves 6
Working time: about 20 minutes
Total time: about 3 hours and 30 minutes (includes cooling)

Calories **120**
Protein **13g**
Cholesterol **30mg**
Total fat **7g**
Saturated fat **3g**
Sodium **40mg**

300 g	*topside or silverside of beef, trimmed of fat*	*10 oz*
1	*onion*	*1*
3	*cloves*	*3*
1	*bay leaf*	*1*
2.5 cm	*piece fresh ginger root, bruised with a pestle or a heavy knife*	*1 inch*
1	*leek, washed and trimmed*	*1*
2	*small carrots, washed*	*2*
1	*sweet red pepper, skinned and seeded (page 11), cut into long thin strips*	*1*
2	*black olives, stoned, sliced into rings*	*2*
	mustard and cress or alfalfa sprouts, for garnish	
	Mustard dressing	
1 tsp	*Dijon mustard*	*1 tsp*
⅛ tsp	*paprika*	*⅛ tsp*
1 tbsp	*finely cut chives*	*1 tbsp*
250 g	*thick Greek yogurt*	*8 oz*

Place the beef in a saucepan, cover with about 90 cl (1½ pints) of water and bring it to the boil. Simmer for 10 minutes, removing the grey scum that rises to the surface of the liquid. Stud the onion with the cloves. When the froth is clear, add the aromatics — the bay leaf, ginger root, clove-studded onion, leek and carrots. Cover the saucepan, reduce the heat to medium low, and simmer the meat for 20 minutes.

Remove the pan from the heat, keep it covered, and let the beef cool in its cooking liquid for 2 to 3 hours. Cut the beef into six slices; the meat should still be moist and pink in the centre.

Arrange the beef on a platter and top each slice with three strips of sweet red pepper. Garnish with the sliced olives and the mustard and cress.

To make the dressing, place the mustard, paprika, chives and yogurt in a small bowl and stir to mix. Serve the salad with the dressing on the side.

EDITOR'S NOTE: *Leftover roast or boiled beef can be used in place of the poached beef in this recipe.*

Raw Beef Salad

CHILLING THE BEEF IN THE FREEZER FOR A BRIEF PERIOD FIRMS IT, MAKING IT POSSIBLE TO CUT THE MEAT INTO VERY THIN SLICES.

Serves 4
Working time: about 25 minutes
Total time: about 1 hour (includes chilling)

Calories **120**
Protein **12g**
Cholesterol **30mg**
Total fat **6g**
Saturated fat **3g**
Sodium **50mg**

75 g	*young leeks, white and green parts, cut into fine strips about 3 cm (1¼ inches) long*	*2½ oz*
175 g	*fillet of beef, trimmed of all fat, wrapped in plastic film and chilled in the freezer for 30 minutes*	*6 oz*
8	*small spinach or rocket leaves, washed and dried*	*8*
75 g	*young carrots, cut into fine strips about 3 cm (1¼ inches) long*	*2½ oz*
¼	*cucumber, seeds removed, cut into thin strips with a vegetable peeler*	*¼*
4	*radishes, trimmed and cut into thin rounds*	*4*
1	*lemon, cut into thin wedges*	*1*
	Horseradish dressing	
1 tsp	*prepared horseradish*	*1 tsp*
75 g	*thick Greek yogurt*	*2½ oz*

First make the dressing. In a small bowl, blend the horseradish into the yogurt. Cover the sauce with plastic film and place it in the refrigerator to chill.

Blanch the leek strips for 10 seconds in boiling water, drain them in a colander and refresh them in cold water. Dry them thoroughly on kitchen paper.

Remove the fillet of beef from the freezer. Using a long, sharp, flexible knife or a meat slicing machine, cut the fillet into very thin slices. Arrange the meat on four chilled plates.

Assemble the spinach or rocket, the carrots, the blanched leeks, the cucumber and the radishes in separate piles round the sliced beef. Divide the dressing among the plates, and serve the salad immediately with the lemon wedges.

Pears with Prosciutto

Serves 4
Working time: about 15 minutes
Total time: about 25 minutes

Calories **55**
Protein **3g**
Cholesterol **10mg**
Total fat **5g**
Saturated fat **1g**
Sodium **195mg**

4	*ripe pears*	4
125 g	*curly endive, washed and dried*	4 oz
1	*bunch watercress, stems removed, leaves washed and dried*	1
4	*slices prosciutto (about 60 g/2 oz), halved lengthwise*	4
	Lemon dressing	
1 tbsp	*virgin olive oil*	1 tbsp
2 tsp	*fresh lemon juice*	2 tsp
	freshly ground black pepper	
2 tsp	*chopped parsley*	2 tsp

To make the dressing, put the olive oil and the lemon juice in a small bowl, stir with a fork to blend thoroughly, and stir in some black pepper and the chopped parsley. Peel, quarter and core the pears, and toss them gently in the dressing to coat them thoroughly. Leave them to steep for 10 minutes.

Arrange the curly endive and the watercress leaves on four serving plates and top them with the prosciutto and the fruit. Sprinkle any remaining dressing over the salad and serve it immediately.

2 *Crêpes prepared with a skimmed-milk batter envelop a piquant filling of crab meat and cucumber, spiked with chopped onion and fresh ginger (recipe, page 83).*

Hot First Courses

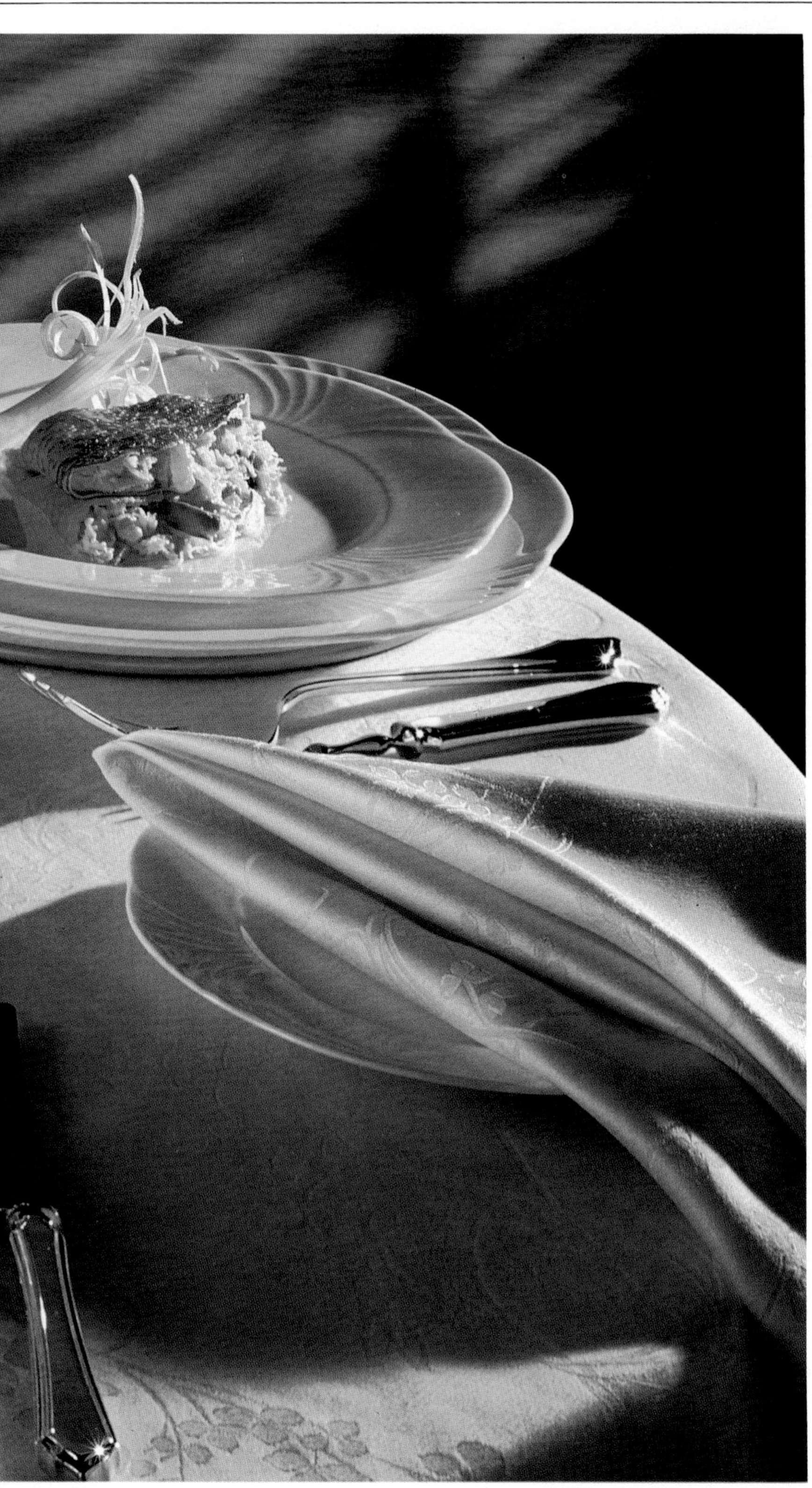

For guests who have braved the elements on a cold winter evening to travel to your home, the finest welcome you can provide is a hot hors-d'oeuvre straight from the oven or pan. A parchment packet, slit with a knife, releases the fragrance of the delicacies that have steamed inside it; a soufflé rises golden above the rim of its dish; brochettes of marinated duck sizzle on their plates. Appetite is whetted, conversation aroused, and the evening is already suffused with warmth and enjoyment.

Wintry weather is not the only factor that may lead you to prefer a hot hors-d'oeuvre to a cold one. A light or cold main course invites indulgence in a rich, hot hors-d'oeuvre, such as a warm salad of pigeon breasts that have been steeped in a Madeira-flavoured vinaigrette and tossed with wild mushrooms *(page 110)*. Other filling hors-d'oeuvre include risottos *(pages 72-73)*, shortcrust tartlets and crêpes stuffed with savoury fillings.

A hot hors-d'oeuvre may also precede a substantial hot main course, provided you plan the meal to offer a contrast of ingredients, textures and cooking methods. Before a plain roast, offer a sauced or dressed hors-d'oeuvre, such as asparagus with tarragon dressing *(page 60)* or seafood wonton with mango and ginger sauce *(page 96)*. If the main course is rich or creamy, choose a simple grilled, baked or steamed first course, such as the chicken and mango brochettes on page 109, or the stuffed vine leaves on page 70. If the main course is a complex assemblage of ingredients, select a less elaborate first course, such as the grilled goat cheese rounds on page 81, or the miniature beef meatballs on page 119.

Whichever your final choice, the ingredients and cooking method in every recipe in this chapter have been carefully planned to keep fat, calories and cholesterol low. In addition, step-by-step photographs throughout the chapter illustrate techniques that will expand any cook's repertoire of hors-d'oeuvre. These make light work of the creation of soufflés, the carving of bread cases, the formation of airy mixtures of seafood or poultry into elegant, oval quenelles, and the crafting of Middle-Eastern pastries, Chinese dumplings and other enticing preludes to a meal.

Asparagus with Tarragon Dressing

Serves 4
Working (and total) time: about 20 minutes

Calories **85**
Protein **3g**
Cholesterol **0mg**
Total fat **8g**
Saturated fat **1g**
Sodium **100mg**

500 g	*fresh asparagus, stalks trimmed and peeled to about 2.5 cm (1 inch) below the tips*	*1 lb*
1 tbsp	*fresh lemon juice*	*1 tbsp*
¼ tsp	*salt*	*¼ tsp*
	white pepper	
2 tbsp	*virgin olive oil*	*2 tbsp*
1 tbsp	*chopped fresh tarragon*	*1 tbsp*

To cook the asparagus, pour water into a large frying pan to a depth of 2.5 cm (1 inch), and bring the liquid to the boil. Line up the asparagus on the bottom of the pan, with all the tips facing in one direction. Position the pan so the thicker ends of the stalks lie over the centre of the heat source. Cook the asparagus until it is tender but still crisp — about 5 to 7 minutes.

While the spears are cooking, make the dressing. Mix together the lemon juice, the salt and some white pepper in a small bowl. When the salt has dissolved, whisk in the olive oil.

With a fish slice, lift the asparagus gently out of the water, place it in a colander and refresh it briefly under cold running water. Drain the asparagus a second time and pat it dry with a clean tea towel. Arrange the spears on individual warmed dishes, spoon the dressing over them and sprinkle with the chopped tarragon.

EDITOR'S NOTE: *Peeling the asparagus ensures that the stalks cook at the same rate as the tender tips.*

Parcels of Spring Vegetables with Lemon Butter

Serves 4
Working time: about 40 minutes
Total time: about 1 hour

Calories **70**
Protein **3g**
Cholesterol **20mg**
Total fat **6g**
Saturated fat **4g**
Sodium **70mg**

16	*small young carrots about 9 cm (3½ inches) long, scraped, with about 4 cm (1½ inches) of green tops retained*	*16*
150 g	*mange-tout, topped and tailed, strings removed*	*5 oz*
20	*thin asparagus spears, trimmed*	*20*
12	*spring onions, trimmed and cut into 10 cm (4 inch) lengths*	*12*
½	*sweet yellow pepper, seeded, deribbed and cut into thin strips*	*½*
4 tsp	*thinly cut chives*	*4 tsp*
4 tsp	*chopped fresh chervil*	*4 tsp*
4 tsp	*chopped fresh tarragon*	*4 tsp*
	Lemon butter	
30 g	*unsalted butter, softened*	*1 oz*
1 tsp	*grated lemon rind*	*1 tsp*
1 tsp	*fresh lemon juice*	*1 tsp*
⅛ tsp	*salt*	*⅛ tsp*
	freshly ground black pepper	

In a small bowl, mix together all the ingredients for the lemon butter, cover the bowl with plastic film and place it in the refrigerator to chill. Preheat the oven to 220°C (425°F or Mark 7).

Pour enough water into a saucepan to fill it about 2.5 cm (1 inch) deep. Put a steamer in the pan and bring the water to the boil. Add the carrots, cover them tightly and steam them until they are partially cooked, but still firm — about 8 minutes. Drain them in a colander and transfer them to a large bowl. Toss in the mange-tout, asparagus, spring onions and pepper.

Cut out four circles about 25 cm (10 inches) in diameter from parchment paper. Fold each circle in half, crease the parchment, then open it out. Brush each circle lightly with oil.

Spoon a quarter of the vegetables on to a paper circle, keeping the filling to one side of the crease and forming a neat rectangle lying parallel to the fold. Dot the vegetables with a little lemon butter, sprinkle them with 1 teaspoon of each of the herbs and fold over the other half of the paper to enclose the filling.

Crimp the edges of the paper, in overlapping double folds, until the package is sealed. Fill and seal the remaining three parcels in the same way.

Brush the outside of the packages with a little oil, to prevent the paper from becoming soggy in the oven. Place the parcels on a baking sheet and bake them in the oven for 12 minutes. Serve the sealed packets on individual plates and let the diners pierce and cut open their own parcels to savour the aroma.

Celeriac Timbales with Wild Mushrooms and Madeira Sauce

THE GNARLED CELERIAC, WITH ITS SUBTLE FLAVOUR REMINISCENT OF CELERY, IS AT ITS BEST IN AUTUMN AND WINTER.

Serves 4
Working time: about 35 minutes
Total time: about 1 hour and 10 minutes

Calories **140**
Protein **4g**
Cholesterol **0mg**
Total fat **5g**
Saturated fat **1g**
Sodium **60mg**

500 g	*celeriac, peeled, cut into 1 cm (½ inch) cubes*	*1 lb*
2 tsp	*fromage frais*	*2 tsp*
1	*egg white*	*1*
	freshly ground black pepper	
1 tbsp	*walnut oil*	*1 tbsp*
	Wild mushroom filling	
12.5 cl	*Madeira*	*4 fl oz*
12.5 cl	*unsalted chicken stock (recipe, page 9)*	*4 fl oz*
125 g	*chanterelles or oyster mushrooms*	*4 oz*
1 tbsp	*fromage frais*	*1 tbsp*
¼ tsp	*chopped fresh thyme or ⅛ tsp dried thyme*	*¼ tsp*
	Madeira sauce	
8 cl	*Madeira*	*3 fl oz*
35 cl	*unsalted chicken stock (recipe, page 9)*	*12 fl oz*
	small thyme sprigs, for garnish	

Put a little water — about 2.5 cm (1 inch) — in a saucepan, place a steamer in the pan and bring the water to the boil. Steam the celeriac until tender — about 9 to 10 minutes — and purée it by passing it through a sieve or a food mill. Transfer the purée to a heavy saucepan, and cook it gently for 1 to 2 minutes to evaporate any excess moisture, stirring constantly to prevent it from sticking. Remove the purée from the heat and beat in the *fromage frais*, the egg white and some black pepper. Cover the mixture and chill it for 30 minutes in the refrigerator.

Preheat the oven to 200°C (400°F or Mark 6).

Meanwhile, prepare the mushroom filling. Place the Madeira and the stock in a saucepan, bring them to the boil, and cook them over high heat until the liquid is reduced to 3 cl (1 fl oz). Set aside eight small, unblemished mushrooms (if the caps are large, break off eight nicely shaped pieces) and chop the remainder finely with a sharp knife. Stir the chopped mushrooms, *fromage frais* and thyme into the stock mixture and set the filling aside to cool.

Brush four 12.5 cl (4 fl oz) ramekin dishes lightly with the walnut oil. Spoon about three quarters of the celeriac purée into the ramekins, pressing it into the sides and bottom of the dish and forming a well in the centre of each one. Spoon the mushroom filling into these hollows, and cover with the remaining purée.

Arrange the ramekins in a deep roasting tin or baking dish, and pour in enough boiling water to come half way up their sides. Bake the ramekins for about 10 minutes, remove them from the oven and set them aside to rest while you prepare the sauce.

In a saucepan, bring the Madeira and the stock to the boil and continue to cook them over high heat until the liquid is reduced to 12.5 cl (4 fl oz). Reduce the

heat, add the reserved mushroom caps to the sauce and simmer for about 1 minute.

To unmould the timbales, run a palette knife round the inside edges of the ramekins, and turn them out carefully on to warmed serving plates. If necessary, smooth the surfaces of the timbales with the palette knife. Using a slotted spoon, remove the mushroom caps from the sauce, and place two next to each timbale. Spoon the sauce round the timbales and serve them warm, garnished with the thyme sprigs.

EDITOR'S NOTE: *If chanterelles or oyster mushrooms are unavailable, a mixture of 90 g (3 oz) of button mushrooms and 15 g (½ oz) of dried wild mushrooms, soaked for 20 minutes and drained, may be substituted.*

Steamed Cucumber with Herb and Yogurt Sauce

Serves 4
Working (and total) time: about 20 minutes

Calories **50**
Protein **3g**
Cholesterol **0mg**
Total fat **3g**
Saturated fat **2g**
Sodium **40mg**

1	*large cucumber*	1
	freshly ground black pepper	
250 g	*thick Greek yogurt*	*8 oz*
1 tbsp	*chopped fresh dill*	*1 tbsp*
1 tbsp	*chopped parsley*	*1 tbsp*
½ tbsp	*chopped fresh tarragon*	*½ tbsp*
4	*fresh tarragon sprigs*	4

With a sharp knife, peel the cucumber and chop it into 2.5 cm (1 inch) pieces. Remove the seeds from the centre of each piece with an apple corer. Pour enough water into a saucepan to fill it about 2.5 cm (1 inch) deep. Set a vegetable steamer in the pan and bring the water to the boil. Place the cucumber pieces in the steamer, season with some black pepper, cover the saucepan and steam until the cucumber is just heated through — 3 to 4 minutes.

While the cucumber is steaming, prepare the sauce by mixing together the Greek yogurt, dill, parsley and chopped tarragon in a small saucepan. Heat the mixture over very low heat until the yogurt is warm, but not hot — about 1 minute.

Using a slotted spoon, transfer the cucumber pieces to warmed plates. Garnish the cucumber with the tarragon sprigs and serve with the warm yogurt sauce.

Baby Baked Potatoes with Celeriac-Watercress Purée

Serves 6
Working time: about 20 minutes
Total time: about 1 hour

Calories **100**
Protein **3g**
Cholesterol **10mg**
Total fat **8g**
Saturated fat **2g**
Sodium **100mg**

6	*new potatoes, washed*	6
1 tsp	*safflower oil*	1 tsp
250 g	*celeriac, peeled and roughly chopped*	8 oz
15 g	*unsalted butter*	½ oz
60 g	*watercress, tough stems removed*	2 oz
1 tbsp	*thick Greek yogurt*	1 tbsp
1½ tbsp	*skimmed milk*	1½ tbsp
⅛ tsp	*salt*	⅛ tsp
	freshly ground black pepper	
6	*red endive or red lollo lettuce leaves, washed and dried*	6
24	*lamb's lettuce leaves, washed and dried*	24
	Vinaigrette dressing	
2 tsp	*white wine vinegar*	2 tsp
⅛ tsp	*salt*	⅛ tsp
	freshly ground black pepper	
6 tsp	*safflower oil*	6 tsp

Preheat the oven to 220°C (425°F or Mark 7).

With a sharp knife, make a shallow slit lengthwise down the centre of each potato. Rub the skins of the potatoes with the oil, and place them on a rack in the oven to bake for 35 to 40 minutes.

While the potatoes are baking, cook the celeriac in a large saucepan of boiling water until it is soft — about 30 minutes. Meanwhile, melt the butter in a non-reactive saucepan and cook the watercress over low heat until it wilts — about 1 minute.

Drain the celeriac in a colander and place it in a food processor or blender together with the watercress, yogurt and milk. Process the mixture until it forms a purée, and season it with the salt and some pepper. Place the purée in a small saucepan and warm it through over very low heat while you make the vinaigrette dressing.

In a small bowl, stir together the vinegar, the salt and some pepper. Blend in the oil.

Arrange the lettuce leaves on a serving platter. Remove the potatoes from the oven, and use a spoon or a knife to open up the central slits a little wider. Place the potatoes on the bed of salad, and spoon the celeriac-watercress purée into the openings in the potatoes. Dribble the vinaigrette over the salad leaves, and serve the potatoes immediately, with any remaining purée on the side.

EDITOR'S NOTE: *For a special occasion, garnish the potatoes with a few spoonfuls of the bright orange salmon roe known as keta, which is available from delicatessens.*

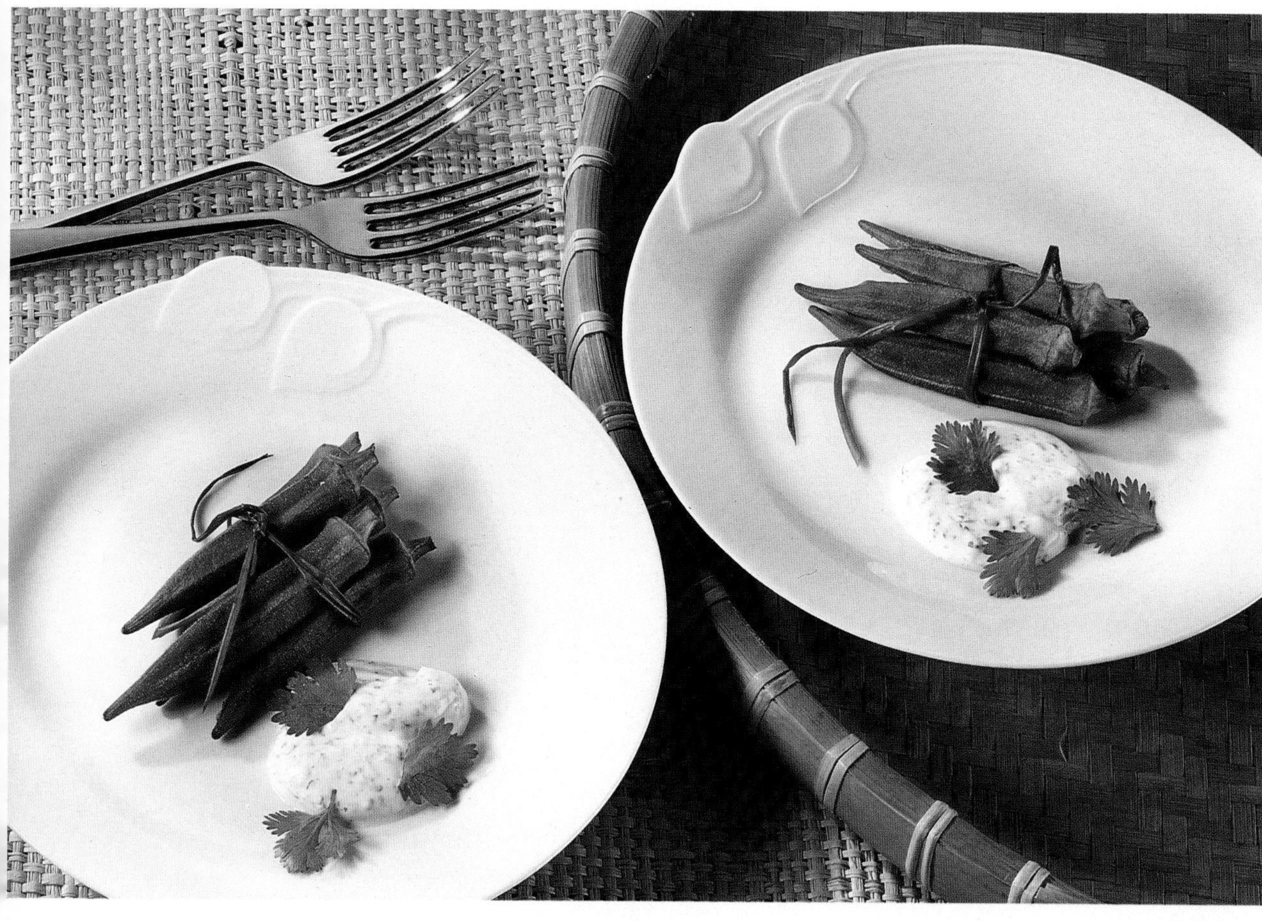

Okra Stuffed with Indian Spices

CHOOSE PLUMP, UNBLEMISHED OKRA PODS FOR STUFFING.

Serves 4
Working (and total) time: about 40 minutes

Calories **60**
Protein **6g**
Cholesterol **10mg**
Total fat **2g**
Saturated fat **1g**
Sodium **125mg**

20	*okra*	20
1 tsp	*coriander seeds*	1 tsp
½ tsp	*yellow mustard seeds*	½ tsp
4	*garlic cloves*	4
¼ tsp	*turmeric*	¼ tsp
½ tsp	*freshly ground black pepper*	½ tsp
1 tbsp	*finely cut chives plus four whole chives, about 18 cm (7 inches) long*	1 tbsp
2½ tbsp	*cottage cheese*	2½ tbsp
	Coriander-yogurt sauce	
½ tsp	*yellow mustard seeds*	½ tsp
6 tbsp	*thick Greek yogurt*	6 tbsp
1½ tbsp	*chopped fresh coriander leaves*	1½ tbsp
¼ tsp	*white pepper*	¼ tsp
½	*garlic clove, crushed*	½
1 tsp	*fresh lemon juice*	1 tsp

First make the sauce. Toast the mustard seeds in a dry, heavy frying pan over medium heat for a few seconds until they begin to pop, then crush them in a mortar with a pestle. In a small bowl, stir together the yogurt, coriander leaves, crushed mustard seeds, pepper, garlic and the lemon juice. Set the sauce aside to allow its flavours to blend while you stuff the okra.

With a sharp knife, make a slit along the length of each okra pod, being careful not to split the ends of the vegetable. Using a small knife or the tips of your fingers, remove the seeds from the okra.

Toast the coriander seeds and the mustard seeds in a dry, heavy frying pan over medium heat for a few seconds until the seeds pop and begin to release their aroma. Place the seeds in a mortar with the garlic, turmeric and black pepper and, using a pestle, pound them to a paste. Stir in the finely cut chives and the cottage cheese and continue pounding the mixture until all the ingredients are well blended.

Stuff each okra pod with a little of the paste, pressing the edges of the slit together so the stuffing will not leak out as it cooks. Wipe off any paste that still clings to the outside of the vegetables. Tie five of the stuffed okra pods together in a bundle with a long piece of chive. Repeat the process to form four bundles of the vegetables. Tuck the loose ends of the chives neatly underneath the okra parcels and place them in a steamer. Steam the okra over boiling water until they are tender and bright green — about 5 minutes.

Serve the okra bundles immediately on individual plates, accompanied by the coriander-yogurt sauce.

Mint-Stuffed Courgettes with Tomato Coulis

Serves 6
Working time: about 30 minutes
Total time: about 50 minutes

Calories **55**
Protein **5g**
Cholesterol **5mg**
Total fat **2g**
Saturated fat **1g**
Sodium **180mg**

6	*small courgettes, halved lengthwise*	*6*
45 g	*fresh mint, leaves only*	*1½ oz*
125 g	*low-fat curd cheese*	*4 oz*
2 tbsp	*breadcrumbs*	*2 tbsp*
¼ tsp	*salt*	*¼ tsp*
	freshly ground black pepper	
2	*egg whites*	*2*
	Tomato coulis	
500 g	*fresh tomatoes, skinned, seeded (page 10) and chopped, or 400 g (14 oz) canned plum tomatoes*	*1 lb*
1	*garlic clove, chopped*	*1*
1 tsp	*chili powder*	*1 tsp*
15 g	*unsalted butter*	*½ oz*
¼ tsp	*salt*	*¼ tsp*

Cook the courgette halves in salted boiling water until they are just tender — about 5 minutes. Drain them in a colander, rinse them under cold running water, and leave them to cool on paper towels.

Preheat the oven to 200°C (400°F or Mark 6). When the courgettes are cool enough to handle, scoop out their centres with a teaspoon and transfer the flesh to a food processor or blender. Add the mint leaves and purée the mixture. Place the purée in a large bowl and add the curd cheese, breadcrumbs, salt and plenty of black pepper. In another bowl, beat the egg whites until they are stiff; fold them into the stuffing.

Arrange the hollowed-out courgette halves on a greased baking sheet and fill their centres with the stuffing. Bake the courgettes for about 25 minutes, until the stuffing acquires a golden tinge.

Meanwhile, bring the tomatoes to the boil in a heavy-bottomed saucepan. Add the garlic and the chili powder, and simmer the mixture for 15 minutes. Put the tomatoes into the food processor or blender with the butter and the salt, and blend until the tomatoes break down to a purée and the butter is thoroughly incorporated. If you are using canned tomatoes, pass the sauce through a sieve. Return the sauce to the pan and cook over gentle heat until it is heated through — about 5 minutes. Serve the courgettes hot, accompanied by the tomato coulis.

Herbed Vegetable Brochettes

Serves 6
Working time: about 25 minutes
Total time: about 6 hours and 30 minutes
(includes marinating)

Calories **115**
Protein **2g**
Cholesterol **0mg**
Total fat **10g**
Saturated fat **2g**
Sodium **230mg**

2	*small courgettes, trimmed and cut into 1 cm (½ inch) rounds*	*2*
12	*small button mushrooms*	*12*
12	*baby sweetcorn cobs, each cut into two or three pieces*	*12*
½	*sweet pepper, cut into 12 squares*	*½*
12	*cherry tomatoes*	*12*
6	*lime wedges, for garnish*	*6*
	Herb marinade	
4 tbsp	*virgin olive oil*	*4 tbsp*
2 tbsp	*fresh lemon juice*	*2 tbsp*
½ tsp	*grated lemon rind*	*½ tsp*
1	*garlic clove, crushed*	*1*
1 tsp	*Dijon mustard*	*1 tsp*
3 tbsp	*chopped mixed fresh herbs, such as basil, marjoram and thyme*	*3 tbsp*

In a bowl, whisk together all the marinade ingredients to blend them thoroughly. Add the vegetables to the marinade, turning them to coat them evenly. Cover the bowl with plastic film and set it aside for at least 6 hours, stirring the vegetables occasionally.

Twenty minutes before you plan to cook the brochettes, soak 12 bamboo skewers in water: this keeps them moist and prevents them from burning under the grill.

Preheat the grill. With a slotted spoon, remove the vegetables from the bowl, reserving the marinade. Thread a selection of vegetables on to each skewer. Grill the brochettes, about 10 cm (4 inches) from the source of heat, turning them occasionally until the vegetables begin to brown — about 10 minutes. Serve the brochettes hot, with the reserved marinade spooned over them. Garnish with the lime wedges.

SUGGESTED ACCOMPANIMENT: *saffron rice.*

Devilled Mushroom Tartlets

Serves 8
Working time: about 50 minutes
Total time: about 1 hour and 20 minutes

Calories **225**
Protein **5g**
Cholesterol **40mg**
Total fat **15g**
Saturated fat **5g**
Sodium **130mg**

600 g	*small button mushrooms, trimmed and wiped clean*	*1¼ lb*
1 tbsp	*fresh lemon juice*	*1 tbsp*
¼ tsp	*salt*	*¼ tsp*
	freshly ground black pepper	
15 cl	*soured cream*	*¼ pint*
1 tsp	*prepared English mustard*	*1 tsp*
⅛ tsp	*cayenne pepper*	*⅛ tsp*
15 g	*plain flour*	*½ oz*
2 tbsp	*finely cut chives*	*2 tbsp*
1 tbsp	*chopped parsley*	*1 tbsp*
	Shortcrust pastry	
175 g	*plain flour*	*6 oz*
⅛ tsp	*salt*	*⅛ tsp*
90 g	*polyunsaturated margarine*	*3 oz*
1	*large egg, beaten*	*1*

Put the mushrooms, lemon juice, salt and some pepper into a saucepan. Cover the pan with a tightly fitting lid and cook gently over low heat until the mushrooms are soft — 10 to 15 minutes.

Drain the mushrooms in a colander set over a bowl. Pour the liquid back into the saucepan, bring it to the boil, then lower the heat and simmer until it is reduced by half — about 5 minutes.

Meanwhile, combine the soured cream, mustard, cayenne pepper and flour in a small bowl, and blend with a wire whisk until the mixture is smooth. Stir this cream into the mushroom juices and cook gently, stirring constantly, until the sauce thickens. Stir in the mushrooms and the chives and remove the pan from the heat. Cover the pan with plastic film to prevent a skin forming on the surface of the sauce, and set the mixture aside to cool for about 20 minutes.

While the filling cools, prepare the pastry. Preheat the oven to 220°C (425°F or Mark 7). Sift the flour and salt into a bowl. Rub the margarine into the flour until the mixture resembles fine breadcrumbs. Reserve 1 teaspoon of the beaten egg and mix the remainder with the dry ingredients and 2 teaspoons of cold water to make a firm dough. Knead the dough lightly on a floured surface until it is smooth.

Roll the pastry out thinly. With a plain round cutter, cut out eight rounds large enough to fit 9.5 cm (3¾ inch) fluted tartlet tins. Line the tins with the pastry rounds. Gather up the trimmings of the dough into a ball, knead them again, and roll them out to form a rectangle measuring about 20 by 10 cm (8 by 4 inches).

Cutting across the short end of the rectangle, slice the dough into strips about 5 mm (¼ inch) wide.

Fill the pastry-lined tins with the mushroom mixture. Moisten the dough strips with cold water and arrange four of them in a lattice pattern on the top of each tartlet. Press the strips firmly into position, then trim them to fit the tins exactly.

Brush the lattices with the reserved beaten egg to glaze them. Place the tartlets on a baking sheet, and bake until golden-brown — 20 to 25 minutes.

With the aid of a palette or table knife, carefully remove the tartlets from their baking tins and transfer them to heated serving plates. Serve the tartlets hot, sprinkled with the chopped parsley.

Hot Chick-Pea Salad

THE EARTHY SAVOUR OF HOT, FRESHLY COOKED CHICK-PEAS MINGLED WITH THE FRUITY FRAGRANCE OF GOOD-QUALITY OLIVE OIL PRODUCES A SIMPLE BUT AROMATIC SALAD, RICH IN PROTEIN.

Serves 6
Working time: about 20 minutes
Total time: 2 hours and 10 minutes (includes soaking)

Calories **240**
Protein **12g**
Cholesterol **0mg**
Total fat **8g**
Saturated fat **1g**
Sodium **160mg**

350 g	*chick-peas, picked over to remove any grit and stones*	*12 oz*
6 tbsp	*finely chopped flat-leaf parsley*	*6 tbsp*
2 tbsp	*finely chopped fresh oregano*	*2 tbsp*
1	*onion, finely chopped*	*1*
	virgin olive oil	
	red wine vinegar	
	salt	
	freshly ground black pepper	

Rinse the chick-peas under cold running water, then put them in a large, heavy-bottomed saucepan and pour in enough cold water to cover them by about 7.5 cm (3 inches). Discard any that float to the surface. Cover the pan, leaving the lid ajar, and slowly bring the liquid to the boil over medium-low heat. Boil the chick-peas for 2 minutes, then turn off the heat and soak them for at least 1 hour. (Alternatively, soak the peas overnight in cold water.) Drain the peas; return them to the pan and cover with at least twice their volume of fresh water. Bring the liquid to the boil, reduce the heat to maintain a strong simmer, and cook the peas until they are tender — about 1 hour.

Meanwhile, combine the parsley and oregano in a small bowl, and put the chopped onion in a second bowl. When the chick-peas are cooked, drain them in a colander, and transfer them to a warmed serving dish. Serve them immediately, accompanied by cruets of oil and vinegar, the bowls of chopped herbs and onion, and the seasonings. The salad can be dressed individually to taste.

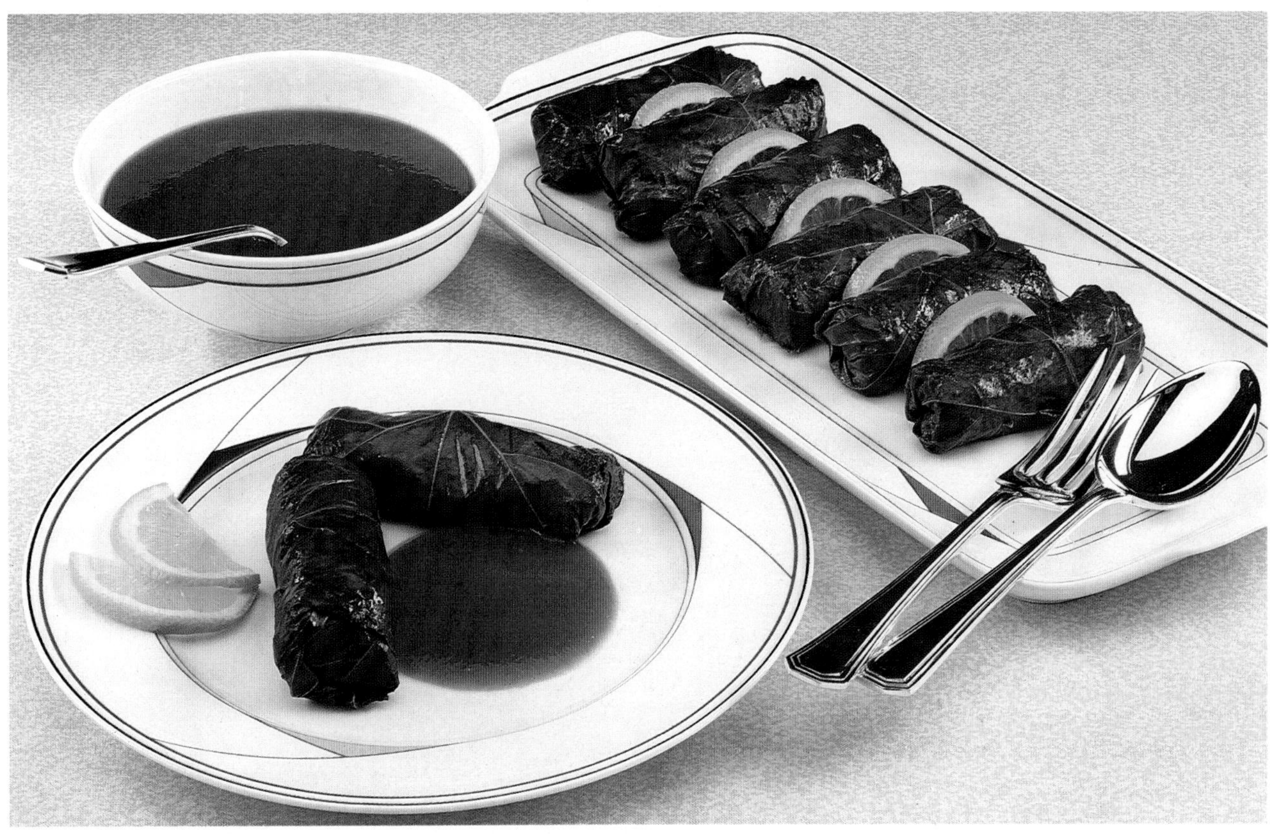

Vine Leaves with a Rice and Date Stuffing

VINE LEAVES SERVED HOT WITH A SAVOURY STUFFING ARE CLASSICS OF EASTERN MEDITERRANEAN CUISINES. THIS RECIPE INCORPORATES A MEATLESS FILLING.

Serves 4
Working time: about 35 minutes
Total time: about 1 hour

Calories **170**
Protein **5g**
Cholesterol **0mg**
Total fat **2g**
Saturated fat **0mg**
Sodium **90mg**

90 g	*round-grain brown rice*	3 oz
125 g	*fresh dates, stoned and chopped*	4 oz
1 tbsp	*pine-nuts, tossed in a frying pan over medium heat until golden, coarsely chopped*	1 tbsp
1	*lemon, grated rind and juice of one half, the remainder halved vertically and thinly sliced*	1
1 tbsp	*chopped parsley*	1 tbsp
	freshly ground black pepper	
8	*large fresh vine leaves, blanched for a few seconds in boiling water, patted dry*	8
	Tomato sauce	
1	*small onion, chopped*	1
250 g	*ripe tomatoes, skinned, seeded (page 10) and chopped*	8 oz
15 cl	*tomato juice*	¼ pint
6 tbsp	*unsalted chicken stock (recipe, page 9) or water*	6 tbsp
⅛ tsp	*sugar*	⅛ tsp
1	*bay leaf*	1
1	*fresh thyme sprig*	1
	freshly ground black pepper	

Bring ½ litre (16 fl oz) of water to the boil in a saucepan. Boil the rice until it is tender — 25 to 30 minutes. Drain it thoroughly in a colander.

Meanwhile, place all the sauce ingredients in a small saucepan. Bring the mixture to the boil, cover the pan and simmer over low heat for 15 minutes. Remove the bay leaf and the thyme sprig and purée the sauce in a food processor or blender until it achieves a smooth consistency. (For an even smoother texture, rub the purée through a sieve as well.) Preheat the oven to 190°C (375°F or Mark 5).

Put the rice in a bowl and stir in the dates, pine-nuts, lemon rind and juice, parsley and some pepper. Lay the vine leaves flat on the work surface. Place a spoonful of the rice mixture in the centre of each leaf. Fold the stem end up over the filling, fold both sides towards the middle, then roll into a small, tight parcel. Lay the parcels on a sheet of foil and wrap them tightly. Bake until heated through — about 15 minutes.

Just before serving, reheat the sauce over gentle heat. Serve the parcels accompanied by a pool of the sauce and one or two lemon slices.

EDITOR'S NOTE: *Preserved vine leaves may be used if fresh leaves are not available. Wash them in cold water to rid them of excess salt, then drain them thoroughly on a folded tea towel. Preserved vine leaves can be tougher than fresh ones: after stuffing them, bake them for about 30 minutes.*

Rice-Coated Fish Balls with Mange-Tout

Serves 4
Working (and total) time: about 35 minutes

Calories **105**
Protein **14g**
Cholesterol **50mg**
Total fat **1g**
Saturated fat **0g**
Sodium **60mg**

45 g	*long-grain rice*	*1½ oz*
300 g	*white fish fillet (such as cod, haddock or plaice), skinned*	*10 oz*
4	*spring onions, finely sliced*	*4*
1	*garlic clove, crushed*	*1*
2.5 cm	*piece fresh ginger root, grated*	*1 inch*
1 tsp	*fresh lemon juice*	*1 tsp*
	freshly ground black pepper	
90 g	*mange-tout, topped and tailed*	*3 oz*
4	*lemon slices, for garnish*	*4*

Cook the rice in boiling water for 5 minutes. Drain it in a colander and set it aside.

In a food processor, process the fish for about 10 seconds until it begins to break down. Place it in a mixing bowl with the spring onion, garlic, ginger, lemon juice and some black pepper, and mix well.

Divide the fish mixture into eight equal portions. Moisten your hands with a little water and shape each portion into a ball. Roll each ball in the parboiled rice so that the rice forms a coating.

Arrange the fish balls in one layer in a steamer and place them over boiling water. Cover the pan and steam the fish balls for 7 minutes.

Just before serving, bring some water to the boil and blanch the mange-tout for 1 minute. Drain them thoroughly in a colander.

Remove the cooked fish balls from the steamer with a slotted spoon. Arrange them on individual serving plates with the mange-tout, garnish with the lemon slices, and serve hot.

Risotto with Carrots and Coriander

Serves 6
Working (and total) time: about 1 hour

Calories **300**
Protein **5g**
Cholesterol **30mg**
Total fat **11g**
Saturated fat **6g**
Sodium **155mg**

45 g	*unsalted butter*	1½ oz
1	*onion, finely chopped*	1
1 litre	*unsalted chicken stock (recipe, page 9)*	1¾ pints
2 tsp	*ground coriander*	2 tsp
300 g	*carrots, peeled and finely diced*	10 oz
350 g	*Italian round-grain rice*	12 oz
	freshly ground black pepper	
45 g	*Parmesan cheese, freshly grated*	1½ oz
1	*small bunch fresh coriander leaves, finely chopped*	1

In a large, heavy-bottomed pan, heat 30 g (1 oz) of the butter, and sauté the onion until it is transparent — 3 to 5 minutes. Meanwhile, bring the stock to the boil in a saucepan, stir in the ground coriander, reduce the heat and keep the liquid simmering gently.

Add the diced carrots to the onion, and sauté them for about 5 minutes. Add the rice, and stir well to ensure that the grains are coated with butter.

Ladle a few spoonfuls of the hot chicken stock into the rice, stir well, and let the mixture cook, stirring occasionally, until most of the liquid has been absorbed by the rice. Continue adding hot stock, a little at a time, stirring the mixture constantly and replenishing the liquid as the rice absorbs it. Cook the rice until it is moist but not swimming in the stock, and the grains have lost their brittleness but still retain a chewy core — about 20 minutes.

Remove the rice from the heat and add the remaining butter, the Parmesan cheese and some pepper. Stir the mixture well, cover the pan, and let the risotto stand for 5 minutes. Stir the rice once more, and sprinkle it with the coriander before serving.

Mushroom Risotto

RISOTTO MADE WITH DRIED MUSHROOMS IS A NORTHERN ITALIAN SPECIALITY. DRIED CEPS, KNOWN IN ITALIAN AS PORCINI, ARE THE VARIETY MOST FAVOURED FOR RISOTTO, BUT ANY OTHER DRIED MUSHROOMS COULD BE SUBSTITUTED.

Serves 8
Working (and total) time: about 1 hour and 20 minutes

alories **285**
rotein **7g**
holesterol **20mg**
otal fat **8g**
aturated fat **4g**
odium **100mg**

60 g	*dried mushrooms*	*2 oz*
45 g	*unsalted butter*	*1½ oz*
1	*onion, finely chopped*	*1*
1 litre	*unsalted chicken stock (recipe, page 9)*	*1¾ pints*
400 g	*round-grain brown rice*	*14 oz*
4 tbsp	*white wine*	*4 tbsp*
45 g	*freshly grated Parmesan cheese*	*1½ oz*
2 tbsp	*chopped parsley*	*2 tbsp*
	freshly ground black pepper	

Soak the dried mushrooms in warm water for 5 minutes to remove grit. Drain them in a colander and soak them again in 60 cl (1 pint) of warm water until they are soft — 10 to 15 minutes. Strain off and reserve their second soaking liquid.

In a large, heavy-bottomed saucepan, heat 30 g (1 oz) of the butter and sauté the onion until it is transparent — 3 to 5 minutes. Meanwhile, bring the chicken stock to the boil in a second pan, add the soaking water from the mushrooms, and simmer the liquid over low heat.

Chop the mushrooms roughly and add them to the onions in the pan. Stir the rice into the onion and mushroom mixture and cook it over a gentle heat for about 5 minutes, stirring constantly, to ensure that the grains are well coated with the butter.

Pour the wine into the rice, then begin adding the hot stock, 2 or 3 ladlefuls at a time, stirring frequently. When one batch of liquid has almost been absorbed by the rice, add another few ladlefuls and continue to stir. Cook the rice until it is moist but not swimming in stock, and the grains are no longer brittle but still retain a chewy core — 25 to 30 minutes.

Remove the rice from the heat and stir in the remaining butter, the Parmesan cheese, 1 tablespoon of the parsley and some pepper. Cover the pan and leave the risotto to rest for 5 minutes before serving it in soup plates, sprinkled with the remaining parsley.

Lighter Ways with Eggs

Airy soufflés, featherlight choux pastry and tende crêpes all depend on eggs. Although eggs are high i fats and cholesterol, these undesirable element reside in the yolk alone. The recipes on the followin pages, and the step-by-step demonstrations here have been devised to produce good results with fewe yolks than usual, or with egg whites only.

Crêpes for Wrapping Round a Filling

1 *MIXING THE BATTER. Put the flour in a large mixing bowl. Make a well in the centre of the flour and break in the egg. Beat the egg into the flour. Whisk in the milk, a little at a time, working from the centre of the bowl outwards. When the batter is smooth, stir in the melted butter.*

2 *STARTING TO COOK A CRÊPE. Brush a little oil over the base of a small frying pan. Place the pan over medium heat until the oil is smoking hot — 2 to 3 minutes. Lift the pan and ladle in enough batter to thinly coat the base. As you pour, tilt and roll the pan to spread the batter evenly. Pour any excess batter back into the bowl.*

3 *TURNING THE CRÊPE. Cook the crêpe until its underside is evenly coloured and its edges curling — about 30 seconds. Slip a palette knife under the crêpe and quickly lift it up and flip it over (above).*

4 *COMPLETING THE CRÊPE. Cook the underside until it is dry and lightly speckled — about 20 seconds — then slide the crêpe on to a plate. Stack the crêpes as you cook them. If not using immediately, wrap the crêpes in plastic film and refrigerate for up to two days.*

Whipping Up a Soufflé

1 *MAKING A THICKENED SAUCE. Melt butter in a heavy pan over medium heat. Stir in the flour and cook the roux for 2 to 3 minutes. Add the liquid — here, a vegetable purée — to the roux and whisk briskly to prevent lumps from forming. Continue whisking over low heat until the mixture is thick — about 10 minutes. Cool for a moment, then mix in any cheese or seasonings.*

2 *BEATING THE EGG WHITES. Separate the whites from the yolks of room temperature eggs. Drop the whites into a clean, dry copper, glass or china bowl; grease lingering in the bowl will prevent the whites from mounting, so plastic must not be used. Using a wire whisk, beat the whites with a regular figure-of-eight motion. Continue to whisk until the whites form stiff peaks.*

3 *FOLDING IN THE EGG WHITES. Gently blend a quarter of the egg whites into the sauce with a metal spoon. Spoon the sauce into the remaining egg whites. With a metal spoon, gently fold the whites into the sauce. Do not over mix: a few streaks of unmixed egg white are preferable to a heavy soufflé. The soufflé mixture is now ready to spoon into greased baking dishes.*

Making Choux Dough

1 *BLENDING FAT AND FLOUR. Sift the flour on to a piece of greaseproof paper. Pour the water or milk into a heavy-bottomed saucepan over medium heat and add the margarine or butter. As soon as the margarine has melted and the liquid is boiling, remove the saucepan from the heat and slide the flour into the liquid.*

2 *BEATING THE MIXTURE. Stir the mixture with a wooden spoon until it is well blended. Return the pan to a medium heat and beat the dough vigorously. When it forms a solid mass that comes away cleanly from the sides of the pan — after about 1 minute — remove it from the heat and allow it to cool for a few minutes.*

3 *ADDING EGGS. Beat the eggs in a small bowl. Add the eggs to the dough a little at a time, beating after each addition, until all the eggs are thoroughly incorporated and the dough holds small peaks.*

4 *FINISHING THE DOUGH. Continue to beat the dough with a wooden spoon until the ingredients are well blended and the dough forms a smooth, firm mass that will drop very slowly from the spoon. Use the dough immediately; if it is allowed to stand, it will stiffen.*

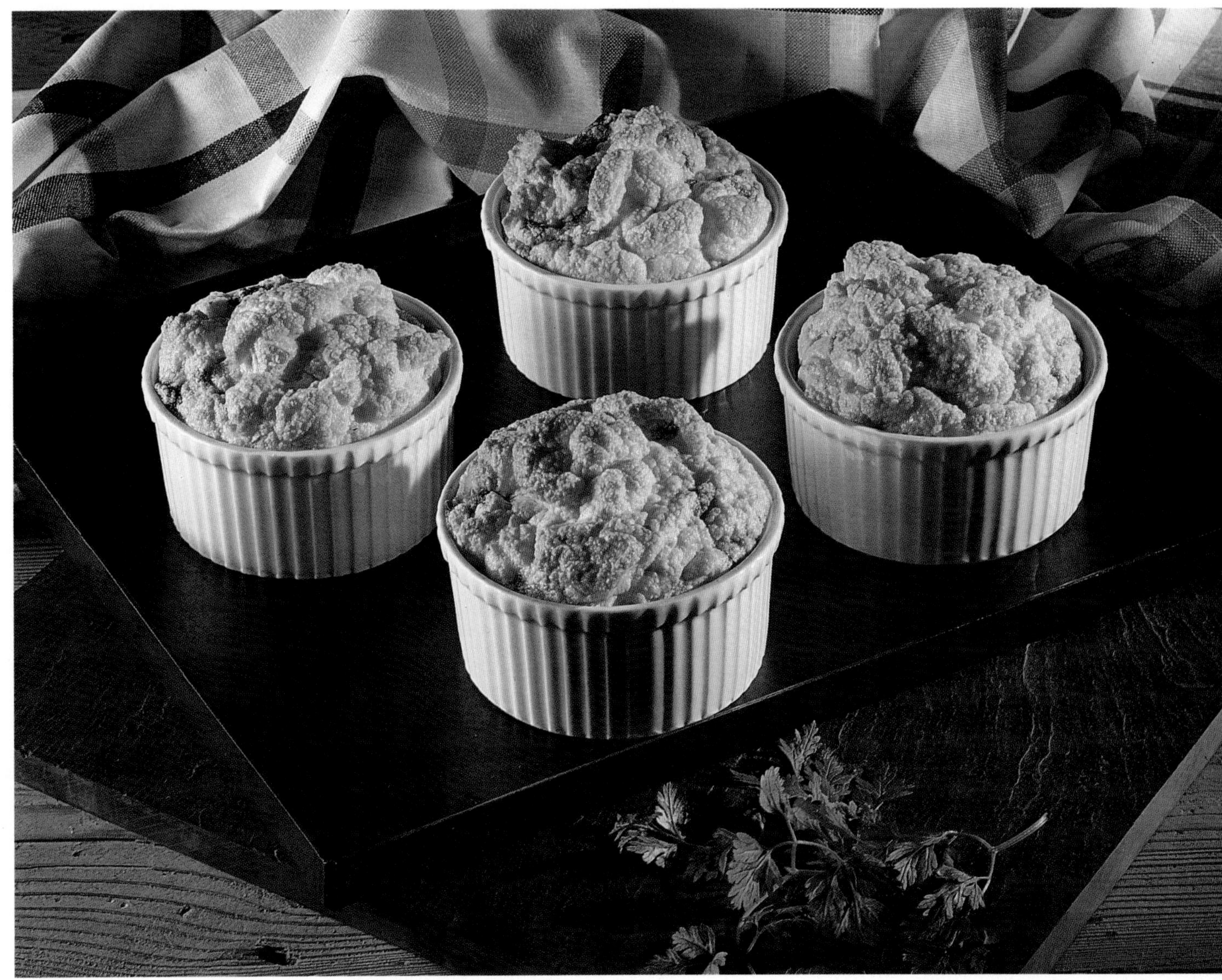

Oyster Mushroom Ramekins

Serves 4
Working time: about 20 minutes
Total time: about 35 minutes

Calories **45**
Protein **3g**
Cholesterol **55mg**
Total fat **3g**
Saturated fat **1g**
Sodium **75mg**

1 tsp	*safflower oil*	*1 tsp*
1	*small onion, finely chopped*	*1*
2 tsp	*chopped fresh chervil*	*2 tsp*
250 g	*oyster mushrooms, finely chopped*	*8 oz*
1	*egg, separated, plus one egg white*	*1*
1 tbsp	*double cream*	*1 tbsp*
⅛ tsp	*salt*	*⅛ tsp*
	freshly ground black pepper	
	fresh chervil sprigs, for garnish	

Preheat the oven to 180°C (350°F or Mark 4).

In a heavy-bottomed saucepan, heat the oil. Add the onion, and sauté until soft — about 3 minutes. Stir the chopped chervil into the onion then, using a slotted spoon, transfer the mixture to a bowl and set aside.

In the same pan, sauté the mushrooms for 2 minutes. Remove about two thirds of the mushrooms from the pan with a slotted spoon and combine them with the onion and the chervil. Divide the mixture among four 12.5 cl (4 fl oz) ramekins.

In a colander set over a bowl, drain the remaining mushrooms; reserve their cooking juices for another use. Put the mushrooms in a bowl with the egg yolk and cream and stir well with a wooden spoon.

In a clean bowl, whisk the egg whites until they are stiff *(page 75)*. Fold them gently into the egg yolk and mushroom mixture. Season the mixture with the salt and some pepper and spoon it into the ramekins.

Bake the ramekins in the oven until the filling is puffed up, firm to the touch and lightly browned — about 15 minutes. Serve the soufflés immediately, garnished with the fresh chervil sprigs.

SUGGESTED ACCOMPANIMENT: *Melba toast triangles.*

Asparagus Soufflés

THE TECHNIQUE FOR PREPARING SOUFFLÉS IS ILLUSTRATED ON PAGE 75.

Serves 6
Working time: about 45 minutes
Total time: about 1 hour

alories **75**
otein **5g**
holesterol **20mg**
otal fat **6g**
aturated fat **3g**
odium **30mg**

350 g	*medium asparagus, trimmed and peeled to about 2.5 cm (1 inch) below the tips*	*12 oz*
30 g	*unsalted butter*	*1 oz*
30 g	*plain flour*	*1 oz*
125 g	*low-fat ricotta cheese*	*4 oz*
¾ tsp	*Dijon mustard*	*¾ tsp*
¼ tsp	*freshly grated nutmeg*	*¼ tsp*
	freshly ground black pepper	
4	*egg whites*	*4*

Preheat the oven to 190°C (375°F or Mark 5).

Cut off six of the asparagus tips, reserving the stalks. Bring a large saucepan of water to the boil, add the six tips and simmer until just tender — about 4 minutes. Remove the tips with a slotted spoon, refresh them under cold running water and set aside. Add the reserved stalks and remaining whole spears to the pan and simmer until very tender — about 15 minutes.

While the asparagus is cooking, butter six 12.5 cl (4 fl oz) ramekin dishes. Drain the asparagus stalks and put them in a food processor. Blend them until smooth, then rub the purée through a sieve placed over a bowl; discard the pulp left in the sieve.

Melt the butter in a saucepan. When it bubbles, add the flour and stir until the butter has been incorporated *(page 75, Step 1)*. Whisk in the asparagus purée, which will be thin. Continue whisking over low heat until the mixture is thick and bubbling. While the sauce cools, push the ricotta cheese through a nylon sieve. Add the ricotta cheese to the sauce together with the mustard, nutmeg and some pepper, and stir with a wooden spoon until smooth.

Beat the egg whites until nearly stiff and beginning to form peaks. Add a large spoonful of the whites to the asparagus purée and whisk it in to lighten the mixture, then use a metal spoon to fold in the remaining whites, cutting and folding until evenly blended. Spoon the mixture into the prepared ramekins.

Insert one reserved asparagus tip into the centre of each ramekin, making sure it just clears the surface of the soufflé mixture. Arrange the ramekins on a baking sheet and bake the soufflés until they are puffed up and just tinged golden-brown, with their centres still soft and not firmly set — 15 to 20 minutes. Serve hot.

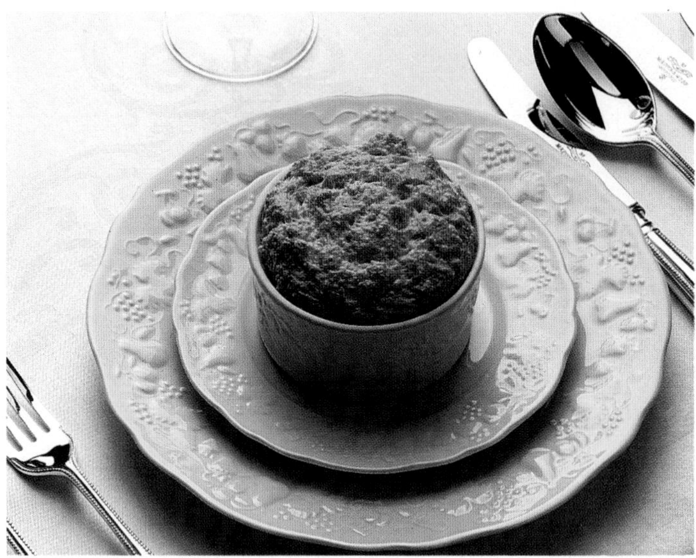

Crab and Paprika Soufflés

Serves 6
Working time: about 15 minutes
Total time: about 35 minutes

Calories **55**
Protein **8g**
Cholesterol **55mg**
Total fat **2g**
Saturated fat **1g**
Sodium **150mg**

175 g	*cooked crab meat, picked over, chilled*	*6 oz*
1	*egg yolk*	*1*
½ tsp	*fresh lemon juice*	*½ tsp*
175 g	*fromage frais*	*6 oz*
2 tsp	*paprika*	*2 tsp*
¼ tsp	*salt*	*¼ tsp*
5	*egg whites*	*5*

Preheat the oven to 180°C (350°F or Mark 4).

In a large bowl, combine the chilled crab meat, egg yolk, lemon juice and *fromage frais*. Add the paprika and the salt to the mixture.

Whisk the egg whites until they are stiff but not dry *(page 75)*, then fold them gently into the crab meat mixture. Divide the mixture among six 12.5 cl (4 fl oz) very lightly oiled ramekin dishes and place them in a baking tin. Bake the soufflés until they are lightly set and golden-coloured — about 17 minutes — and serve immediately.

Gougère with a Pepper and Tomato Filling

THE TECHNIQUE FOR MAKING A CHOUX PASTRY IS DEMONSTRATED ON PAGE 75.

Serves 8
Working time: about 55 minutes
Total time: about 1 hour and 30 minutes

Calories **185**
Protein **7g**
Cholesterol **60mg**
Total fat **10g**
Saturated fat **3g**
Sodium **175mg**

60 g	*polyunsaturated margarine*	*2 o*
75 g	*plain flour*	*2½ o*
75 g	*wholemeal flour*	*2½ o*
¼ tsp	*cayenne pepper*	*¼ ts*
2	*eggs, plus one egg white*	
2 tsp	*Dijon mustard*	*2 ts*
60 g	*Gruyère cheese, coarsely grated*	*2 o*
1 tbsp	*freshly grated Parmesan cheese*	*1 tbs*
	Pepper and tomato filling	
1	*onion, thinly sliced*	
1	*garlic clove, crushed*	
1	*sweet red pepper, seeded, deribbed and cut into thin strips*	
1	*sweet yellow pepper, seeded, deribbed and cut into thin strips*	
500 g	*ripe tomatoes, skinned (page 10) and chopped, or 400 g (14 oz) canned tomatoes, chopped, with their juice*	*1*
2 tbsp	*chopped mixed fresh herbs, such as basil, parsley, thyme and oregano*	*2 tbs*

Preheat the oven to 190°C (375°F or Mark 5).

Draw a circle measuring about 20 cm (8 inches) i diameter on a sheet of non-stick parchment paper an transfer it to a baking sheet.

To prepare the choux dough, put the margarine an 30 cl (½ pint) of water in a saucepan. Cook the mixtur over low heat until the margarine is melted, then in crease the heat and bring the liquid to the boil.

Sift the plain and wholemeal flours and the cayenn pepper on to a sheet of greaseproof paper, reservin the bran that remains in the sieve. Slide the spice flour all at once into the saucepan and stir briskly wit a wooden spoon until the dough is well combined an beginning to draw away from the sides of the pan Remove the pan from the heat.

In a small bowl, lightly beat the eggs with the eg white and Dijon mustard. Gradually beat the egg mix ture into the dough in the pan. Cool the mixture briefl then stir in the Gruyère cheese.

Drop heaped tablespoons of the dough on to th outline of the circle on the parchment paper: keep th dollops close together. With a dampened finger, joi up the pieces of dough to make a ring. Mix th Parmesan with the reserved bran and sprinkle it over th ring. Bake the gougère until it is risen, browned and just firm to the touch — 40 to 45 minutes.

While the gougère bakes, prepare the filling. Put the onion, garlic, peppers and tomatoes in a heavy-bottomed sauté pan and cook, covered, over low heat until tender — 20 to 25 minutes — stirring occasionally. If the tomatoes release a large amount of moisture, uncover the pan for the last 5 minutes of cooking to evaporate the excess liquid. Remove the vegetables from the heat, stir in the fresh herbs, cover and keep the filling warm while you finish the gougère.

Turn off the oven and remove the gougère. With the tip of a sharp knife, pierce the sides of the ring six to eight times, and return it to the oven for 10 minutes to allow steam to escape, keeping the pastry light and airy. With the aid of a spatula, slide the gougère on to a serving platter and fill the centre of the ring with the pepper and tomato mixture. Serve immediately.

Phyllo Triangles with Spinach and Feta Cheese

THESE LITTLE GREEK-STYLE PASTRIES, USING TWO DIFFERENT FILLINGS, MAKE AN INTERESTING STARTER FOR A LARGE DINNER PARTY. FOR A SMALLER GATHERING OR A FAMILY MEAL, HALVE THE QUANTITY OF PHYLLO AND FILL THE TRIANGLES WITH EITHER THE SPINACH MIXTURE OR THE FETA CHEESE AND DILL. THE UNCOOKED PASTRIES CAN BE FROZEN AND SERVED ON ANOTHER OCCASION.

Serves 12
Working time: about 1 hour and 30 minutes
Total time: about 2 hours

Calories **140**
Protein **6g**
Cholesterol **25mg**
Total fat **8g**
Saturated fat **3g**
Sodium **155mg**

12	*sheets phyllo pastry, each 30 cm (12 inches) square*	*12*
30 g	*unsalted butter, melted*	*1 oz*
3 tbsp	*virgin olive oil*	*3 tbsp*
	Spinach filling	
350 g	*fresh spinach, stemmed, washed but not dried, coarsely chopped*	*12 oz*
1 tbsp	*virgin olive oil*	*1 tbsp*
1	*large onion, finely chopped*	*1*
1	*garlic clove, finely chopped*	*1*
60 g	*feta cheese, crumbled*	*2 oz*
150 g	*quark*	*5 oz*
2 tbsp	*chopped parsley*	*2 tbsp*
1 tbsp	*chopped fresh oregano, or 1 tsp dried oregano*	*1 tbsp*
1½ tsp	*chopped fresh mint*	*1½ tsp*
	freshly ground black pepper	
	Dill and feta cheese filling	
150 g	*feta cheese*	*5 oz*
150 g	*silken tofu*	*5 oz*
1	*egg*	*1*
3 tbsp	*chopped fresh dill*	*3 tbsp*
	freshly ground black pepper	

To make the spinach filling, put the spinach in a saucepan and cook it over medium heat in the water that clings to its leaves. Stir occasionally until it wilts and is tender — about 6 minutes. Drain the spinach well in a colander, pressing out all excess liquid with the back of a wooden spoon.

In a small, heavy-bottomed sauté pan, heat the oil and cook the onion and the garlic, covered, over low heat until they are soft — about 10 minutes. Turn them into a bowl, add the spinach, feta, quark, parsley, oregano, mint and some pepper, and mix well.

To make the cheese filling, place the feta cheese in a small bowl, mash it with a fork, then mix in the tofu, egg, dill and some pepper.

Preheat the oven to 180°C (350°F or Mark 4).

To form the pastry triangles, stack up the sheets of phyllo and cut them into four strips. Take one strip and place it on a dry work surface; cover the remaining strips with a dampened tea towel to prevent them from drying out. Combine the melted butter with the oil and brush a little very lightly over the pastry strip.

Put a heaped teaspoon of one of the fillings near the bottom of the strip and fold one corner over the filling to form a triangle. Press lightly to spread out the filling within the triangle, then fold the stuffed portion over again, keeping its three-cornered shape. Continue folding up the strip to its end, making a neat triangular pastry. Form 23 more triangles in the same way; then use the second filling to make 24 more triangles from the remaining strips.

Lightly grease a baking sheet with the oil and butter mixture. Arrange the pastry triangles on the sheet, leaving space between the pastries. Brush the pastries with the remaining oil and butter, and bake them until they are puffed up, crisp and golden-brown — 15 to 20 minutes. Allow them to cool slightly before serving.

Grilled Goat Cheese Rounds

Serves 4
Working time: about 20 minutes
Total time: about 30 minutes

Calories **210**
Protein **6g**
Cholesterol **30mg**
Total fat **12g**
Saturated fat **6g**
Sodium **30mg**

4	*large garlic cloves, unpeeled*	4
1	*small sweet red pepper*	1
1 tbsp	*virgin olive oil*	1 tbsp
4	*thin slices wholemeal bread*	4
2 tsp	*grainy mustard*	2 tsp
100 g	*goat cheese, sliced into four rounds*	3½ oz
4 tsp	*freshly grated Parmesan cheese*	4 tsp
1	*ripe tomato, cut into wedges*	1
4	*lettuce leaves, washed and dried*	4
8	*small fresh basil sprigs*	8

Preheat the oven to 190°C (375°F or Mark 5). Place the garlic and red pepper with the olive oil in a small baking dish, and roast the vegetables until they are soft — about 15 minutes. Remove the dish from the oven and set it aside until the garlic and the pepper are cool enough to handle.

Meanwhile, from each slice of bread cut out a circle slightly larger than the cheese rounds. Toast both sides of the bread rounds very lightly. Spread them with the mustard and place a slice of goat cheese on top of each round.

Sprinkle the Parmesan over the slices of goat cheese, and place the bread and cheese under a hot grill until it is golden-brown — about 5 minutes. While the cheese grills, peel the garlic cloves and strip the transparent skin off the pepper, quarter it, and remove the ribs and seeds. Place the bread and cheese rounds on four small plates, and garnish with the quartered pepper, roasted garlic cloves, tomato wedges, lettuce and basil. Serve immediately.

Salmon Soufflé Crêpes with Watercress Sauce

Serves 8
Working time: about 1 hour
Total time: about 2 hours and 10 minutes

Calories **225**
Protein **15g**
Cholesterol **120mg**
Total fat **15g**
Saturated fat **5g**
Sodium **185mg**

60 g	*plain flour*	*2 oz*
⅛ tsp	*salt*	*⅛ tsp*
1	*egg*	*1*
15 cl	*skimmed milk*	*¼ pint*
15 g	*unsalted butter, melted*	*½ oz*
1 tsp	*safflower oil*	*1 tsp*
15 g	*freshly grated Parmesan cheese*	*½ oz*
	Salmon filling	
2	*fresh salmon steaks, about 200 g (7 oz) each*	*2*
15 cl	*unsalted fish stock (recipe, page 9)*	*¼ pint*
1	*slice onion*	*1*
1	*bay leaf*	*1*
1	*parsley sprig*	*1*
1	*marjoram sprig*	*1*
2 tsp	*fresh lemon juice*	*2 tsp*
15 g	*unsalted butter*	*½ oz*
15 g	*plain flour*	*½ oz*
¼ tsp	*salt*	*¼ tsp*
	freshly ground black pepper	
1	*egg yolk*	*1*
3	*egg whites*	*3*
	Watercress sauce	
2	*bunches watercress, trimmed, washed and finely chopped*	*2*
1	*small onion, very finely chopped*	*1*
30 cl	*unsalted chicken stock (recipe, page 9)*	*½ pint*
1 tbsp	*plain flour*	*1 tbsp*
2 tbsp	*soured cream*	*2 tbsp*

To make the crêpe batter, sift the flour and salt into a bowl and make a well in the centre. Break the egg into the well. Using a wire whisk, gradually whisk the egg into the flour. As the mixture thickens, whisk in the milk a little at a time *(page 74, Step 1)*. When all the milk is incorporated, whisk in the melted butter. Cover the bowl with plastic film and set it aside in a cool place for about 30 minutes to rest.

Meanwhile, prepare the crêpe filling. Place the salmon steaks in a shallow saucepan with the fish stock, onion slice, bay leaf, parsley, marjoram and lemon juice. Cover the pan and cook the salmon just until the flesh begins to flake easily — 5 to 6 minutes; take care not to overcook the fish or it will be dry. Transfer the salmon to a plate with a slotted spatula, remove the remaining skin and bone from the fish, and flake the flesh gently with a fork.

Melt the butter in a saucepan and stir in the flour. Gradually stir in the reserved cooking liquid and bring the mixture to the boil, stirring constantly until the sauce thickens. Remove the sauce from the heat, add the salt and some freshly ground pepper, and let it cool for 2 minutes. Beat the egg yolk into the sauce and fold in the flaked fish. Cover the sauce closely with plastic film to prevent a skin from forming on its surface and set it aside in the refrigerator until you are ready to assemble the crêpes.

Brush a little of the oil over the base of a 15 cm (6 inch) crêpe pan, or small frying pan, and make eight crêpes using the method described on page 74, Steps 2 to 4. Stack the crêpes on a plate and set them aside while you prepare the watercress sauce.

Preheat the oven to 190°C (375°F or Mark 5).

Put the watercress, chopped onion and chicken stock in a small saucepan. Bring the mixture to the boil, reduce the heat and simmer, uncovered, until the onion is well cooked — 20 to 30 minutes. While the sauce simmers, assemble the crêpes.

In a clean bowl, whisk the egg whites until they are stiff but not dry. Fold one third of the egg whites into the salmon mixture to lighten it, then carefully fold in the rest of the egg whites.

Lay the crêpes out flat on the work surface. Spoon one eighth of the salmon mixture on to the centre of a crêpe. Bring one side of the crêpe over the filling, then bring over the other side until the two overlap. Fill the remaining crêpes in the same way and place them side by side in a large, well-buttered ovenproof dish. Sprinkle the crêpes with the Parmesan cheese and bake until the soufflé filling is heated through and well puffed up — about 20 minutes.

While the crêpes bake, purée the watercress sauce in a food processor or blender and return it to the saucepan. In a small bowl, whisk together the flour and the soured cream, then whisk this mixture, a little at a time, into the sauce. Stir the sauce over low heat until it thickens, but do not allow it to boil. Remove the sauce from the heat and cover to keep warm until the filled crêpes are ready. Serve the crêpes hot, accompanied by the watercress sauce.

Gingered Crab Meat Crêpes

Serves 8
Working (and total) time: about 45 minutes

Calories **140**
Protein **9g**
Cholesterol **75mg**
Total fat **8g**
Saturated fat **2g**
Sodium **195mg**

60 g	*plain flour*	*2 oz*
⅛ tsp	*salt*	*⅛ tsp*
1	*egg*	*1*
15 cl	*skimmed milk*	*¼ pint*
15 g	*unsalted butter, melted*	*½ oz*
8	*small spring onions (optional)*	*8*
1 tsp	*safflower oil*	*1 tsp*
	Gingered crab meat filling	
15 g	*unsalted butter*	*½ oz*
1	*onion, very finely chopped*	*1*
5 cm	*piece fresh ginger root, peeled and very finely chopped*	*2 inch*
20 cm	*piece cucumber, cut into 5 cm by 5 mm (2 by ¼ inch) sticks*	*8 inch*
250 g	*fresh crab meat, picked over*	*8 oz*
8 cl	*single cream*	*3 fl oz*
	freshly ground black pepper	

To make the crêpe batter, sift the flour and salt into a bowl and make a well in the centre. Break the egg into the well in the flour then, using a wire whisk, gradually whisk the egg into the flour. As the mixture thickens, begin whisking in the milk *(page 74, Step 1)*. Continue to add the milk, a little at a time, until all the milk is incorporated into the batter. Whisk in the melted butter, then cover the bowl and set the batter aside in a cool place for about 30 minutes to rest.

Meanwhile, trim the spring onions, if using, to 7.5 cm (3 inch) lengths, discarding the green tops and the root tips. To fashion onion brushes, make four short cuts at each end of the spring onion, turning the onion after each cut and being careful to leave the mid-section of the onion intact. Place the spring onions in a bowl of iced water and leave in the refrigerator for about 30 minutes, until the ends curl.

To prepare the crab meat filling, melt the butter in a frying pan, add the finely chopped onion and cook gently until the onion is softened but not browned — 5 to 6 minutes. Add the ginger and the cucumber sticks and continue cooking the mixture until the cucumber softens — about 5 minutes. Stir in the crab meat and the single cream and season the mixture with freshly ground black pepper.

To cook the crêpes, brush a little of the oil over the base of a 15 cm (6 inch) crêpe pan, or small frying pan. Heat the oil until it is smoking hot and make eight crêpes, using the method described on page 74, Steps 2 to 4. Stack the crêpes on a plate and keep them warm in a low oven.

Set the crab filling over medium heat and stir until it is thoroughly heated through, but do not allow it to boil.

Working quickly, spoon an eighth of the crab filling on to one half of a crêpe, fold the other side of the crêpe over to enclose the filling, then fold it in half again. Fill the remaining seven crêpes in the same way and serve them immediately, garnished with the spring onion brushes.

EDITOR'S NOTE: *The crêpes may be prepared in advance, put into a buttered dish and covered with foil. They should be reheated in a 180°C (350°F or Mark 4) oven for about 30 minutes before serving.*

Cornmeal Pancakes Filled with Chicken Picadillo

PICADILLO IS A HIGHLY SPICED MEXICAN DISH WITH A MINCED MEAT OR POULTRY BASE.

Serves 8
Working and total time: about 1 hour and 15 minutes

Calories **190**
Protein **14g**
Cholesterol **20mg**
Total fat **5g**
Saturated fat **2g**
Sodium **65mg**

75 g	*cornmeal*	*2½ oz*
60 g	*plain flour*	*2 oz*
1	*egg*	*1*
30 cl	*skimmed milk*	*½ pint*
2 tsp	*corn oil*	*2 tsp*
225 g	*fromage frais*	*7½ oz*
3 tbsp	*chopped fresh coriander*	*3 tbsp*
1 tsp	*safflower oil*	*1 tsp*
	Chicken picadillo	
500 g	*ripe tomatoes, skinned (page 10) and chopped, or 400 g (14 oz) canned tomatoes, chopped, with their juice*	*1 lb*
1	*onion, finely chopped*	*1*
1	*large garlic clove, crushed*	*1*
1 tbsp	*red wine vinegar*	*1 tbsp*
1 tbsp	*mild chili powder*	*1 tbsp*
2 tsp	*fresh oregano, or 1 tsp dried oregano*	*2 tsp*
½ tsp	*ground cumin*	*½ tsp*
	freshly ground black pepper	
45 g	*raisins*	*1½ oz*
30 g	*stoned green olives, quartered*	*1 oz*
30 g	*flaked almonds*	*1 oz*
2 tsp	*capers, coarsely chopped (optional)*	*2 tsp*
250 g	*cooked chicken, diced*	*8 oz*

To make the pancake batter, combine the cornmeal and flour in a bowl and make a well in the centre. Break the egg into the well. Using a wire whisk, gradually beat the egg into the flour. As the mixture thickens, whisk in the milk a little at a time *(page 74, Step 1)*. When it is all incorporated, whisk in the corn oil. Cover and set aside in a cool place for 30 minutes.

While the batter rests, prepare the picadillo. Put the tomatoes, onion and garlic in a heavy-bottomed saucepan and stir in the vinegar, chili powder, oregano, cumin and some pepper. Cook the mixture, covered, over low heat until the onion is soft and the sauce is quite thick — about 20 minutes. Stir occasionally, and add a few tablespoons of water if the mixture begins to stick to the pan. Add the raisins, olives, almonds, capers if using, and chicken, and stir everything well. Cover and cook gently until the mixture is heated through — about 10 minutes.

Meanwhile, make the pancakes. Brush a little of the safflower oil over the base of a 15 cm (6 inch) pancake pan, or small frying pan. Heat the oil until it is smoking hot. Stir the batter well, then pour 2 to 3 tablespoons into the centre of the pan and make eight pancakes as demonstrated on page 74, Steps 2 to 4, stirring the batter well between pancakes to keep the cornmeal from sinking to the bottom. The cornmeal pancakes will be speckled brown on one side.

Lay out the cooked pancakes, speckled side down, on a flat surface. Spoon a little of the picadillo on to a pancake and roll it up; repeat until all the pancakes are filled. Place the pancakes on warmed individual plates and top with the *fromage frais*. Sprinkle the chopped coriander over the pancakes and serve them hot.

EDITOR'S NOTE: *The pancakes can be made ahead of time, then filled and reheated in a lightly oiled baking dish, covered with foil, in a 180°C (350°F or Mark 4) oven for 30 minutes.*

Buckwheat Blinis with Caviare

THESE LITTLE PANCAKES, USUALLY PARTNERED WITH CAVIARE TO MAKE A CLASSIC RUSSIAN HORS-D'OEUVRE, ARE HERE GARNISHED WITH LOW-FAT *FROMAGE FRAIS* INSTEAD OF SOURED CREAM.

Serves 10
Working time: about 30 minutes
Total time: about 2 hours and 30 minutes

Calories **145**
Protein **11g**
Cholesterol **85mg**
Total fat **6g**
Saturated fat **3g**
Sodium **325mg**

1 tsp	*caster sugar*	*1 tsp*
2 tsp	*dried yeast*	*2 tsp*
300 g	*buckwheat flour*	*10 oz*
¼ tsp	*salt*	*¼ tsp*
35 cl	*tepid milk*	*12 fl oz*
1	*egg, separated, plus one egg white*	*1*
125 g	*caviare or black lumpfish roe*	*4 oz*
500 g	*fromage frais*	*1 lb*
6	*spring onions, chopped*	*6*

Combine the sugar and 15 cl (¼ pint) of tepid water in a bowl and stir to dissolve the sugar, then whisk in the dried yeast until it has dissolved. Add the buckwheat flour and the salt, and mix well, then whisk in the tepid milk and the egg yolk. Cover the bowl and leave the batter in a warm place to rise until it has doubled in bulk — 1½ to 2 hours.

Whisk the yeast batter lightly until it becomes liquid again. In another bowl, whisk the egg whites until they are stiff. Fold them into the batter with a metal spoon. Let the batter stand for 10 minutes.

Heat a non-stick frying pan or griddle over medium heat. Drop the batter from a large spoon on to the pan to make little pancakes about 6 cm (2½ inches) in diameter. Cook the blinis until they are golden-brown on both sides — 1½ to 2 minutes in all. As the blinis cook, remove them from the pan and keep them hot in a folded tea towel.

Top each blini with a teaspoon of the caviare or lumpfish roe, a tablespoon of the *fromage frais* and a generous sprinkling of the spring onions. Serve hot.

EDITOR'S NOTE: *Buckwheat flour is more variable in consistency than other sorts of flour. When combining it with milk, you may have to alter the quantity of liquid specified here to produce a batter that drops easily from a spoon.*

Quick Fried Scallops

Serves 4
Working (and total) time: about 30 minutes

Calories **225**
Protein **29g**
Cholesterol **50mg**
Total fat **9g**
Saturated fat **1g**
Sodium **450mg**

2 tbsp	*almond oil*	*2 tbsp*
1	*bulb lemon grass, crushed in a mortar or a garlic press*	*1*
2.5 cm	*piece fresh ginger root, crushed in a mortar or a garlic press*	*1 inch*
6	*kumquats, finely sliced into rings and seeded*	*6*
2 tsp	*rice vinegar*	*2 tsp*
¼ tsp	*salt*	*¼ tsp*
	white pepper	
12	*cos lettuce leaves, washed and dried*	*12*
1 tbsp	*mint leaves, torn into small pieces*	*1 tbsp*
1 tbsp	*fresh coriander leaves*	*1 tbsp*
500 g	*shelled scallops, bright white connective tissue removed*	*1 lb*

In a heavy, non-stick frying pan, warm 1 tablespoon of the almond oil over low heat. Remove the pan from the heat and place the lemon grass and the ginger in the warm oil to infuse it with their flavours for at least 5 minutes. Meanwhile, blanch the kumquat rings in boiling water until they are soft — about 5 minutes — and drain them in a colander. Strain the flavoured oil, discarding the ginger and lemon grass.

Combine the remaining tablespoon of almond oil, 1 teaspoon of the rice vinegar, a little of the salt and some pepper in a large mixing bowl. Place the lettuce leaves in the bowl and toss them gently to coat them lightly with the dressing. Mix in the mint and the coriander leaves, and transfer the salad to four individual serving dishes.

Rinse the scallops under cold running water and pat them dry. Detach the corals and chop them finely. Slice large scallops horizontally in three; leave smaller scallops whole.

In the frying pan, heat the flavoured oil until it is fairly hot, but not sizzling. Toss the whites of the scallops in the oil, and cook them, stirring gently, for 1 minute. Lower the heat, add the kumquat rings, and cook gently for another minute. Stir in the chopped coral,

cook the mixture for 30 seconds more and remove it from the heat. Sprinkle the remaining rice vinegar over the scallops, and season them lightly with the remaining salt and some pepper.

Arrange the scallops and kumquats on the four individual beds of salad, and serve them warm.

EDITOR'S NOTE: *Fresh lemon grass is available in Oriental food shops and some supermarkets. If it is unobtainable, infuse two strips of lemon rind in the oil.*

Almond oil is used here for its delicate and distinctive flavour, but if it is unavailable, substitute a neutral oil such as safflower oil.

Stir-Fried Prawns with Mango and Ginger

Serves 4
Working time: about 20 minutes

Calories **180**
Protein **6g**
Cholesterol **70mg**
Total fat **8g**
Saturated fat **2g**
Sodium **70mg**

2 tbsp	*safflower oil*	*2 tbsp*
3	*garlic cloves, peeled and finely chopped*	*3*
7.5 cm	*piece fresh ginger root, peeled and grated*	*3 inch*
6	*spring onions*	*6*
125 g	*shelled prawns*	*4 oz*
2	*mangoes, peeled and stoned, flesh sliced into 1 cm (½ inch) wide strips*	*2*
1 tbsp	*low-sodium soy sauce or shoyu*	*1 tbsp*

In a wok or a heavy frying pan, heat the sunflower oil over high heat, and stir-fry the chopped garlic, grated ginger and spring onions for 2 minutes. Add the prawns, mangoes and soy sauce. Cook, stirring frequently, until the prawns and fruit are heated through — 5 to 6 minutes. Serve immediately.

Mushrooms with Mussels

Serves 4
Working (and total) time: about 35 minutes

Calories **90**
Protein **11g**
Cholesterol **30mg**
Total fat **5g**
Saturated fat **2g**
Sodium **130mg**

16	*mussels, scrubbed and debearded*	*16*
4	*large cup mushrooms (about 175 g/ 6 oz), wiped clean, stalks finely chopped, caps left whole*	*4*
1 tbsp	*finely chopped shallot*	*1 tbsp*
12.5 cl	*dry white wine*	*4 fl oz*
15 g	*unsalted butter, diced*	*½ oz*
2 tbsp	*torn basil leaves*	*2 tbsp*
	freshly ground black pepper	
8	*opal basil leaves (four large and four small)*	*8*

Pour 4 tablespoons of water into a large saucepan. Add the mussels, cover the pan and bring the water to the boil. Steam the mussels until their shells open — 4 to 5 minutes. Transfer the opened mussels to a shallow dish; discard any that remain closed.

Place the mushroom caps dome side uppermost on a piece of greaseproof paper and set them on the rack of a steamer or a colander placed over a saucepan of boiling water. Cover the mushrooms with a lid and steam them for 5 minutes; remove them from the heat and keep them warm.

Put the mushroom stalks and the shallots into a small saucepan, pour in the wine and simmer gently until the vegetables are tender — 3 to 4 minutes. Increase the heat and boil the mushroom stalks and shallot until the liquid has reduced by half. Reduce the heat to very low and gradually stir in the diced butter, piece by piece. Add the torn basil leaves, the mussels and some black pepper; keep the mixture warm over a very low heat.

Place the large opal basil leaves on four plates and place a mushroom cap upside down on each one. Pile the mussel mixture into the mushrooms, top with a small opal basil leaf and serve hot.

EDITOR'S NOTE: *Opal basil is a red-leafed variety of basil with a lemony scent. If it is unobtainable, substitute lemon balm, oakleaf lettuce or other attractive salad leaves.*

Seafood Brochettes with Dill Sauce

Serves 8
Working time: about 45 minutes
Total time: about 2 hours and 15 minutes (includes chilling)

Calories **70**
Protein **6g**
Cholesterol **45mg**
Total fat **4g**
Saturated fat **1g**
Sodium **115mg**

8	*fresh scallops (about 350 g/12 oz), bright white connective tissue removed*	*8*
175 g	*large uncooked prawns, peeled*	*6 oz*
175 g	*large mussels, scrubbed and debearded*	*6 oz*
	Lemon and dill marinade	
1 tbsp	*virgin olive oil*	*1 tbsp*
1 tbsp	*fresh lemon juice*	*1 tbsp*
1 tbsp	*chopped fresh dill*	*1 tbsp*
⅛ tsp	*cayenne pepper*	*⅛ tsp*
	freshly ground black pepper	
	Dill sauce	
½ tbsp	*virgin olive oil*	*½ tbsp*
1	*shallot, finely chopped*	*1*
1 tbsp	*plain flour*	*1 tbsp*
30 cl	*unsalted fish stock (recipe, page 9)*	*½ pint*
1 tbsp	*chopped fresh dill*	*1 tbsp*
1 tbsp	*single cream*	*1 tbsp*
1 tsp	*Dijon mustard*	*1 tsp*
¼ tsp	*salt*	*¼ tsp*
	freshly ground black pepper	

Separate the corals from the scallops. With a sharp knife, slice the white cushions in half horizontally, and set both corals and cushions aside.

To prepare the prawns, first devein them; make a shallow incision with a sharp knife along the centre of the back and pull out the veinlike intestine. Then slice the prawns in half lengthwise along the incision and set them aside.

Put 3 tablespoons of water into a small saucepan. Add the mussels, cover the pan and bring the water to the boil. Steam the mussels until their shells open — about 4 minutes. Transfer the opened mussels to a shallow dish, discarding any that remain closed. As soon as they are cool enough to handle, remove the mussels from their shells.

To prepare the marinade, mix the olive oil, lemon juice, dill, cayenne and some black pepper in a bowl. Add the scallops and their corals, the mussels and the prawns, turning them in the marinade until they are evenly coated. Cover the dish with plastic film and refrigerate it for 2 hours.

About 30 minutes before you are ready to cook the brochettes, prepare the dill sauce. Heat the oil in a saucepan, add the shallot and cook gently until it is softened, but not browned — about 5 minutes. Stir in the flour and add the stock. Stirring all the time, bring the mixture to the boil. Add the dill, then reduce the heat to low. Simmer the sauce, uncovered, for 20 minutes, stirring frequently; skim the surface from time to time with a metal spoon to remove any scum. Stir in the cream, mustard, salt and some pepper. Keep the sauce hot while you grill the brochettes.

Preheat the grill to high. Thread the marinated mussels, prawns, corals and scallops on to eight skewers. Cook the brochettes on a rack under the grill for 1 to 2 minute on each side.

Serve the seafood brochettes hot, on a large platter, with the dill sauce on the side.

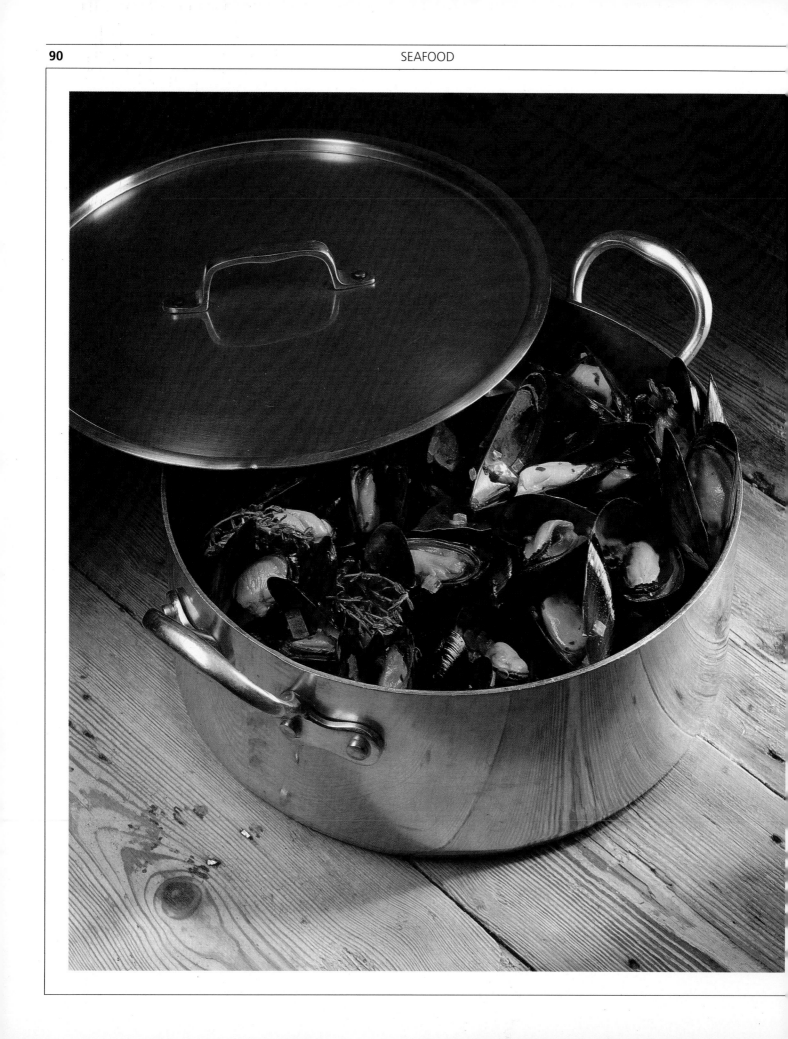

Mussels in White Wine

Serves 8
Working (and total) time: about 30 minutes

Calories **120**
Protein **13g**
Cholesterol **30mg**
Total fat **5g**
Saturated fat **3g**
Sodium **195mg**

2 kg	*mussels, scrubbed and debearded*	*4 lb*
1	*onion, chopped*	*1*
3	*garlic cloves, crushed*	*3*
2	*bay leaves*	*2*
60 g	*parsley, finely chopped*	*2 oz*
3	*thyme sprigs*	*3*
30 g	*unsalted butter*	*1 oz*
	freshly ground black pepper	
¼ litre	*white wine*	*8 fl oz*

Place the mussels in a large, heavy-bottomed saucepan with the onions, garlic, bay leaves, parsley and thyme. Add the butter and some pepper, and pour in the white wine. Cover the pan and cook the mussels over high heat, lifting and shaking the pan several times, until the shells have opened — 3 to 5 minutes, depending on the size and number of mussels.

With a slotted spoon, transfer the mussels to individual soup plates, discarding the bay leaves and any mussels that remain closed. Pour the cooking liquid through a strainer into the soup plates, and serve the mussels hot in their broth.

SUGGESTED ACCOMPANIMENT: *crusty bread.*

Steamed Clams with Spinach

Serves 4
Working (and total) time: about 20 minutes

Calories **115**
Protein **9g**
Cholesterol **20mg**
Total fat **4g**
Saturated fat **2g**
Sodium **100mg**

1 tbsp	*unsalted butter*	*1 tbsp*
1	*onion, finely chopped*	*1*
1	*garlic clove, finely chopped*	*1*
12.5 cl	*white wine*	*4 fl oz*
1 tbsp	*chopped parsley*	*1 tbsp*
½ tsp	*freshly ground black pepper*	*½ tsp*
750 g	*small clams in their shells*	*1½ lb*
250 g	*fresh spinach, washed, stems removed, leaves shredded*	*8 oz*
1	*lemon, quartered*	*1*

Melt the butter in a deep, non-reactive saucepan, add the onion and garlic, and cook, stirring continuously, until the onion is soft but not coloured — about 5 minutes. Stir in the wine, parsley and pepper, and bring the mixture to the boil. Add the clams and cook them for 5 minutes, covered, until their shells begin to open. With a slotted spoon, remove the clams from the pan and discard the loose top half of each shell. Place the clams in a warmed dish and cover with a tea towel.

Simmer the spinach in the wine and onion mixture for 2 minutes over moderate heat. When the spinach is cooked, drain it thoroughly in a colander set over a bowl. Press the spinach to drain off any excess liquid. Return the liquid to the pan. Divide the spinach among four plates, and place an equal number of clams on top of each portion.

Bring the reserved pan juices to the boil and cook over high heat for 1 minute to reduce them. Spoon the juices over the clams and spinach, and serve them garnished with the lemon wedges.

EDITOR'S NOTE: *Cockles may be substituted for the clams.*

Sardines in Vine Leaves

Serves 4
Working time: about 15 minutes
Total time: about 1 hour and 15 minutes (includes marinating)

Calories **140**
Protein **8g**
Cholesterol **30mg**
Total fat **11g**
Saturated fat **2g**
Sodium **225mg**

8	*small sardines (about 125 g/4 oz each), gutted*	8
2 tbsp	*virgin olive oil*	2 tbsp
1	*lemon, juice only*	1
1	*garlic clove, finely chopped*	1
¼ tsp	*salt*	¼ tsp
8	*fresh thyme sprigs, or 1 tsp dried thyme*	8
8	*fresh oregano sprigs, or 1 tsp dried oregano*	8
8	*fresh vine leaves, or preserved vine leaves, rinsed*	8

Rinse the sardines and pat them dry. In a dish large enough to hold all the fish in a single layer, mix together the olive oil, lemon juice, chopped garlic and salt. Place the fish in the dish, turning them in the marinade. Cover the dish with a lid or plastic film and place in the refrigerator for 1 hour. Turn the sardines once while they are marinating.

Preheat the grill to high. Remove the fish from the marinade and place each one on a vine leaf, together with a sprig of thyme and a sprig of oregano, or a sprinkling of dried thyme and oregano. Roll up the sardines in the vine leaves, tuck the ends of the leaves underneath the fish to form secure parcels and place them on the grill rack.

Grill the sardines for 3 minutes on each side, watching carefully to make sure the parcels do not burn. Place two of the wrapped sardines on each plate and serve the fish immediately, to be unwrapped at the table. When the leaves are pulled off, the fish skins and scales will come away with them.

EDITOR'S NOTE: *The technique described for grilling sardines can also be used with small red mullet.*

Oriental Fish Parcels

STEAMING FOOD IN PAPER PACKAGES IS A TECHNIQUE COMMON TO CHINESE AND OTHER ORIENTAL CUISINES.

Serves 4
Working (and total) time: about 20 minutes

Calories **80**
Protein **11g**
Cholesterol **35mg**
Total fat **3g**
Saturated fat **1g**
Sodium **85mg**

150 g	*carrots, cut into fine julienne*	*5 oz*
3	*spring onions, cut into fine julienne*	*3*
2 tsp	*chopped fresh coriander*	*2 tsp*
300 g	*white fish fillet (such as cod, or haddock), skinned*	*10 oz*
2 tsp	*sesame oil*	*2 tsp*
	freshly ground black pepper	
1	*lime, cut into thin wedges, for garnish*	*1*

Cut out four 25 cm (10 inch) squares of greaseproof paper. In a small bowl, mix together the carrot and spring onion strips and the chopped coriander. Divide the mixture of vegetables and herbs equally among the paper squares.

With a sharp knife, slice the fish thinly into strips and divide the strips evenly among the squares. Sprinkle each portion with the sesame oil and some freshly ground black pepper.

Fold a paper square to enclose the fish and vegetables: bring two sides of the square up over the filling, allowing one side to overlap the other. Fold over a margin of about 1 cm (½ inch) on both remaining sides. Fold each of the margins over once again to enclose the packet completely, pressing down on the creases to seal them. Repeat the process to wrap the remaining three parcels. Arrange the fish parcels in a single layer on a steamer rack.

Place the rack over boiling water, cover the pan and steam the fish parcels for 5 minutes. Place each parcel, still wrapped, on a serving dish, and garnish with wedges of lime.

Brill and Leek Croustades

TRADITIONALLY, CROUSTADE CASES ARE SATURATED WITH BUTTER BEFORE BEING CRISPED IN THE OVEN. HERE THEY ARE LIGHTLY BRUSHED WITH OIL BEFORE BAKING.

Serves 4
Working (and total) time: about 50 minutes

Calories **200**
Protein **10g**
Cholesterol **10mg**
Total fat **8g**
Saturated fat **1g**
Sodium **300mg**

½	*large day-old loaf white bread, crust removed*	½
1 tbsp	*safflower oil*	*1 tbsp*
125 g	*leeks, trimmed cleaned and cut into 1 cm (½ inch) cubes*	*4 oz*
12.5 cl	*medium dry white wine*	*4 fl oz*
125 g	*skinned brill fillets, cut into strips about 6 cm by 5 mm (2½ by ¼ inch)*	*4 oz*
½ litre	*unsalted fish stock (recipe, page 9)*	*16 fl oz*
60 g	*fromage frais*	*2 oz*
1 tbsp	*finely cut chives*	*1 tbsp*

Cut the bread into four 4 cm (1½ inch) thick slices, about 7.5 cm (3 inches) square, and prepare the croustade cases as demonstrated on the opposite page. While the croustades bake, prepare the filling.

In a saucepan, simmer the leeks in the wine until they are tender and the wine is almost completely evaporated. Place the strips of brill on top of the leeks, pour in the stock, which should just cover the fish, reduce the heat so that the liquid barely moves in the pan and poach the fish for 30 seconds.

Remove the fish from the stock with a slotted spoon and place it in a dish. Transfer the leeks in the same way to a separate heated dish, and cover to keep warm. Boil the stock until it is reduced to 4 tablespoons. Reduce the heat to very low and stir in the *fromage frais*. Lightly fold the brill into the sauce and gently heat through — being careful not to boil.

Place a quarter of the leeks in each croustade, spoon on the brill, sprinkle with the chives and serve.

Making Croustades

1 CUTTING THE CASES. *Trim the crust off a sandwich loaf. If the bread is soft, put it in the freezer for a few minutes. Cut 4 cm (1½ inch) thick slices. Using a small sharp knife, carefully cut a square in the top of each slice, 5 mm (¼ inch) in from each edge and within 5 mm of the base.*

2 LOOSENING THE CENTRES. *Insert the knife horizontally 5 mm (¼ inch) above the base of one corner and swivel it; the knife point should penetrate beyond the centre of the square. Withdraw it and insert it into the diagonally opposite corner. Swivel the knife again to loosen the centre.*

3 HOLLOWING OUT THE CASES. *Use the tip of the knife to lever out the centre section of each square. Turn the cases upside down and gently shake out any remaining crumbs. Place the cases on a lightly greased baking sheet.*

4 BAKING THE CASES. *Pour the oil into a small bowl and, with a pastry brush, apply a scant coating of oil to the bread case surfaces. Place the cases in a preheated 170°C (325°F or Mark 3) oven and bake until crisp and golden — about 40 minutes; turn occasionally so they colour evenly.*

Sole and Cucumber Croustades

Serves 4
Working (and total) time: about 25 minutes

Calories **140**
Protein **8g**
Cholesterol **15mg**
Total fat **4g**
Saturated fat **2g**
Sodium **180mg**

4	*slices white bread*	4
15 g	*unsalted butter, melted*	½ oz
4 tsp	*dry vermouth*	4 tsp
35 cl	*unsalted fish stock (recipe, page 9)*	12 fl oz
175 g	*sole fillets, skinned and cut into 2.5 cm (1 inch) cubes*	6 oz
100 g	*fromage frais*	3½ oz
1 tbsp	*coarsely chopped fresh dill*	1 tbsp
	white pepper	
5 cm	*piece cucumber, halved lengthwise, seeded, each half cut into eight thin wedges*	2 inch

Preheat the oven to 190°C (375°F or Mark 5). Trim the bread into rounds about 10 cm (4 inches) in diameter. Lightly grease four 7.5 cm (3 inch) tartlet moulds, press the bread slices into the containers, top with squares of greaseproof paper and weight them down with baking beans. Bake the cases for 5 minutes, to set their shape. Remove the baking beans and carefully lift the baked bread cases out of their moulds with the tip of a blunt knife.

Brush the bread cases lightly with the butter on all sides, put them back in their moulds and return to the oven until golden-brown — about 15 minutes.

Meanwhile, prepare the filling. In a small saucepan, boil the vermouth until it is almost completely evaporated. Stir in the stock and heat the mixture until it barely simmers. Add the sole pieces and poach for 15 seconds. Using a slotted spoon, lift out the fish, drain it on absorbent paper towels, and keep it warm while you complete the sauce.

Return the stock to the boil and cook it until it is reduced to about 2 tablespoons. Reduce the heat to very low and stir in the *fromage frais.* Heat the sauce through, stirring, but do not allow it to boil. Add the dill and a little white pepper.

Gently stir the fish strips and cucumber pieces into the sauce. Remove the bread cases from the oven, spoon the filling into them and serve hot.

EDITOR'S NOTE: *The croustade cases for this recipe may also be prepared using the technique demonstrated above.*

Seafood Wonton with Mango and Ginger Sauce

WONTON IN CHINESE MEANS "A MOUTHFUL OF CLOUD"; IT IS TRADITIONALLY MADE WITH A PASTA DOUGH, AND IS OFTEN DEEP FRIED IN OIL. IN THIS LIGHTER VERSION, PHYLLO PASTRY IS USED FOR THE CONTAINERS, AND THE WONTONS ARE BAKED IN THE OVEN INSTEAD OF DEEP FRIED.

Serves 6
Working (and total) time: about 1 hour and 30 minutes

Calories **240**
Protein **20g**
Cholesterol **85mg**
Total fat **9g**
Saturated fat **2g**
Sodium **230mg**

1 kg	*sole or haddock, skinned and filleted, covered with plastic film and chilled*	*2 lb*
2	*egg whites*	*2*
⅛ tsp	*white pepper*	*⅛ tsp*
⅛ tsp	*cayenne pepper*	*⅛ tsp*
2 tbsp	*dry sherry*	*2 tbsp*
¼ tsp	*fresh lime juice*	*¼ tsp*
350 g	*fresh prawns, shelled, diced, covered with plastic film and refrigerated*	*12 oz*
5	*shallots, finely chopped*	*5*
4	*sheets phyllo pastry, each 30 cm (12 inches) square*	*4*
2 tbsp	*safflower oil*	*2 tbsp*
2 tbsp	*shelled peas, cooked, for garnish*	*2 tbsp*
	Mango and ginger dipping sauce	
30 cl	*unsalted fish stock (recipe, page 9)*	*½ pint*
15 g	*concentrated butter*	*½ oz*
1 tsp	*finely grated fresh ginger root*	*1 tsp*
1	*ripe mango (about 375g/13 oz), skinned, seeded and roughly chopped*	*1*
½	*lime, juice only*	*½*
¼ tsp	*salt*	*¼ tsp*
12	*fresh coriander leaves, for garnish*	*12*

Place the chilled fish in a food processor with the egg whites, pepper, cayenne pepper, sherry and lime juice, and process until it forms a smooth purée. Put the purée in a bowl and stir in the prawns and shallots. Cover the bowl with plastic film and chill it in the refrigerator while you prepare the phyllo pastry.

Preheat the oven to 180°C (350°F or Mark 4).

Spread out a phyllo sheet on a floured surface. Brush it lightly with a little of the oil and place a second sheet on top of it. Using a ruler and a sharp knife, cut the double layer of phyllo into 10 cm (4 inch) squares. Repeat the process with the remaining phyllo sheets to form 18 squares.

Rub a little oil on a baking sheet. Brush both sides of the sandwiched pastry squares lightly with the remaining oil. Remove the filling from the refrigerator and put a tablespoon of seafood mixture in the centre of a square, gather up the corners and pinch them gently round the filling to form a parcel. With the aid of a sharp knife, separate the tips of the pastry corners and pull them apart to form petals. Prepare the remaining wontons in the same way and transfer them to the oiled baking sheet.

Place the baking sheet on the middle rack of the

oven and bake the wontons until they are golden-brown — 15 to 20 minutes. Check them after the first 10 minutes of baking: if their tips are browning too quickly, cover the wontons with a sheet of foil.

Meanwhile, prepare the sauce. In a saucepan, boil the fish stock over high heat until it is reduced by half. In a second saucepan, melt the butter and fry the ginger until it is slightly golden. Add the chopped mango, stir until the fruit is soft — about 2 minutes — then add the reduced stock and simmer the mixture for 5 minutes. Purée the sauce in a blender, returning it afterwards to the pan to keep warm. Add the lime juice and salt.

Just before serving, place a few of the peas in the centre of each wonton and garnish the sauce with the coriander leaves.

EDITOR'S NOTE: *The fish bones and trimmings and the heads and shells of the prawns can be reserved and used to make a shellfish-flavoured fish stock (recipe, page 9).*

Sea Trout and Sweetcorn Papillotes

Serves 6
Working (and total) time: about 35 minutes

Calories **150**
Protein **8g**
Cholesterol **35mg**
Total fat **9g**
Saturated fat **1g**
Sodium **290mg**

30	*baby sweetcorn cobs*	*30*
2¼ tbsp	*sesame oil*	*2¼ tbsp*
2.5 cm	*piece fresh ginger root, peeled and finely grated*	*1 inch*
60 g	*chives, finely cut*	*2 oz*
350 g	*sea trout fillet, boned, skinned and cut into six pieces*	*12 oz*
¼ tsp	*salt*	*¼ tsp*
	mixed green, pink, white and black peppercorns, coarsely ground	
2 tbsp	*fresh lemon juice*	*2 tbsp*

Preheat the oven to 240°C (475°F or Mark 9).

In a saucepan, bring 60 cl (1 pint) of lightly salted water to the boil, add the baby sweetcorn cobs and cook them until they are tender — about 5 minutes. Drain the cobs in a colander, and set aside to cool.

Meanwhile, cut out six 20 cm (8 inch) squares of greaseproof paper, and grease the centre of each square with a little sesame oil, leaving an ungreased outer rim of about 4 cm (1½ inches) on all sides.

Put four baby sweetcorns in the centre of each square and sprinkle the ginger over them. Place the chives on a flat plate and roll the fish in the chives until well coated. Top each pile of sweetcorn and ginger with a piece of fish, then set a final sweetcorn on top of the fish. Season each papillote assemblage with a little of the salt, a generous grinding of mixed peppercorns, and 1 teaspoon each of the sesame oil and lemon juice. Bring two opposite sides of the paper together and pleat them to enclose the fish. Make a 1 cm (½ inch) fold in each of the ends and fold over twice, pressing down firmly to seal the parcel. Repeat the process to make five more papillotes.

Place the parcels on a baking sheet, and bake them for 7 minutes. Serve them immediately, letting the diners open their own papillotes at table to savour the aroma that emerges as the package is unwrapped.

EDITOR'S NOTE: *For a more economical dish, pink trout may be substituted for the sea trout in this recipe.*

Salmon-Filled Choux Buns

CHOUX DOUGH IS MORE COMMONLY USED FOR SWEET PASTRIES SUCH AS ÉCLAIRS OR PROFITEROLES. HERE IT FORMS THE BASIS OF AN ELEGANT, BUT SIMPLE, HORS-D'OEUVRE. THE TECHNIQUE FOR MAKING CHOUX DOUGH IS DEMONSTRATED ON PAGE 75.

Serves 6
Working (and total) time: about 1 hour and 30 minutes

Calories **225**
Protein **12g**
Cholesterol **90mg**
Total fat **13g**
Saturated fat **4g**
Sodium **295mg**

60 cl	*unsalted fish stock (recipe, page 9)*	*1 pint*
15 cl	*dry white wine*	*¼ pint*
⅛ tsp	*salt*	*⅛ tsp*
	freshly ground black pepper	
½	*small lemon, juice only*	*½*
175 g	*salmon tail, skinned, filleted and cut into six equal portions*	*6 oz*
175 g	*fine French beans*	*6 oz*
15 g	*polyunsaturated margarine, chilled and cut into small cubes*	*½ oz*
	Choux dough	
45 g	*polyunsaturated margarine*	*1½ oz*
75 g	*plain flour, sifted*	*2½ oz*
2	*eggs, beaten*	*2*
30 g	*smoked salmon, finely chopped*	*1 oz*
1 tbsp	*finely chopped fresh dill or fennel leaves*	*1 tbsp*

Preheat the oven to 200°C (400°F or Mark 6). To make the choux dough, put the margarine in a small saucepan with 12.5 cl (4 fl oz) of water, and cook over medium heat just until the liquid comes to the boil. Remove the pan from the heat and quickly beat in the flour, all at once. Continue beating until the mixture holds together and is free of lumps. Return the pan to a low heat and cook the dough gently for about 1 minute to dry it out a little.

Remove the pan from the heat and add the beaten eggs, a little at a time, beating well after each addition. Stir in the smoked salmon and the dill or fennel leaves.

Grease a baking sheet and spoon the choux mixture on to the sheet, forming six small piles. Place the choux buns in the oven and bake them until they are well risen and golden all over — about 25 to 30 minutes. Meanwhile, prepare a sauce for the beans.

In a saucepan, combine 45 cl (¾ pint) of the fish stock with the white wine and boil the mixture over high heat to reduce it by two thirds of its volume. Season the mixture with the salt and some pepper, stir in the lemon juice, and set the sauce aside.

When the choux buns are cooked, slit them horizontally to form six lids and six bases. Turn the oven down to its lowest setting and return the lids and bases to the oven to dry out slightly.

Meanwhile, poach the salmon fillet pieces in the remaining 15 cl (¼ pint) of fish stock until they turn pale pink — 3 to 5 minutes.

Fill a saucepan with a large quantity of boiling water, plunge in the French beans and boil them until they are cooked but still crunchy — 2 to 5 minutes. Set them aside and keep them warm.

Reheat the fish stock and wine mixture over gentle heat and whisk in the cold margarine cubes to thicken it. Keep the sauce warm while you fill the buns.

Place one portion of the poached salmon fillet in each choux bun and set the pastry lid on top. Toss the French beans in the sauce and serve them alongside the filled buns.

Spiced Crab Puffs

THESE HIGHLY FLAVOURED SEAFOOD PUFFS ARE A MARRIAGE OF CHINESE FLAVOURINGS, SUCH AS GINGER, SOY SAUCE AND FIVE-SPICE POWDER, WITH A LOW-FAT ADAPTATION OF CLASSIC FRENCH CHOUX DOUGH.

Serves 4
Working time: about 30 minutes
Total time: about 55 minutes

Calories **245**
Protein **10g**
Cholesterol **80mg**
Total fat **12g**
Saturated fat **3g**
Sodium **200mg**

1 tbsp	*safflower oil*	*1 tbsp*
1	*large garlic clove, finely chopped*	*1*
1 tsp	*grated fresh ginger root*	*1 tsp*
3	*spring onions, chopped*	*3*
100 g	*white crab meat, picked over and flaked*	*3½ oz*
1 tbsp	*rice vinegar*	*1 tbsp*
1 tsp	*low-sodium soy sauce or shoyu*	*1 tsp*
¼ tsp	*hot red pepper flakes*	*¼ tsp*
1 tbsp	*chopped fresh coriander*	*1 tbsp*
	Choux dough	
30 g	*polyunsaturated margarine*	*1 oz*
15 cl	*skimmed milk*	*¼ pint*
75 g	*plain flour*	*2½ oz*
¼ tsp	*five-spice powder*	*¼ tsp*
⅛ tsp	*cayenne pepper*	*⅛ tsp*
1	*egg*	*1*
1	*egg white*	*1*

Preheat the oven to 190°C (375°F or Mark 5). To make the choux dough, put the margarine and the milk in a saucepan. Cook over low heat until the margarine melts, then bring the liquid to the boil. Meanwhile, sift the flour, five-spice powder and cayenne pepper on to a sheet of greaseproof paper. Add the spiced flour to the saucepan and stir briskly with a wooden spoon until the mixture is well amalgamated and beginning to draw away from the sides of the pan *(page 75, Steps 1 and 2).* Remove the pan from the heat.

In a small bowl, lightly beat the egg with the egg white, then add the egg mixture to the dough in the pan, beating it in a little at a time. Using a spoon or a piping bag, drop the dough in eight dollops on to a dampened baking sheet. Bake the choux pastries until they are risen, golden-brown and crisp — 20 to 25 minutes. Turn off the oven.

Make a slit in the side of each puff to allow steam to escape, then return the puffs to the oven to keep warm while you prepare the filling.

Heat the oil in a small, heavy frying pan over medium-high heat. Add the garlic and ginger, and stir-fry for 30 seconds. Add the spring onions and crab meat, and stir-fry for 1 minute. Stir in the vinegar, soy sauce and red pepper flakes, and cook for another 30 seconds. Remove the filling from the heat and stir in the chopped coriander. Spoon about a tablespoon of filling into each puff through the slit you cut. Serve the crab puffs warm.

Warm Skate Salad with Red Pepper Vinaigrette

WARM SALADS, OR *TIÈDE* AS THEY ARE KNOWN IN FRENCH CUISINE, ARE COMPOSED OF FRESHLY COOKED SEAFOOD OR MEAT IN A LIGHT DRESSING. THEY APPEAR WITH INCREASING FREQUENCY ON RESTAURANT MENUS, BUT THEY MAKE AN EXCELLENT ADDITION TO THE REPERTOIRE OF THE HOME COOK, EITHER AS IMPRESSIVE DINNER-PARTY STARTERS, OR AS LIGHT MAIN COURSES FOR FAMILY MEALS.

Serves 6
Working (and total) time: about 45 minutes

Calories **95**
Protein **8g**
Cholesterol **25mg**
Total fat **6g**
Saturated fat **1g**
Sodium **100mg**

500 g	*skate wings, skinned*	*1 lb*
30 cl	*white wine*	*½ pint*
1	*small onion, cut in half*	*1*
1	*garlic clove, unpeeled*	*1*
1	*small carrot, peeled*	*1*
1	*parsley sprig*	*1*
1	*fresh thyme sprig*	*1*
1	*bay leaf*	*1*
175 g	*mange-tout, topped, strings removed*	*6 oz*
	Red pepper vinaigrette	
1 tbsp	*red wine vinegar*	*1 tbsp*
¼ tsp	*salt*	*¼ tsp*
2	*sweet red peppers, skinned and sieved (page 11)*	*2*
	freshly ground black pepper	
2 tbsp	*virgin olive oil*	*2 tbsp*

Rinse the skate wings well under cold running water. In a large non-reactive frying pan, combine the wine, 1 litre (1¾ pints) of water, the onion, garlic, carrot, parsley, thyme and bay leaf. Bring to the boil, then reduce the heat to medium low and add the skate. Poach the fish until the flesh is opaque and cooked through at the thickest part — about 15 minutes.

While the skate cooks, prepare the red pepper vinaigrette. In a small bowl, combine the wine vinegar with the salt, and stir until the salt dissolves. Stir in the sieved red pepper and some black pepper, then whisk in the oil until the dressing is thoroughly blended.

Lift the poached skate wings from their cooking liquid with a slotted spoon, and transfer them to a plate. Blanch the mange-tout in rapidly boiling water for 30 seconds. Drain and refresh briefly under cold running water, then drain again. Arrange the mange-tout on six serving plates.

As soon as the fish is cool enough to handle, use your finger to lift the flesh, in strips, from the cartilage. Place a portion of skate on each bed of mange-tout. Stir the red pepper vinaigrette well with a fork, and serve it alongside the warm skate

EDITOR'S NOTE: *If the skate wings have not been skinned by the fishmonger, slip a sharp, thin-bladed knife between the skin and the flesh. Pressing the blade of the knife against the skin and working towards the edge of the wing, cut away the skin with short slicing strokes. Turn the wing over and repeat the process to remove the skin from the other side.*

Smoked Haddock in Leek Wrappers

Serves 6
Working time: about 35 minutes
Total time: about 55 minutes

Calories **90**
Protein **10g**
Cholesterol **30mg**
Total fat **4g**
Saturated fat **2g**
Sodium **450mg**

3	*large leeks, two outermost layers only, ends trimmed*	*3*
250g	*smoked haddock fillet, all skin and bones removed*	*8 oz*
1	*egg*	*1*
4 tbsp	*plain low-fat yogurt*	*4 tbsp*
	freshly ground black pepper	
12.5 cl	*dry white wine*	*4 fl oz*
1 tbsp	*fresh lemon juice*	*1 tbsp*
1	*shallot, finely chopped*	*1*
15g	*unsalted butter, cut into small pieces*	*½ oz*
2 tsp	*finely cut chives*	*2 tsp*
1 tsp	*finely chopped parsley*	*1 tsp*
⅛ tsp	*cayenne pepper*	*⅛ tsp*
½	*lemon, thinly sliced*	*½*

To prepare the leek wrappers, bring a large saucepan of water to the boil, add the outer leek layers and blanch them for 2 minutes. Drain the layers, refresh them under cold running water, then pat them dry with paper towels. Trim each layer to a neat rectangle 20 by 10 cm (8 by 4 inches), and set the wrappers aside.

Preheat the oven to 220°C (425°F or Mark 7). In a food processor, blend the smoked haddock fillet, egg, yogurt and pepper to create a smooth purée.

Lay out the leek wrappers on a flat surface. Place 2 teaspoons of the smoked haddock filling on the dark green end of each wrapper. Roll up the packages, pressing them slightly to seal in the filling *(above)*.

Arrange the leek rolls seam side down in a shallow baking dish, just large enough to accommodate them comfortably. Pour the wine and lemon juice over the leeks and cover the dish tightly with dampened greaseproof paper. Bake the rolls until the filling is just set — 15 to 20 minutes. Using a slotted spatula, transfer the leek rolls to a warmed platter and keep them hot while you prepare the sauce.

Strain the juices from the baking dish into a small saucepan and add the shallot. Bring the liquid to the boil over high heat and boil it for 1 minute in order to reduce it slightly.

Remove the pan from the heat and briskly stir in the butter, one piece at a time. When all the butter has been incorporated, spoon the sauce over the leek rolls. Add a sprinkling of chives and parsley, and a small pinch of cayenne, to each serving. Garnish the rolls with the lemon slices, and serve.

EDITOR'S NOTE: *Use the biggest leeks you can find to provide the wrappers. The inner parts of the leeks can be reserved for another use.*

Wine-Glazed Red Mullet

Serves 4
Working (and total) time: about 45 minutes

Calories **140**
Protein **13g**
Cholesterol **25mg**
Total fat **6g**
Saturated fat **1g**
Sodium **160mg**

1	*large red mullet (about 300 g/ 10 oz), cleaned and filleted but not skinned*	*1*
¼ tsp	*salt*	*¼ tsp*
	freshly ground black pepper	
4 tbsp	*red wine*	*4 tbsp*
½	*small red onion*	*½*
6	*pink or black peppercorns*	*6*
2 tbsp	*red wine vinegar*	*2 tbsp*
2 tsp	*light unrefined granulated sugar*	*2 tsp*
125 g	*red grapes, halved and seeded*	*4 oz*
2	*small hearts of radicchio, weighing 90 to 125 g (3 to 4 oz) each, quartered*	*2*
1 tbsp	*grapeseed or safflower oil*	*1 tbsp*

Remove the fine bones from the centre of the fish fillet with tweezers. Season the skin-free side of each mullet fillet lightly with the salt and some freshly ground pepper, and set them aside.

Put the red wine, onion and peppercorns in a small non-reactive saucepan. Bring the mixture to the boil, lower the heat and simmer gently until the liquid reduces to about 2 tablespoons. With a slotted spoon, remove and discard the onion and the peppercorns. Add the wine vinegar and sugar to the saucepan and cook the mixture over high heat until it reduces to about 2 tablespoons of syrupy glaze.

Preheat the grill.

Set aside 1 teaspoon of the glaze for the salad dressing and coat the skin side of each fillet with half of the glaze from the saucepan, keeping the remainder in the pan. Brush the grill pan and rack with a little oil and arrange the fish fillets on the rack in the pan, skin side upwards.

In a small bowl, whisk together the oil and the reserved teaspoon of glaze to form the salad dressing. Toss the grapes and radicchio quarters in this mixture and place them in a fireproof dish, ready to heat through under the grill.

Grill the red mullet, skin side upwards, 8 to 10 cm (3½ to 4 inches) below the heat source — never allowing the skin to blister — for 3 to 5 minutes. Half way through the grilling process, brush the fillets with the remaining glaze.

When the fish fillets are fully cooked, remove them from the grill and set them aside while you heat through the grape and radicchio salad for about 30 seconds under the grill.

Remove the fish from the grill pan and slice each fillet diagonally into three or four pieces. Arrange the fish pieces on individual plates with the warm salad, and serve immediately.

Squid in a Spanish Sauce

THIS SPANISH DELICACY IS A CLASSIC *TAPA* — ONE OF A VARIETY OF SMALL DISHES SERVED AS A SNACK WITH A GLASS OF SHERRY, OR AS A PRELUDE TO AN EVENING MEAL.

Serves 6
Working time: about 25 minutes
Total time: about 1 hour and 10 minutes

Calories **135**
Protein **14g**
Cholesterol **100mg**
Total fat **6g**
Saturated fat **1g**
Sodium **220mg**

2 tbsp	*virgin olive oil*	*2 tbsp*
1	*onion, halved and sliced thinly*	*1*
750 g	*small squid, cleaned, pouches cut into 1.5 cm (¾ inch) slices, small tentacles left whole, large tentacles sliced*	*1½ lb*
2	*garlic cloves, chopped*	*2*
12.5 cl	*red wine*	*4 fl oz*
4	*tomatoes, skinned, seeded (page 10) and chopped*	*4*
1 tbsp	*tomato paste*	*1 tbsp*
1	*bay leaf*	*1*
1	*thyme sprig*	*1*
¼ tsp	*salt*	*¼ tsp*
	freshly ground black pepper	
1 tbsp	*chopped parsley*	*1 tbsp*
	lemon wedges, for garnish	

Heat the oil in a heavy-bottomed saucepan and fry the onion until it is softened. Add the squid and the garlic and cook them for about 4 minutes, turning them occasionally, until the squid is firm and opaque.

Add the wine, tomatoes, tomato paste, bay leaf, thyme, salt and some pepper. Cover the pan and cook the squid until it is tender — about 45 minutes. Remove the bay leaf and the thyme sprig, then stir in the chopped parsley.

Turn the sauced squid into a serving dish and garnish with the lemon wedges.

SUGGESTED ACCOMPANIMENT: *crusty bread.*

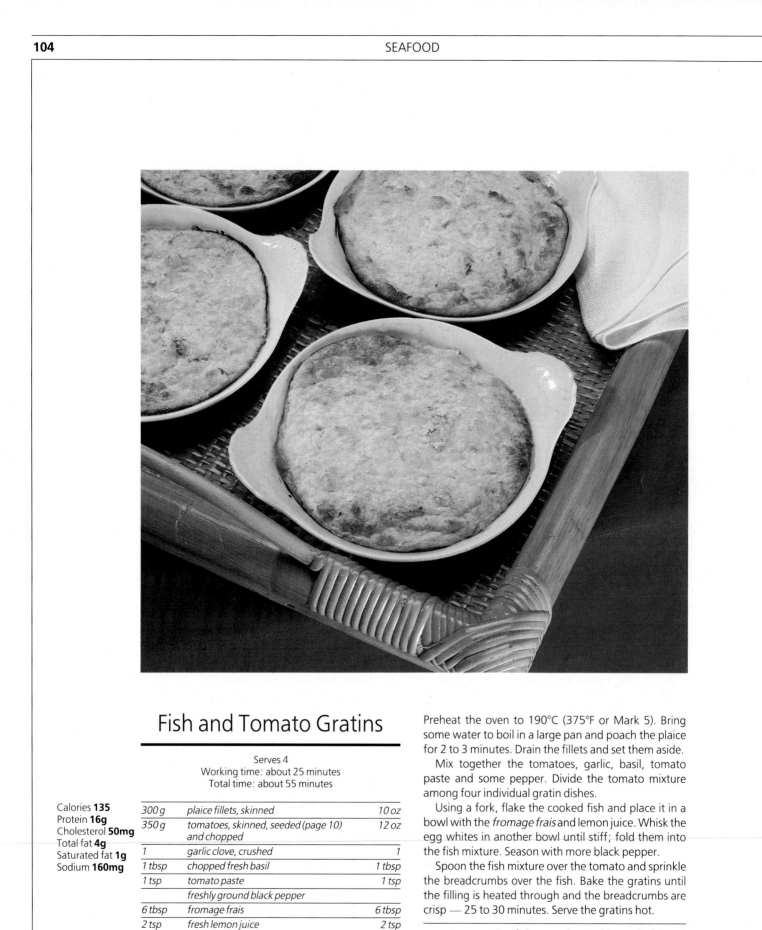

Fish and Tomato Gratins

Serves 4
Working time: about 25 minutes
Total time: about 55 minutes

Calories **135**
Protein **16g**
Cholesterol **50mg**
Total fat **4g**
Saturated fat **1g**
Sodium **160mg**

300 g	*plaice fillets, skinned*	*10 oz*
350 g	*tomatoes, skinned, seeded (page 10) and chopped*	*12 oz*
1	*garlic clove, crushed*	*1*
1 tbsp	*chopped fresh basil*	*1 tbsp*
1 tsp	*tomato paste*	*1 tsp*
	freshly ground black pepper	
6 tbsp	*fromage frais*	*6 tbsp*
2 tsp	*fresh lemon juice*	*2 tsp*
2	*egg whites*	*2*
3 tbsp	*fresh white breadcrumbs*	*3 tbsp*

Preheat the oven to 190°C (375°F or Mark 5). Bring some water to boil in a large pan and poach the plaice for 2 to 3 minutes. Drain the fillets and set them aside.

Mix together the tomatoes, garlic, basil, tomato paste and some pepper. Divide the tomato mixture among four individual gratin dishes.

Using a fork, flake the cooked fish and place it in a bowl with the *fromage frais* and lemon juice. Whisk the egg whites in another bowl until stiff; fold them into the fish mixture. Season with more black pepper.

Spoon the fish mixture over the tomato and sprinkle the breadcrumbs over the fish. Bake the gratins until the filling is heated through and the breadcrumbs are crisp — 25 to 30 minutes. Serve the gratins hot.

EDITOR'S NOTE: *Oat flakes may be used instead of breadcrumbs for topping the gratins. Other white fish fillets, such as sole or haddock, are an alternative to the plaice.*

Courgettes Filled with Crab

Serves 6
Working time: about 30 minutes
Total time: about 1 hour and 10 minutes

Calories **80**
Protein **2g**
Cholesterol **35mg**
Total fat **3g**
Saturated fat **1g**
Sodium **25mg**

6	*courgettes, about 125 g (4 oz) each, trimmed, washed and patted dry*	6
15 g	*unsalted butter*	½ oz
1	*very small onion, finely chopped*	1
15 g	*plain flour*	½ oz
15 cl	*dry white wine*	¼ pint
175 g	*fresh crab meat*	6 oz
1 tbsp	*single cream*	1 tbsp
1 tsp	*fresh lemon juice*	1 tsp
¼ tsp	*salt*	¼ tsp
	freshly ground black pepper	
15 g	*fresh white breadcrumbs*	½ oz
1	*small carrot, finely julienned, for garnish*	1

Preheat the oven to 190°C (375°F or Mark 5).

Cut the courgettes in half lengthwise and score the cut sides lightly with the tines of a fork or a sharp knife. Grease a large, shallow ovenproof dish, and place the courgettes in the dish, cut side down. Cover them with aluminium foil and bake the courgettes until they are cooked through — 45 to 50 minutes.

About 15 minutes before the courgettes are ready, melt the butter in a saucepan, then add the onion and cook it gently until it is very soft but not browned — 3 to 4 minutes. Stir the flour into the onion and cook for 1 minute. Gradually stir the wine into the flour and onion roux, then bring the mixture to the boil, stirring all the time until the sauce becomes very thick. Remove the saucepan from the heat, and stir in the crab meat, cream, lemon juice, salt and some pepper.

Preheat the grill.

When the courgettes are cooked, turn them over so the cut sides are uppermost. Divide the crab mixture evenly among the courgettes, spooning it neatly on top of the halves. Sprinkle the breadcrumbs evenly over the top and place the dish under the grill until the crab mixture is heated through and the breadcrumbs are golden-brown. Serve the courgettes hot, garnished with the carrot julienne.

EDITOR'S NOTE: *The courgettes may be stuffed in advance. When you are ready to serve them, top with the breadcrumbs and heat through under a hot grill.*

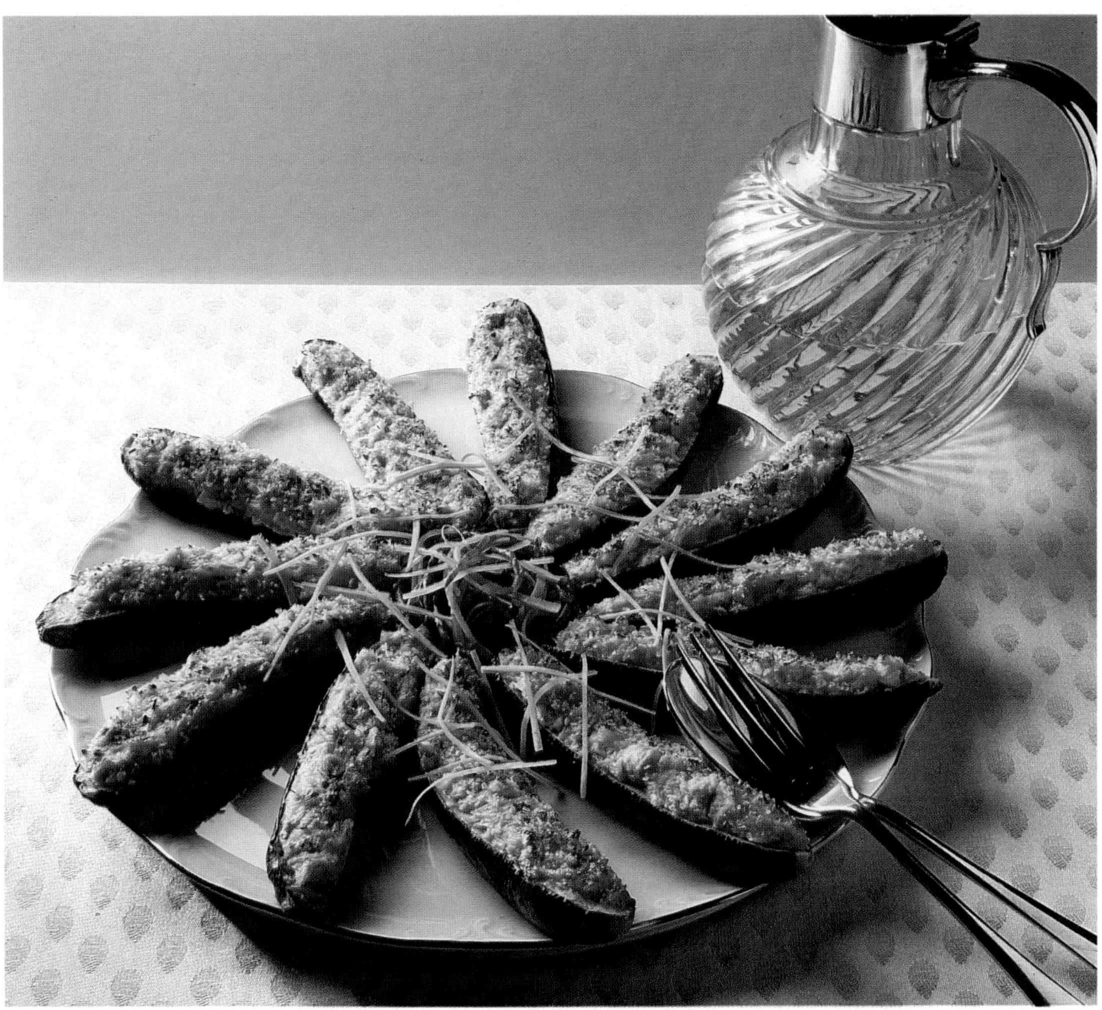

Quenelles with Rosé Wine Sauce

THE FISH FOR THESE QUENELLES MUST BE WELL CHILLED: THE COLDER THE FISH, THE MORE EASILY IT WILL ABSORB THE *CRÈME FRAÎCHE*, GIVING A BETTER TEXTURE TO THE FINISHED DISH.

Serves 6
Working time: about 45 minutes
Total time: about 2 hours and 30 minutes (includes chilling)

Calories **155**
Protein **4g**
Cholesterol **70mg**
Total fat **8g**
Saturated fat **3g**
Sodium **95mg**

350 g	*skinless, boneless whiting fillet, well chilled*	*12 oz*
2	*egg whites*	*2*
⅛ tsp	*grated nutmeg*	*⅛ tsp*
⅛ tsp	*cayenne pepper*	*⅛ tsp*
¼ tsp	*salt*	*¼ tsp*
	white pepper	
125 g	*crème fraîche*	*4 oz*
175 g	*fromage frais*	*6 oz*
	Rosé wine sauce	
1 tbsp	*safflower oil*	*1 tbsp*
1	*shallot, finely chopped*	*1*
175 g	*tomatoes, skinned, seeded (page 10) and chopped*	*6 oz*
30 cl	*rosé wine*	*½ pint*
2 tbsp	*fromage frais*	*2 tbsp*
¼ tsp	*salt*	*¼ tsp*
	freshly ground black pepper	

Put the fish, egg whites, nutmeg, cayenne pepper, salt and some white pepper in a food processor and blend to a smooth paste. With the machine still running, add the *crème fraîche* and the *fromage frais*, a little at a time, and process until the ingredients are thoroughly blended. Turn the mixture into a bowl, cover with plastic film, and refrigerate for about 2 hours.

While the fish mixture is chilling, begin the sauce. Heat the oil in a small saucepan and cook the shallot over moderate heat for 30 seconds. Stir in the tomatoes and the wine, bring the mixture to the boil and cook, stirring occasionally, until the liquid is reduced to about 35 cl (12 fl oz) — about 8 minutes.

Remove the wine sauce from the heat and set it aside.

Choose a shallow non-stick pan at least 30 cm (12 inches) in diameter in which to cook the quenelles. Using two large, deep-bowled dessertspoons, shape the fish mixture into 12 quenelles *(box, opposite page)* and place them in the pan. Do not let the quenelles touch one another, or they may stick together as they cook. Pour boiling water slowly down the side of the pan until the quenelles are just covered, and simmer them gently until just firm — about 10 minutes.

While the quenelles are cooking, reheat the sauce over low heat. Stir in 1 tablespoon of the *fromage frais*, the salt and some pepper. In a small bowl, mix 1 tablespoon of the wine sauce with the remaining *fromage frais*. Distribute the rest of the sauce among six heated serving plates.

Using a slotted spoon, lift the quenelles out of the water. Drain them on paper towels. Place two quenelles on each plate. Dribble the reserved blend of sauce and *fromage frais* between and around the quenelles. Draw out the paler sauce with the edge of a spoon to create a marbled effect, and serve.

Chicken and Spinach Quenelles

Serves 4
Working time: about 35 minutes
Total time: about 1 hour and 30 minutes (includes freezing)

Calories **175**
Protein **16g**
Cholesterol **30mg**
Total fat **7g**
Saturated fat **2g**
Sodium **350mg**

175 g	*skinned and boned chicken breast, all sinew and tendon removed*	*6 oz*
750 g	*spinach, washed and stemmed*	*1½ lb*
2	*egg whites*	*2*
½ tsp	*salt*	*½ tsp*
	freshly ground black pepper	
175 g	*quark*	*6 oz*
	Tomato-basil concasse	
4	*large tomatoes, blanched for 10 to 15 seconds, skinned, seeded (page 10) and diced*	*4*
6	*shallots, finely chopped*	*6*
½	*garlic clove, crushed*	*½*
12	*large basil leaves, cut into thin strips*	*12*
⅛ tsp	*salt*	*⅛ tsp*
	freshly ground black pepper	
½ tbsp	*safflower oil*	*½ tbsp*

In a food processor, reduce the chicken breast to a smooth paste — about 1 minute. Blanch the spinach leaves for 1 minute in 4 litres (7 pints) of boiling water.

Shaping Quenelles

MOULDING WITH SPOONS. Wet two large, deep-bowled dessertspoons in cold water and scoop up some of the quenelle mixture in one of them. Slice the other spoon between the first spoon and the mixture, then turn the mixture back on to the first spoon. Repeat the process until the quenelle is smooth.

Set a colander over a bowl and drain the spinach, reserving its cooking liquid. Squeeze it dry in a tea towel. Add half the cooked spinach leaves to the chicken along with the egg whites, some pepper and ¼ teaspoon of the salt, and process the mixture for another minute, stopping once to scrape down the bowl with a rubber spatula. Scrape down the bowl again and continue processing until the mixture turns deep green — about 15 seconds. Put the food processor bowl in the freezer for about 15 minutes so that the mixture becomes firm.

Meanwhile, begin the tomato-basil concasse. In a small bowl, combine the tomatoes, shallots, garlic, basil, salt and some pepper, and set the bowl aside while you finish preparing the quenelles.

Remove the chicken and spinach mixture from the freezer and blend in 60 g (2 oz) of the quark. Return the bowl to the freezer for another 10 minutes.

In a blender, purée the remaining spinach together with another 60 g (2 oz) of the quark, and add the remaining salt and some more pepper. If the purée is too thick, thin it down a little with the reserved spinach cooking liquid, blending until the sauce is smooth and pours easily. Set the sauce aside.

Remove the chicken and spinach mixture from the freezer, beat in the remaining quark, and freeze the mixture for a final 15 minutes.

At the end of this time, remove the chicken mixture from the freezer. Using two large, deep-bowled dessertspoons, shape the mixture into eight quenelles, as demonstrated above.

Lightly oil a large frying pan, and arrange the quenelles in the pan without touching each other. Slowly and carefully pour enough boiling water down the side of the pan to cover the quenelles. Cover, and simmer the quenelles until they are cooked through and begin to float — 8 to 10 minutes. Take care not to overcook the quenelles or they will become tough.

Meanwhile, warm the spinach purée in a small saucepan over low heat. In another saucepan, heat the safflower oil and lightly toss the tomato-basil mixture until it is hot.

Arrange a circle of the tomato-basil concasse on each serving plate. Remove the quenelles from the water with a slotted spoon and place them on paper towels to drain for a moment before setting them on top of the concasse. Coat each quenelle with a little of the hot spinach purée.

Garlicky Chicken Wings

GARLICKY CHICKEN WINGS ARE A FAVOURITE *MEZZE* (HORS-D'OEUVRE) THROUGHOUT THE EASTERN MEDITERRANEAN.

Serves 6
Working time: about 20 minutes
Total time: about 7 hours and 30 minutes (includes marinating)

Calories **110**
Protein **12g**
Cholesterol **55mg**
Total fat **8g**
Saturated fat **2g**
Sodium **165mg**

1 tsp	*coriander seeds*	*1 tsp*
½ tsp	*cumin seeds*	*½ tsp*
¼ tsp	*fennel seeds*	*¼ tsp*
2 or 3	*large garlic cloves, peeled*	*2 or 3*
½ tsp	*salt*	*½ tsp*
2	*lemons, juice only*	*2*
2 tbsp	*virgin olive oil*	*2 tbsp*
12	*chicken wings*	*12*

Place the seeds in a small, dry frying pan and toast them over medium heat until they begin to brown and smell fragrant — about 1 minute. Tip them into a mortar and crush them with a pestle. Add the garlic and salt and crush them finely with the seeds. Mix in the lemon juice and oil. Pour this mixture into a baking dish large enough to fit the chicken wings comfortably.

Fold the small wing tips under the large bones of each chicken wing so that they will lie flat in the dish. Place the wings in the dish and turn them to coat them thoroughly with the spice and garlic mixture. Cover the dish with plastic film and leave the wings to marinate in the refrigerator for at least 6 hours, turning them over from time to time.

When you are ready to cook the chicken, preheat the oven to 200°C (400°F or Mark 6). Remove the dish from the refrigerator and turn the wings over to be sure they are well coated with the marinade. Bake the wings, uncovered, for 30 minutes, then turn them over and bake them until they are thoroughly cooked and golden-brown on all sides — about 40 minutes more. Serve the chicken wings hot or cold.

SUGGESTED ACCOMPANIMENT: *yogurt mixed with diced cucumber and crushed garlic.*

Chicken and Mango Brochettes with Honey-Lime Sauce

Serves 8
Working time: about 1 hour
Total time: about 2 hours and 30 minutes (includes marinating)

Calories **110**
Protein **15g**
Cholesterol **40mg**
Total fat **2g**
Saturated fat **1g**
Sodium **110mg**

500 g	*chicken breast fillets, skinned, cut into neat 2.5 cm (1 inch) cubes*	*1 lb*
2	*firm ripe mangoes*	*2*
1	*lime, thinly sliced*	*1*
	Spicy marinade	
1	*small onion, very finely chopped*	*1*
5 cm	*piece fresh ginger root, peeled and very finely chopped*	*2 inch*
15 cl	*plain low-fat yogurt*	*¼ pint*
½ tsp	*ground cardamom*	*½ tsp*
½ tsp	*ground cumin*	*½ tsp*
½ tsp	*ground coriander*	*½ tsp*
1 tsp	*ground turmeric*	*1 tsp*
2	*garlic cloves, crushed*	*2*
¼ tsp	*salt*	*¼ tsp*
	Honey-lime sauce	
4 tbsp	*clear honey*	*4 tbsp*
2	*limes, finely grated rind and juice*	*2*

Put all of the ingredients for the marinade into a large bowl and mix them well together. Add the chicken cubes, turning them until they are completely coated with the marinade. Cover the dish and allow the chicken to marinate at room temperature for 2 hours.

About 30 minutes before you are ready to serve the brochettes, prepare the sauce. Put the honey into a small saucepan with the lime rind and juice. Bring the mixture to the boil, reduce the heat and simmer gently until the sauce turns syrupy — about 20 minutes.

While the sauce simmers, remove the skin from the mangoes and cut the flesh cleanly away from the stones with a small, sharp knife. Cut the flesh into neat 2.5 cm (1 inch) cubes. Thread the marinated chicken and the mango on to eight skewers, alternating cubes of chicken with pieces of fruit. Preheat the grill to high.

Place the brochettes on a rack and grill them until the chicken is cooked through — about 2 minutes on each side. The chicken needs only brief grilling; if it is overcooked, its lean flesh will quickly dry out.

To serve the brochettes, pour the lime sauce over them, and garnish them with the lime slices.

SUGGESTED ACCOMPANIMENT: *boiled rice.*

Squab Salad with Wild Mushrooms

TO KEEP PIGEON BREASTS TENDER AND JUICY, THEY SHOULD BE SAUTÉED ONLY BRIEFLY AND SERVED WHILE STILL PINK.

Serves 6
Working time: about 35 minutes
Total time: about 9 hours (includes marinating)

Calories **165**
Protein **12g**
Cholesterol **35mg**
Total fat **12g**
Saturated fat **2g**
Sodium **70mg**

4 tsp	*balsamic vinegar*	*4 tsp*
2 tsp	*dry Madeira*	*2 tsp*
4 tsp	*walnut oil*	*4 tsp*
½ tsp	*Sichuan peppercorns, toasted and crushed (optional)*	*½ tsp*
½ tsp	*black peppercorns, coarsely ground*	*½ tsp*
6	*pigeon squab breasts, skinned, sinews removed*	*6*
15 g	*unsalted butter*	*½ oz*
180 g	*fresh wild mushrooms, such as chanterelles, ceps or shiitake, cleaned and trimmed*	*6 oz*
⅛ tsp	*salt*	*⅛ tsp*
2 tsp	*safflower oil*	*2 tsp*
	freshly ground black pepper	
90 g	*salad leaves, such as purslane or lamb's lettuce, washed and dried*	*3 oz*

In a shallow bowl, combine 2 teaspoons of the balsamic vinegar, the Madeira, 2 teaspoons of the walnut oil and the two kinds of peppercorns. Place the pigeon breasts in the marinade and refrigerate them for at least 8 hours, turning the breasts from time to time.

Shortly before serving, melt the butter in a heavy-bottomed saucepan and add the mushrooms. Toss them gently in the pan with a wooden spoon until they begin to release their juices. Remove the mushrooms from the heat while you sauté the pigeon breasts.

Place a large, dry heavy frying pan over high heat until its base becomes very hot. Remove the pigeon breasts from the marinade without draining them, place them in the hot pan and sauté them over very high heat for 2 minutes on each side. Remove the pan from the heat, and cover it to keep the pigeon breasts warm while you prepare the vinaigrette.

In a small bowl, stir the salt into the remaining balsamic vinegar, until it dissolves. Add the remaining walnut oil, the safflower oil and some pepper and whisk the ingredients together until they are thoroughly blended.

Remove the pigeon breasts from the frying pan and slice each one into long, thin slices.

Pour the vinaigrette into the saucepan containing the wild mushrooms to warm through for a few seconds. Arrange the pigeon breasts, mushrooms and salad leaves on individual serving plates. Spoon the vinaigrette from the saucepan over the mushrooms. Serve the salad immediately.

Golden Quail in a Spaghetti Squash Nest

Serves 4
Working (and total) time: about 45 minutes

Calories **195**
Protein **24g**
Cholesterol **70mg**
Total fat **7g**
Saturated fat **2g**
Sodium **70mg**

1	*small spaghetti squash*	*1*
16	*cardamom pods*	*16*
¼ tsp	*saffron threads, pounded to a powder in a mortar with ⅛ tsp coarse salt*	*¼ tsp*
1 tbsp	*honey*	*1 tbsp*
15 cl	*muscat wine*	*¼ pint*
4	*quail, plucked and drawn, stray quills and pinfeathers plucked out*	*4*
½ tsp	*salt*	*½ tsp*
	freshly ground black pepper	
30 g	*pine-nuts, toasted in a small, dry frying pan over medium heat until golden*	*1 oz*

Cook the spaghetti squash whole in a large saucepan of boiling water until a skewer or fork can be inserted into it easily — about 30 minutes. While it cooks, prepare the basting liquid for the quail.

Remove the husks from four of the cardamom pods, place the pods in a mortar and grind them to a powder. In a pan, heat the saffron, ground cardamom, honey and wine over low heat until the honey has dissolved.

Season the cavity of each quail with the salt and some pepper. With a pestle or a heavy knife, lightly crush the 12 remaining cardamom pods and place a quarter of the spice inside each bird. Tie the legs of the quail together with string.

Preheat the grill. Place the quail in a fireproof grill pan, and coat them with a little of the basting liquid. Grill the birds for approximately 1 minute on each side 10 to 15 cm (4 to 6 inches) below the heat source, to brown the skin lightly all over. Reduce the heat and cook the birds gently for a further 15 to 20 minutes, basting them frequently and turning them from time to time. Transfer the quail to a dish, cover it with foil, and set aside to rest for 5 minutes.

Place the grill pan over low heat, and deglaze it by pouring in any remaining basting liquid, stirring and scraping the pan to loosen any browned fragments stuck to the base. Spoon the glaze over the quail. Any remaining glaze can be poured over the pine-nuts to enhance their colour.

When the spaghetti squash is cooked, cut it in half lengthwise and scoop out and discard the seeds and loose fibres. Use a fork to twist out the spaghetti-like strands. Place a small mound of the squash on each of four heated serving plates, and set one grilled bird on each nest. Sprinkle the toasted pine-nuts over the quail and serve them hot.

Duck Brochettes with Spiced Wine Sauce

Serves 4
Working time: about 45 minutes
Total time: about 1 hour and 25 minutes (includes marinating)

Calories **210**
Protein **18g**
Cholesterol **70mg**
Total fat **7g**
Saturated fat **2g**
Sodium **125 mg**

350 g	*boned duck breasts*	*12 oz*
5 tbsp	*red wine*	*5 tbsp*
¼ tsp	*salt*	*¼ tsp*
1 tsp	*mixed dried herbs, such as oregano, thyme and marjoram*	*1 tsp*
½	*small onion, finely chopped*	*½*
125 g	*oyster mushrooms, trimmed and wiped*	*4 oz*
½ tsp	*virgin olive oil*	*½ tsp*
	Red wine sauce	
1 tsp	*grated orange rind*	*1 tsp*
2 tbsp	*fresh orange juice*	*2 tbsp*
60 g	*redcurrant jelly*	*2 oz*
12.5 cl	*red wine*	*4 fl oz*
⅛ tsp	*cayenne pepper*	*⅛ tsp*

Carefully remove the skin and fat from the duck breasts. Cut the flesh into neat 2.5 cm (1 inch) cubes.

Put the red wine, salt, herbs and onion in a bowl and mix them well. Add the cubed duck flesh, turning the pieces in the marinade until they are evenly coated. Cover the bowl and allow the duck to marinate at room temperature for at least 1 hour, turning the duck pieces occasionally.

Meanwhile, prepare the sauce. Combine the orange rind and juice, redcurrant jelly, wine and cayenne pepper in a small saucepan. Bring the mixture to the boil, stirring constantly, then lower the heat and simmer the sauce gently until it is reduced by about half. Strain the sauce, return it to the pan, cover and keep warm over low heat while you grill the brochettes.

Preheat the grill to high. Remove the duck pieces from the marinade with a slotted spoon, and thread them alternately with the mushrooms on to small skewers. Place the brochettes on the grill rack and brush them with the oil. Grill the brochettes, turning them once, until the duck pieces are tender yet still slightly pink inside — 4 to 5 minutes. Serve the brochettes hot, with the wine sauce on the side.

EDITOR'S NOTE: *Other varieties of mushroom, such as chanterelles, ceps or button mushrooms, can be used in place of the oyster mushrooms.*

Lamb and Mange-Tout Brochettes with Cranberry Sauce

Serves 6
Working time: about 35 minutes
Total time: about 2 hours and 30 minutes
(includes marinating)

Calories **175**
Protein **19g**
Cholesterol **45mg**
Total fat **7g**
Saturated fat **3g**
Sodium **110mg**

375 g	*lamb fillet, trimmed of all visible fat*	*12 oz*
2	*lemons, finely grated rind only*	*2*
1	*garlic clove, peeled*	*1*
1 tsp	*salt*	*1 tsp*
½ tsp	*ground cardamom*	*½ tsp*
1 tbsp	*virgin olive oil*	*1 tbsp*
1 tbsp	*chopped parsley*	*1 tbsp*
125 g	*mange-tout, strings removed, blanched for 30 seconds and drained*	*4 oz*
	Cranberry sauce	
125 g	*fresh or frozen cranberries*	*4 oz*
30 g	*demerara sugar*	*1 oz*
½ tsp	*arrowroot*	*½ tsp*

Cut the lamb fillet into four strips lengthwise, then cut each strip into 12 pieces to make forty-eight 2.5 cm (1 inch) cubes. Put the cubes into a bowl.

In a mortar, combine the lemon rind with the garlic and salt. Pound the mixture with a pestle to form a smooth paste. Gradually work in the cardamom, oil and parsley. Toss the lamb well in this marinade to coat the pieces evenly. Cover the lamb and allow it to marinate at room temperature for 2 hours.

While the meat is marinating, make the sauce. Put the cranberries into a saucepan with the sugar and 15 cl (¼ pint) of water and cook gently until the berries are tender — 8 to 10 minutes. Blend the arrowroot with 2 tablespoons of cold water and stir the resulting paste into the cranberries. Bring the mixture to the boil, stirring continuously. When the sauce thickens and clears, reduce the heat. Simmer the sauce gently for 5 minutes, stirring frequently.

Remove the sauce from the heat and let it cool a little, then cover the surface of the sauce closely with plastic film and set it aside until you are ready to serve the lamb brochettes.

Fifteen minutes before serving, preheat the grill to high. Wrap a mange-tout pod round each piece of lamb and thread four of the wrapped cubes on to each of 12 small skewers, arranging them so the mange-tout wrappers lie on alternating sides of the cubes. Grill the brochettes on a rack, turning them over half way through cooking, until the lamb is cooked yet still slightly pink inside — 3 to 4 minutes. Meanwhile, reheat the sauce over low heat.

Serve the brochettes on preheated individual plates with a little cranberry sauce on the side.

EDITOR'S NOTE: *Instead of cranberry sauce, the brochettes may be served with lemon wedges.*

Prosciutto, Mange-Tout and Tomato Croustades

Serves 4
Working (and total) time: about 1 hour

Calories **140**
Protein **6g**
Cholesterol **15mg**
Total fat **7g**
Saturated fat **2g**
Sodium **350mg**

½	*large day-old loaf white bread*	½
1 tbsp	*safflower oil*	1 tbsp
5 tsp	*dry sherry*	5 tsp
45 cl	*unsalted chicken stock (recipe, page 9)*	¾ pint
½ tsp	*herb or Dijon mustard*	½ tsp
60 g	*mange-tout, strings removed, cut diagonally in half*	2 oz
175 g	*ripe tomatoes, skinned, seeded (page 10) and chopped into 5 mm (¼ inch) cubes*	6 oz
60 g	*prosciutto, trimmed of all fat and finely shredded*	2 oz
7 g	*unsalted butter, chilled and cut into cubes*	¼ oz

Trim off the crust from the bread and cut it into four 4 cm (1½ inch) thick slices, about 7.5 cm (3 inches) square. Prepare the croustade cases as on page 95, Steps 1 to 3. Brush with the oil and bake as in Step 4.

In a small saucepan, boil the sherry over high heat until it is reduced to about 2 teaspoons. Stir in the stock and boil the liquid until it is reduced to about 10 cl (3½ fl oz). Add the mustard, lower the heat and keep the liquid warm while you prepare the filling.

Steam the mange-tout for about 1½ minutes, then drain them in a colander. Reserve eight mange-tout for garnish and transfer the remainder to a bowl. Add the tomatoes and prosciutto, and toss them lightly.

Reduce the heat under the saucepan to very low, and swirl in the cold butter cubes to thicken the sauce. Remove the pan from the heat.

Divide the mange-tout, prosciutto and tomato mixture among the four croustades, spoon the sauce over the croustades, and serve warm, garnished with the reserved mange-tout pieces.

Chicken and Asparagus Croustades

Serves 4
Working (and total) time: about 1 hour

Calories **140**
Protein **11g**
Cholesterol **20mg**
Total fat **5g**
Saturated fat **1g**
Sodium **50mg**

½	*large day-old loaf wholemeal bread, crust removed*	½
1 tbsp	*safflower oil*	1 tbsp
125 g	*chicken breast meat, skinned and cut into 4 by 1 cm (1½ by ½ inch) strips*	4 oz
125 g	*thin asparagus spears, trimmed and cut diagonally into 3mm (⅛ inch) slices*	4 oz
6 tbsp	*dry sherry*	6 tbsp
150 g	*thick Greek yogurt*	5 oz
2 tbsp	*fresh orange juice*	2 tbsp
	freshly ground black pepper	
1 tbsp	*marjoram leaves and flowers*	1 tbsp

Cut the bread into four 4 cm (1½ inch) thick slices, about 7.5 cm (3 inches) square, and prepare the croustade cases as on page 95, Steps 1 to 3. Brush with the oil and bake as described in Step 4.

Place the chicken strips and the asparagus pieces in a vegetable steamer. Set it over a pan of boiling water, cover with a lid and steam for about 2 minutes.

Meanwhile, in a small saucepan, boil the sherry until it is reduced to 1 tablespoon. While it reduces, blend the yogurt and orange juice together. Lower the heat under the sherry, stir in the yogurt and orange juice mixture, and heat the sauce over gentle heat, stirring constantly. Season the sauce with some black pepper.

Place the steamed chicken and asparagus in the croustades and spoon the sauce over them. Sprinkle the marjoram leaves and flowers over each filled croustade, and serve immediately.

EDITOR'S NOTE: *As an alternative to the sherry, flavour the sauce with dry vermouth.*

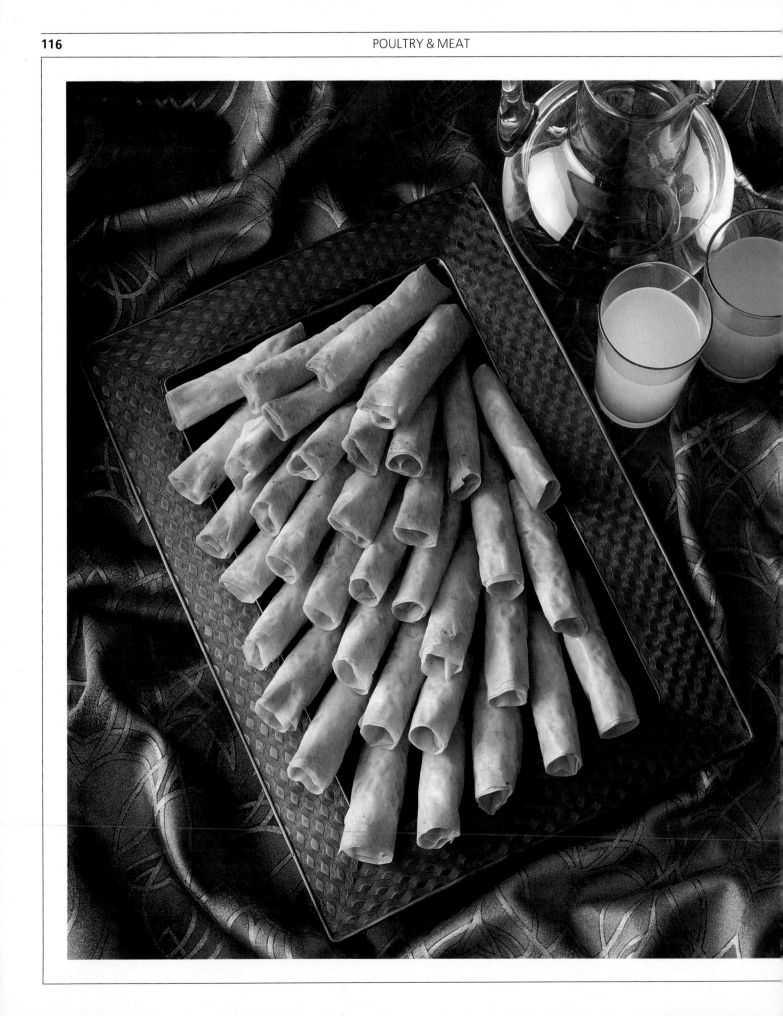

Turkish Beef and Pine-Nut Rolls

Serves 12
Working time: about 30 minutes
Total time: about 45 minutes

alories **115**
rotein **8g**
holesterol **20mg**
otal fat **6g**
aturated fat **2g**
odium **70mg**

1 tbsp	*virgin olive oil*	*1 tbsp*
1	*onion, finely chopped*	*1*
250 g	*lean minced beef*	*8 oz*
1 tsp	*ground cumin*	*1 tsp*
½ tsp	*ground allspice*	*½ tsp*
2 tbsp	*pine-nuts*	*2 tbsp*
¼ tsp	*salt*	*¼ tsp*
2 tbsp	*chopped parsley*	*2 tbsp*
	freshly ground black pepper	
9	*sheets phyllo pastry, each 30 cm (12 inches) square*	*9*
30 g	*unsalted butter, melted*	*1 oz*

Heat the oil in a heavy frying pan and fry the onion until it is soft. Add the beef and fry it until it has lost its red colour, then add the cumin and allspice and fry for another minute. Stir in the pine-nuts, salt, parsley, some pepper and 2 tablespoons of water, and cook the mixture for about 10 minutes. Remove it from the heat and set it aside to cool slightly while you prepare the phyllo pastry.

Preheat the oven to 190°C (375°F or Mark 5). Cut the phyllo pastry into 7.5 cm (3 inch) wide strips and use the beef mixture to make up the rolls as demonstrated below, covering the phyllo you are not working on with a dampened tea towel to prevent it from drying out and becoming brittle.

Place the phyllo rolls on a baking sheet, brush them with the remaining butter, and bake them until they are golden-brown and crisp — about 15 minutes. Serve them immediately.

Perfect Packages from Phyllo Pastry

1 *PREPARING THE PASTRY. Place a teaspoon of filling on the top strip of phyllo pastry 2.5 cm (1 inch) from the end. Starting from the opposite end, lightly brush three quarters of the pastry strip with melted butter.*

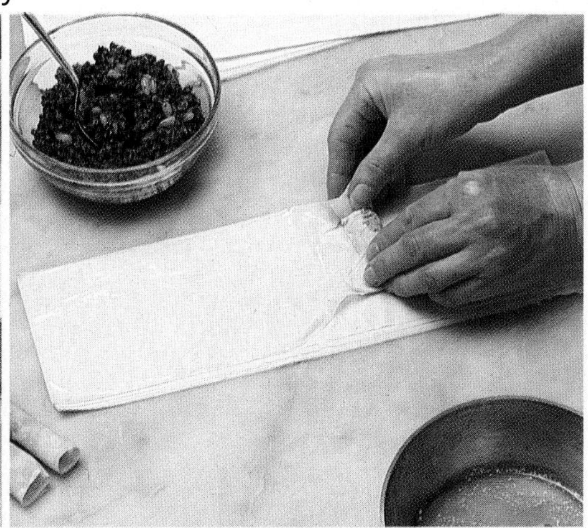

2 *FORMING THE ROLLS. Working from the unbuttered end, fold the pastry over the filling and roll up to the buttered section. Before continuing the roll, fold the sides of the pastry over the filling to seal the ends (above). Continue to roll the cylinder to the end of the pastry strip. Turn the cylinder over so that the seam is underneath.*

Beef and Tofu Satay

IN THIS ADAPTATION OF A SOUTH-EAST ASIAN SPECIALITY, TOFU — OR BEAN CURD — IS ALTERNATED WITH THE TRADITIONAL CUBES OF BEEF TO CREATE LOW-FAT BROCHETTES.

Serves 12
Working time: about 45 minutes
Total time: about 5 hours (includes marinating)

Calories **145**
Protein **7g**
Cholesterol **10mg**
Total fat **8g**
Saturated fat **2g**
Sodium **20mg**

3 tbsp	*low-sodium soy sauce or shoyu*	*3 tbsp*
3 tbsp	*fresh lemon juice*	*3 tbsp*
1	*garlic clove, finely chopped*	*1*
1 cm	*piece fresh ginger root, peeled and finely chopped*	*½ inch*
½ tsp	*light brown sugar*	*½ tsp*
¼ tsp	*hot red pepper flakes*	*¼ tsp*
250 g	*beef fillet, trimmed of fat and cut into 1 cm (½ inch) cubes*	*8 oz*
250 g	*firm tofu, well drained, cut into 1 cm (½ inch) cubes*	*8 oz*
	fresh coriander leaves, for garnish	
	Peanut sauce	
60 g	*shelled peanuts*	*2 oz*
2 tbsp	*groundnut oil*	*2 tbsp*
1	*onion, very finely chopped*	*1*
1	*garlic clove, crushed*	*1*
¾ tsp	*chili powder*	*¾ tsp*
¾ tsp	*ground coriander*	*¾ tsp*
1 tsp	*light brown sugar*	*1 tsp*
2 tsp	*fresh lemon juice*	*2 tsp*
2 tsp	*low-sodium soy sauce or shoyu*	*2 tsp*
1 tsp	*cornflour*	*1 tsp*

In a medium-sized bowl, mix the soy sauce, lemon juice, garlic, ginger, sugar and red pepper flakes, stirring until the sugar has dissolved. Add the beef and the tofu and stir to coat them with the marinade. Cover the bowl closely with plastic film and leave it to marinate in the refrigerator for 4 to 6 hours, turning over the meat and tofu occasionally.

To make the peanut sauce, preheat the oven to 180°C (350°F or Mark 4). Spread out the peanuts on a baking sheet and toast them in the oven for 10 minutes. When they are toasted, tip the nuts on to a tea towel and rub them vigorously in the towel to remove their loose brown skins. Put the nuts in a food processor and grind them finely.

Heat the oil in a non-stick frying pan. Add the onion, garlic, ground peanuts, chili powder and coriander, and fry them for 2 minutes, stirring constantly. Add the brown sugar, lemon juice, soy sauce and ¼ litre (8 fl oz) of water, and bring the mixture to the boil, stirring it well. Simmer the sauce until it is the consistency of cream — about 10 minutes — stirring frequently to prevent it from sticking. While it cooks, place the cornflour in a small bowl, add 1 tablespoon of water and stir them together to make a paste. When the sauce is ready, stir in the cornflour paste; this mixture will serve as a binder, and prevent the sauce from separating. Pour the sauce into a serving dish and leave it to cool.

About 30 minutes before you cook the satay, soak 12 bamboo skewers in cold water. This will keep them moist and prevent them from burning under the grill.

Preheat the grill. Remove the skewers from the water and pat them dry on a tea towel. Thread the beef

and the tofu cubes alternately on to the skewers and grill them 8 to 10 cm (3½ to 4 inches) below the heat source, turning the skewers occasionally to brown the meat evenly, for 5 to 8 minutes.

When the meat is cooked, transfer the skewers to a platter or individual serving plates, and garnish them with the coriander leaves. Serve the satay hot, accompanied by the peanut sauce.

EDITOR'S NOTE: *The red pepper flakes in the marinade make the beef cubes very spicy. For a milder flavour, rub the meat cubes with paper towels after you remove them from the marinade and before threading them on the skewer.*

Miniature Meatballs

Serves 6
Working time: about 40 minutes
Total time: about 1 hour and 30 minutes

Calories **220**
Protein **21g**
Cholesterol **75mg**
Total fat **8g**
Saturated fat **2g**
Sodium **160mg**

400 g	*lean beef, minced*	*14 oz*
90 g	*fresh wholemeal breadcrumbs*	*3 oz*
1 tbsp	*chopped parsley*	*1 tbsp*
1	*garlic clove, finely chopped*	*1*
1	*egg*	*1*
⅛ tsp	*salt*	*⅛ tsp*
	freshly ground black pepper	
½ tbsp	*virgin olive oil*	*½ tbsp*
	Spanish sauce	
1 tbsp	*virgin olive oil*	*1 tbsp*
1	*onion, chopped*	*1*
2	*garlic cloves, chopped*	*2*
1	*small sweet red pepper, chopped*	*1*
250 g	*ripe tomatoes, skinned, seeded (page 10), and chopped, or 200 g (7 oz) canned tomatoes, drained and chopped*	*8 oz*
⅛ tsp	*freshly ground black pepper*	*⅛ tsp*
6 cl	*medium sherry*	*2 fl oz*

To make the sauce, heat the oil in a heavy, fireproof casserole and fry the onion and garlic until they are soft but not browned. Add the chopped red pepper, tomatoes, salt and some freshly ground black pepper, and simmer the mixture over low heat for 20 minutes. While it cooks, prepare the meatballs.

Preheat the oven to 180°C (350°F or Mark 4). Combine the beef, breadcrumbs, parsley, garlic, egg and 2 tablespoons of water in a large mixing bowl. Add the salt and some black pepper and mix the ingredients until they are thoroughly blended. With dampened hands, shape the mixture into 36 miniature meatballs, each slightly smaller than a walnut.

Heat the oil in a heavy frying pan and fry the meatballs, shaking the pan and turning the meatballs constantly to prevent them from sticking, until they are browned all over. Remove the meatballs from the pan with a slotted spoon and drain them on paper towels.

Transfer the sauce to a blender or food processor, add the sherry, and purée the mixture. Return the sauce to the casserole, add the drained meatballs, and bake them for 40 minutes in the oven. Serve hot.

SUGGESTED ACCOMPANIMENT: *crusty bread.*

Home-Made Ravioli Cushions

1 ADDING EGGS TO FLOUR. Sift the flour and the salt on to a work surface, preferably marble as here, and make a well in the centre. Drop the egg and the egg whites into the well, then add the oil to soften the dough and make it easier to manipulate.

2 MIXING THE INGREDIENTS. With one hand, gradually push the flour from around the edge of the well into the eggs and oil. Stir with your fingers to form a batter. Continue to incorporate the flour into the eggs, until the mixture has become a firm paste and can be formed into a ball.

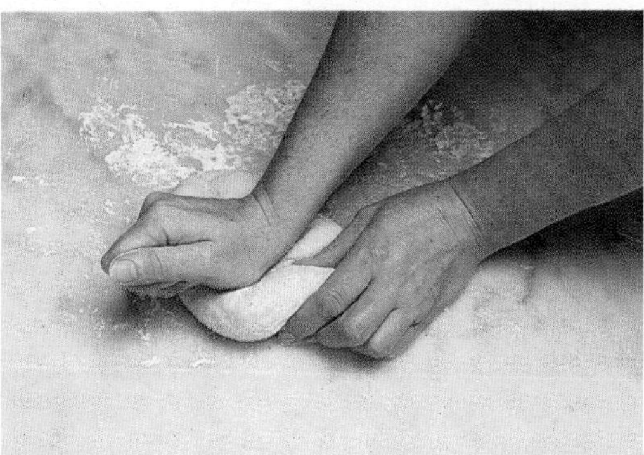

3 KNEADING THE DOUGH. On a lightly floured surface, press the dough flat with the heel of your hand. Fold the dough double then press again. Repeat this procedure for 5 to 10 minutes, until the dough is silky and elastic. Leave the dough, covered with a cloth, for 1 hour to rest.

4 ROLLING THE DOUGH. Divide the dough in half and cover one half with plastic film. On a lightly floured surface, roll out the other half, turning the dough at intervals to produce a round sheet. Continue rolling until the dough is almost translucent. Repeat with the second half.

5 STUFFING THE RAVIOLI. Using a fluted pastry wheel, trim the sheets of pasta into rectangles of equal size. Place teaspoons of the filling in rows on one of the sheets, about 2.5 cm (1 inch) apart. Brush the dough with water round the edges and between the fillings.

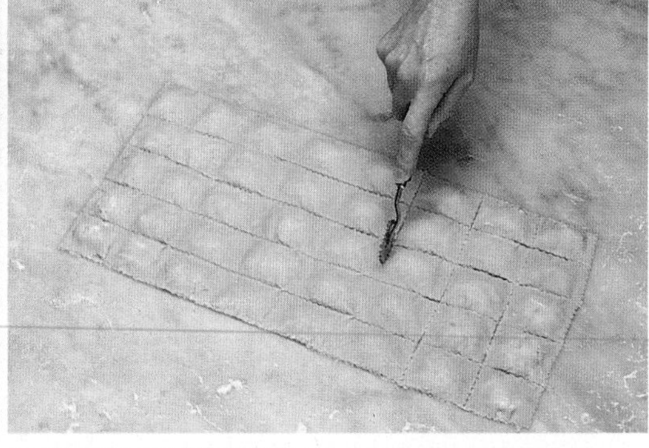

6 CUTTING THE RAVIOLI. Lay the second sheet of pasta over the first one. With your fingers, press the pasta between the mounds of filling and along the edges to stick the sheets together. Using the pastry wheel, cut between the rows of filling to separate the individual ravioli (above).

Fish Ravioli with Basil Dressing

Serves 8
Working time: about 1 hour and 10 minutes
Total time: about 2 hours and 30 minutes (includes chilling)

Calories **225**
Protein **11g**
Cholesterol **55mg**
Total fat **10g**
Saturated fat **3g**
Sodium **130mg**

350 g	*plaice fillets, skinned*	*12 oz*
8 cl	*unsalted fish stock (recipe, page 9)*	*3 fl oz*
2 tsp	*fresh lemon juice*	*2 tsp*
	freshly ground black pepper	
15 g	*unsalted butter*	*½ oz*
15 g	*plain flour*	*½ oz*
1 tsp	*capers, very finely chopped*	*1 tsp*
	Ravioli dough	
250 g	*strong plain flour*	*8 oz*
¼ tsp	*salt*	*¼ tsp*
1	*egg*	*1*
2	*egg whites*	*2*
1 tbsp	*virgin olive oil*	*1 tbsp*
	Basil dressing	
2 tbsp	*virgin olive oil*	*2 tbsp*
2 tbsp	*fresh lemon juice*	*2 tbsp*
2	*garlic cloves, crushed*	*2*
15 g	*Parmesan cheese, freshly grated*	*½ oz*
3 tbsp	*finely shredded basil leaves*	*3 tbsp*

Put the plaice in a saucepan with the stock, lemon juice and some pepper. Cover the pan, heat the stock gently and poach until the fish flakes easily — 4 to 5 minutes. Drain in a sieve set over a bowl, reserving the liquid. Flake the plaice gently with a fork.

In a saucepan, melt the butter and stir in the flour. Gradually pour in the reserved cooking liquid and bring to the boil, stirring until it thickens. Reduce the heat and simmer for 4 to 5 minutes, stirring frequently. Remove from the heat and stir in the plaice and the capers. Cover the filling with plastic film, let it cool, and place it in the refrigerator to chill for about an hour.

Meanwhile, prepare the dough for the ravioli following the instructions on the opposite page, Steps 1 to 3. Then, with the chilled filling, make the ravioli according to the technique described in Steps 4 to 6.

Put all the ingredients for the basil dressing into a large heatproof serving bowl and mix them thoroughly.

Bring a large pan of water to the boil, add the ravioli and cook them until they float on top of the water — 2 to 3 minutes. Pour the ravioli into a colander and drain thoroughly. Add them to the basil dressing and mix gently to coat them well. Serve immediately.

EDITOR'S NOTE: *The ravioli may be prepared in advance. Store them in the refrigerator in single layers, between sheets of waxed paper or plastic film lightly sprinkled with fine semolina.*

Tagliatelle with Spinach and Mushrooms

Serves 8
Working time: about 30 minutes
Total time: about 50 minutes

Calories **255**
Protein **11g**
Cholesterol **20mg**
Total fat **7g**
Saturated fat **4g**
Sodium **140mg**

45 g	*unsalted butter*	*1½ oz*
2	*garlic cloves, finely chopped*	*2*
500 g	*fresh spinach, washed, stems removed, leaves chopped*	*1 lb*
350 g	*button mushrooms, wiped and sliced*	*12 oz*
½ tsp	*salt*	*½ tsp*
	freshly ground black pepper	
	grated nutmeg	
750 g	*fresh tagliatelle, or 350 g (12 oz) dried tagliatelle*	*1½ lb*
45 g	*Parmesan cheese, freshly grated*	*1½ oz*

First, prepare the sauce. In a heavy-bottomed saucepan, melt the butter and add the garlic. Stir for a few seconds, then add the spinach and mushrooms. Cook the sauce over low heat for 3 to 4 minutes. Season it with the salt, some pepper and grated nutmeg, and keep it warm while you cook the pasta.

In a large pan, bring 4 litres (7 pints) of lightly salted water to the boil. Drop the tagliatelle into the water and cook them until they are *al dente* — 2 to 3 minutes for fresh pasta, about 10 minutes for dried.

When the tagliatelle are cooked, drain them thoroughly in a colander. Pour the sauce into a large, warmed serving bowl, and toss in the pasta, mixing well. Serve the pasta hot, accompanied by the Parmesan cheese.

Spinach-Filled Cannelloni Gratins with Tomato Sauce

Serves 4
Working (and total) time: about 1 hour

Calories **165**
Protein **10g**
Cholesterol **15mg**
Total fat **8g**
Saturated fat **4g**
Sodium **385mg**

4	*cannelloni tubes (about 90 g/3 oz)*	*4*
750 g	*spinach leaves, washed, stemmed, blanched in boiling water for 30 seconds, drained and squeezed dry*	*1½ lb*
15 g	*unsalted butter*	*½ oz*
1 tbsp	*single cream*	*1 tbsp*
¼ tsp	*salt*	*½ tsp*
	freshly ground black pepper	
½ tsp	*grated nutmeg*	*½ tsp*
15 g	*Parmesan cheese, freshly grated*	*½ oz*
15 g	*dry wholemeal breadcrumbs*	*½ oz*
1 tbsp	*finely shredded basil leaves*	*1 tbsp*
	Tomato sauce	
½ tbsp	*virgin olive oil*	*½ tbsp*
1	*small onion, very finely chopped*	*1*
1	*garlic clove, crushed*	*1*
750 g	*tomatoes, skinned, seeded (page 10) and chopped, or 400 g (14 oz) canned tomatoes, drained and sieved*	*1½ lb*
2 tbsp	*finely shredded basil leaves*	*2 tbsp*
¼ tsp	*salt*	*¼ tsp*
	freshly ground black pepper	

To make the tomato sauce, heat the oil in a heavy-bottomed saucepan, add the onion, and cook over very low heat until the onion is softened but not browned. Stir in the garlic, tomatoes, basil, salt and some pepper. Cook the mixture very gently, uncovered, until the tomato sauce is thickened and reduced by half — about 30 minutes.

Meanwhile, cook the cannelloni tubes in a large pan of lightly salted boiling water until they are softened — 3 to 4 minutes. Drain the tubes in a colander, rinse them under cold running water, and allow them to drain once more.

To prepare the filling, chop the spinach very finely. Heat the butter in a small frying pan, add the spinach and cook gently until it is heated through. Stir in the cream, the salt, some pepper and the grated nutmeg. Using a large spoon, fill the cannelloni tubes with the spinach mixture and place them in individual, well-buttered gratin dishes.

Preheat the grill to high. Spoon the tomato sauce over the cannelloni, sprinkle them generously with the Parmesan cheese and the breadcrumbs, and cook them under the grill until they are thoroughly heated through and golden-brown — about 5 minutes. Sprinkle the gratins with the shredded basil and serve them immediately.

EDITOR'S NOTE: *The cannelloni gratins may be prepared ahead of time and heated through just before serving.*

Pasta with Fresh Herbs and Garlic

Serves 8
Working time: about 10 minutes
Total time: about 20 minutes

Calories **250**
Protein **5g**
Cholesterol **0mg**
Total fat **7g**
Saturated fat **1g**
Sodium **50mg**

400 g	*fusilli or other spiralled pasta*	*14 oz*
250 g	*fromage frais*	*8 oz*
2 tbsp	*chopped parsley*	*2 tbsp*
1 tbsp	*chopped fresh oregano*	*1 tbsp*
2 tbsp	*chopped fresh thyme*	*2 tbsp*
1 tbsp	*chopped fresh mint*	*1 tbsp*
2 tbsp	*virgin olive oil*	*2 tbsp*
½	*garlic clove, finely chopped*	*½*
¼ tsp	*salt*	*¼ tsp*
	freshly ground black pepper	

Cook the pasta in 4 litres (7 pints) of lightly salted boiling water until it is *al dente* — about 9 minutes. Meanwhile, in a small bowl combine the *fromage frais,* chopped parsley, oregano, thyme and mint with the olive oil and chopped garlic; season the mixture with the salt and some freshly ground pepper.

When the fusilli are cooked, drain them in a colander, but leave a little of the cooking water clinging to the pasta: this will thin down the herb, cheese and garlic mixture to form a sauce. Stir the herb mixture into the pasta and serve it hot.

Wholemeal Spaghetti with Prawn Sauce

THE PRAWNS IN THIS RECIPE ARE COOKED UNSHELLED, RELEASING THEIR FULL FLAVOUR INTO THE TOMATO SAUCE. THE SHELLS ARE THEN REMOVED AT TABLE BY EACH DINER.

Serves 6
Working time: about 15 minutes
Total time: about 45 minutes

Calories **245**
Protein **11g**
Cholesterol **35mg**
Total fat **7g**
Saturated fat **1g**
Sodium **290mg**

2 tbsp	*virgin olive oil*	*2 tbsp*
1	*onion, chopped*	*1*
750 g	*fresh ripe plum tomatoes, skinned, seeded (page 10) and chopped, or 400 g (14 oz) canned plum tomatoes*	*1½ lb*
250 g	*prawns, shells left on*	*8 oz*
3	*garlic cloves, crushed*	*3*
¼ tsp	*salt*	*¼ tsp*
½ tsp	*cayenne pepper*	*½ tsp*
1½ tbsp	*chopped parsley*	*1½ tbsp*
300 g	*wholemeal spaghetti*	*10 oz*

In a large, heavy frying pan, heat the oil and sauté the onion until it is transparent — about 5 minutes. Add the tomatoes and 3 to 4 tablespoons of water, and cook the mixture for 15 minutes over low heat. Stir in the prawns and cook for another 5 minutes, then add the garlic, salt and cayenne pepper. Stir in the parsley, mix well, and keep warm.

Bring 4 litres (7 pints) of lightly salted water to the boil in a large pan. Drop the spaghetti into the water, and cook until *al dente* — about 10 minutes. Drain thoroughly in a colander. Transfer the pasta to a heated platter, then mix in the sauce and serve hot.

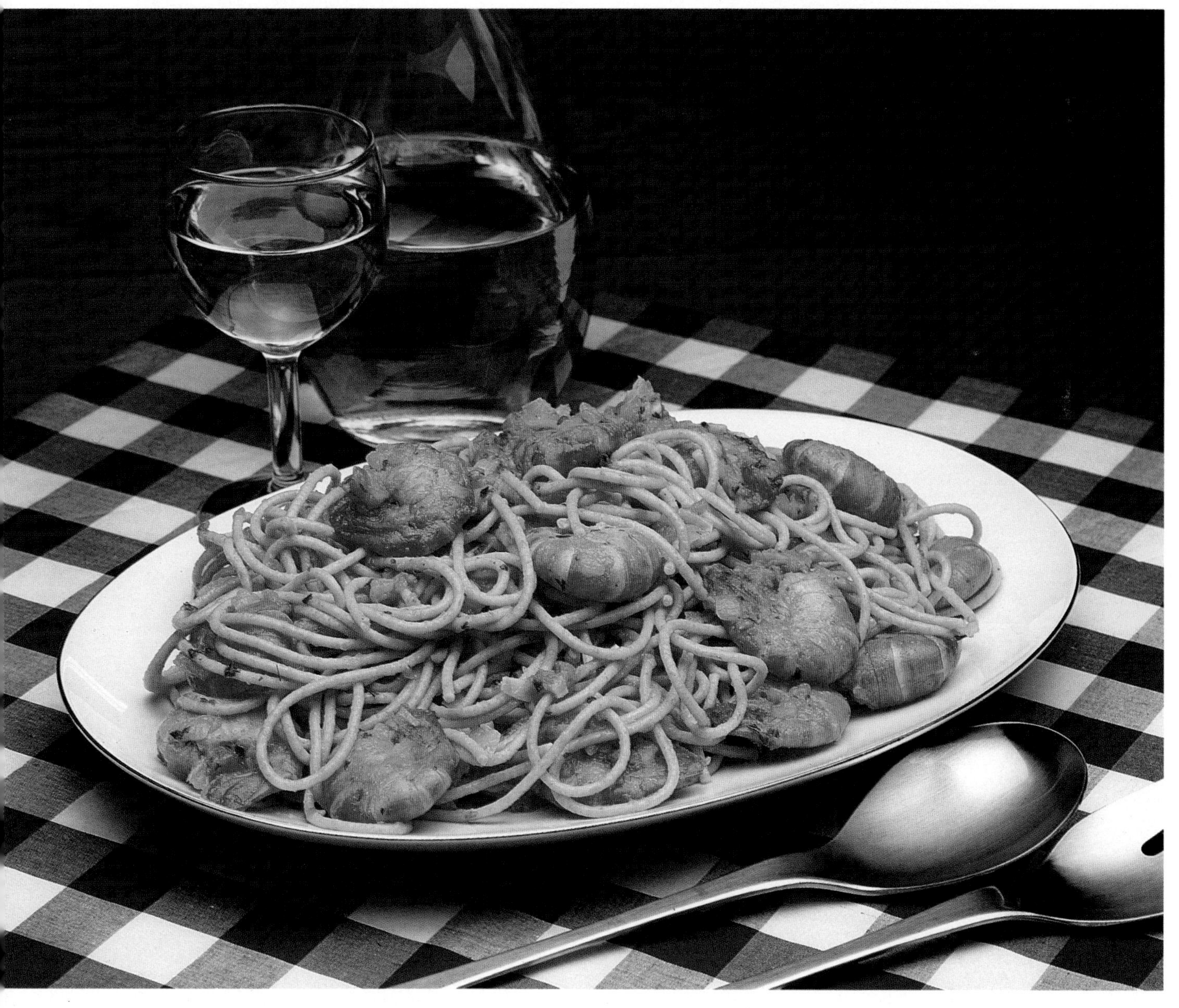

East-West Crab and Vegetable Crescents

Serves 12
Working (and total) time: about 1 hour and 45 minutes

Calories **190**
Protein **10g**
Cholesterol **80mg**
Total fat **4g**
Saturated fat **1g**
Sodium **150mg**

250 g	*strong plain flour*	*8 oz*
¼ tsp	*salt*	*¼ tsp*
1 tbsp	*safflower oil*	*1 tbsp*
2	*eggs*	*2*
⅛ tsp	*saffron threads (loosely packed), macerated for 20 minutes in 10 cl (3½ fl oz) boiling water*	*⅛ tsp*
	Vegetable and crab filling	
1 tbsp	*safflower oil*	*1 tbsp*
3	*spring onions, white and green parts separated and finely chopped*	*3*
185 g	*bamboo shoots, finely diced*	*6½ oz*
2	*parsnips, parboiled for 10 minutes, drained and finely diced*	*2*
20 g	*dried shiitake mushrooms, soaked in 12.5 cl (4 fl oz) cold water for 20 minutes*	*¾ oz*
7 g	*dried ceps, soaked in 4 tbsp cold water for 20 minutes*	*¼ oz*
1 tbsp	*miso*	*1 tbsp*
1	*garlic clove, finely chopped*	*1*
2 tsp	*finely grated fresh ginger root*	*2 tsp*
125 g	*button mushrooms, finely diced*	*4 oz*
1 tsp	*dry sherry*	*1 tsp*
1 tsp	*low-sodium soy sauce or shoyu*	*1 tsp*
⅛ tsp	*cayenne pepper*	*⅛ tsp*
	freshly ground black pepper	
250 g	*fresh crab meat, picked over and flaked*	*8 oz*
90 g	*fresh coriander*	*3 oz*

To make the dough for the dumplings, sieve the flour and the salt on to a cool, lightly floured work surface. Make a well in the centre of the flour, and pour in the oil and the eggs. Pour the saffron water through a small strainer into the well; transfer the saffron threads to a small bowl, and cover them with 2 tablespoons of boiling water.

With your fingertips, work the flour mixture into a soft dough. If the mixture is too dry, add a little more strained saffron water. Knead the dough until it is smooth and elastic, cover it with an inverted bowl, and leave it to rest for 1 hour.

While the dough rests, prepare the filling. In a wok or a heavy frying pan, heat ½ tablespoon of the oil over medium heat and stir-fry the white part of the spring onions until soft — about 30 seconds. Add the bamboo shoots and stir-fry for 1 minute, then add the parsnips and stir-fry for 30 seconds more. Remove the vegetables from the wok and set them aside.

Remove the shiitake mushrooms and the ceps from their soaking liquids with a slotted spoon and finely chop them. Strain the soaking liquids through a fine-meshed sieve into a bowl and stir in the miso.

Heat the remaining oil in the wok, toss in the garlic and the ginger and stir-fry until they are slightly golden; add the ceps, shiitake and button mushrooms and stir-fry for another minute. Pour in the miso mixture, increase the heat, and stir-fry until the liquid is nearly absorbed. Add the sherry, soy sauce, cayenne and some black pepper. Reduce the heat and cook until the mushrooms are dry — about 30 seconds. Remove the wok from the heat. In a large bowl, combine the stir-fried vegetables, the crab meat and the chopped spring onion greens, and set the mixture aside to cool.

Meanwhile, on a floured work surface, divide the dough into four parts with a sharp knife, and roll out each portion as thinly as possible. Using a 7.5 cm (3 inch) round, fluted pastry cutter, cut 15 circles of dough from each sheet.

Using a pastry brush, paint one half of a dough circle with cold water. Put 1 heaped teaspoon of filling on the unmoistened half-circle and place a coriander leaf, shiny side down, on the other half. Fold over the dough to cover the filling and pinch the edges of the circle together to seal them. Bend the dumpling gently into a crescent-moon shape and leave it to dry on a lightly oiled baking sheet. Repeat the process to fill and shape the remaining dumplings.

To cook the dumplings, bring about 2 litres (3½ pints) of water to the boil in a large pan. Add a drop of oil and a pinch of salt, adjust the heat so that the water is just bubbling, and lower 12 to 18 of the crescents carefully into the pan. Poach the dumplings until they float to the surface, then remove them with a slotted spoon. Set them aside in a warm place while you poach the remaining crescents.

Serve the dumplings hot.

SUGGESTED ACCOMPANIMENT: *steamed mange-tout.*

Steamed Chinese Dumplings

THESE DUMPLINGS WERE STEAMED IN A TRADITIONAL TWO-TIER CHINESE BAMBOO STEAMER IN TWO BATCHES. BAMBOO STEAMERS ARE AVAILABLE FROM ORIENTAL GROCERS IN A VARIETY OF SIZES AND TIERS; ALTERNATIVELY, AN ORDINARY STEAMER CAN BE USED.

Serves 8
Working time: about 1 hour and 30 minutes
Total time: about 4 hours

Calories **185**
Protein **10g**
Cholesterol **25mg**
Total fat **4g**
Saturated fat **1g**
Sodium **90mg**

250 g	*strong plain flour*	*8 oz*
15 g	*fresh yeast, or 7 g (¼ oz) dried yeast*	*½ oz*
¼ tsp	*sugar*	*¼ tsp*
½ tbsp	*safflower oil*	*½ tbsp*
⅛ tsp	*salt*	*⅛ tsp*
	Dried prawn and spinach filling	
2 tsp	*sesame seeds*	*2 tsp*
2 tsp	*safflower oil*	*2 tsp*
600 g	*spinach, washed and stemmed*	*1¼ lb*
1	*large onion, finely chopped*	*1*
1	*garlic clove, finely chopped*	*1*
½ tsp	*grated fresh ginger root*	*½ tsp*
2 tsp	*sesame oil*	*2 tsp*
90 g	*dried prawns, soaked for 20 minutes, drained and rinsed*	*3 oz*
	freshly ground black pepper	
16	*fresh coriander leaves*	*16*

Prepare the dough as described on the opposite page.

To make the filling, first toast the sesame seeds in a wok or large heavy-bottomed saucepan over medium-low heat until golden. Remove them from the pan and set aside. In the same pan, heat half the safflower oil, add the spinach, and stir-fry for 30 seconds; cover and steam for a further 30 seconds. Let the spinach cool slightly, then drain it on paper towels, squeeze it dry and chop it finely with a sharp knife. Set aside.

Heat the remaining safflower oil in the wok or saucepan and fry the onion gently until it is golden-brown. Add the garlic and ginger, stir-fry the mixture for 30 seconds, then stir in 1 teaspoon of the sesame oil and the prawns. Cook the mixture gently until it becomes quite dry — 10 to 15 minutes — then transfer it to a small bowl. Add the remaining sesame oil to the pan, heat it and sauté the spinach over low heat to evaporate most of its moisture. Stir in the prawn mixture, the sesame seeds, and some pepper. Remove the filling from the heat and leave it to cool.

Cut out sixteen 5 cm (2 inch) squares of greaseproof paper; rub them lightly with oil and set them aside. On a floured work surface, roll the risen dough into a long sausage, cut it into 16 segments and form each one into a ball. With a rolling pin, roll each ball into a circle measuring 11 cm (4½ inches) across.

Divide the prawn and spinach filling into 16 small balls, place one ball in the centre of a round of dough, and gather up the edges of the circle to enclose it. To seal the dumpling, pinch and twist the edges of the dough together. Place the dumpling on a paper square, and repeat the process to form 16 dumplings. Cover them with a sheet of oiled plastic film and leave

them to rise for 15 minutes at room temperature.

Arrange the dumplings, mounted on their paper squares, on steamer racks and set them over a pan of boiling water. Lay a tea towel over the top tier and put on the lid. Take the loose corners of the tea towel and tie them over the top of the lid: this prevents the heat escaping. Steam the dumplings for 15 minutes over high heat. With a spatula, remove them from the steamer, peel off the paper and transfer them to a heated dish, making sure they do not touch. If cooking in two batches, cover the first batch with a tea towel to keep warm. Serve garnished with the coriander.

SUGGESTED ACCOMPANIMENT: *steamed baby sweetcorns.*

Making Yeast Dough

1 *COMBINING THE INGREDIENTS. Place the flour in a large bowl and put the bowl in the oven at its lowest setting for 3 to 5 minutes; warming the flour will help the dough to rise. Mix the yeast and sugar with the oil and 12.5 cl (4 fl oz) of warm water in a jug. Add the salt to the flour and make a well. Pour the yeast mixture into the well.*

2 *MIXING THE DOUGH. Mix the flour and liquid together with one hand, scooping and turning until they are thoroughly blended and form a shaggy mass. Empty the dough from the bowl on to the work surface. Wash out and dry the mixing bowl.*

3 *KNEADING THE DOUGH. Hold the dough with one hand. With the heel of the other hand, push the dough away from you until it begins to tear (above). At first, the dough will be sticky and will tear very easily. Fold the dough back and at the same time give the mass a slight turn.*

4 *FORMING THE DOUGH INTO A ROUND. Continue to knead the dough with a regular rythmic motion for 10 to 15 minutes. Exerting a light even pressure with the heel of your hand, push away a corner of dough; at the same time give the corner a slight twist, to turn the whole mass of dough slightly.*

5 *FINISHING THE ROUND. Fold the pushed-out piece of dough back into the middle and begin the process again with the adjacent section. Repeat the process with a regular, rhythmic motion until the loaf is rounded. Turn the dough so that its pleats are on the bottom and place it in the mixing bowl.*

6 *LEAVING THE DOUGH TO RISE. To keep the dough moist, cover the bowl with plastic film. Set aside in a warm place until the dough has doubled in bulk — 1½ to 2½ hours. To test that the dough has risen enough, press a finger into it — if the indentation remains, filling in very slowly, the dough is ready.*

3 *Tossed in a microwaved sauce of chanterelles, crème fraîche, fromage frais and mustard seeds, a dish of saffron pasta (recipe, opposite) stands ready to serve.*

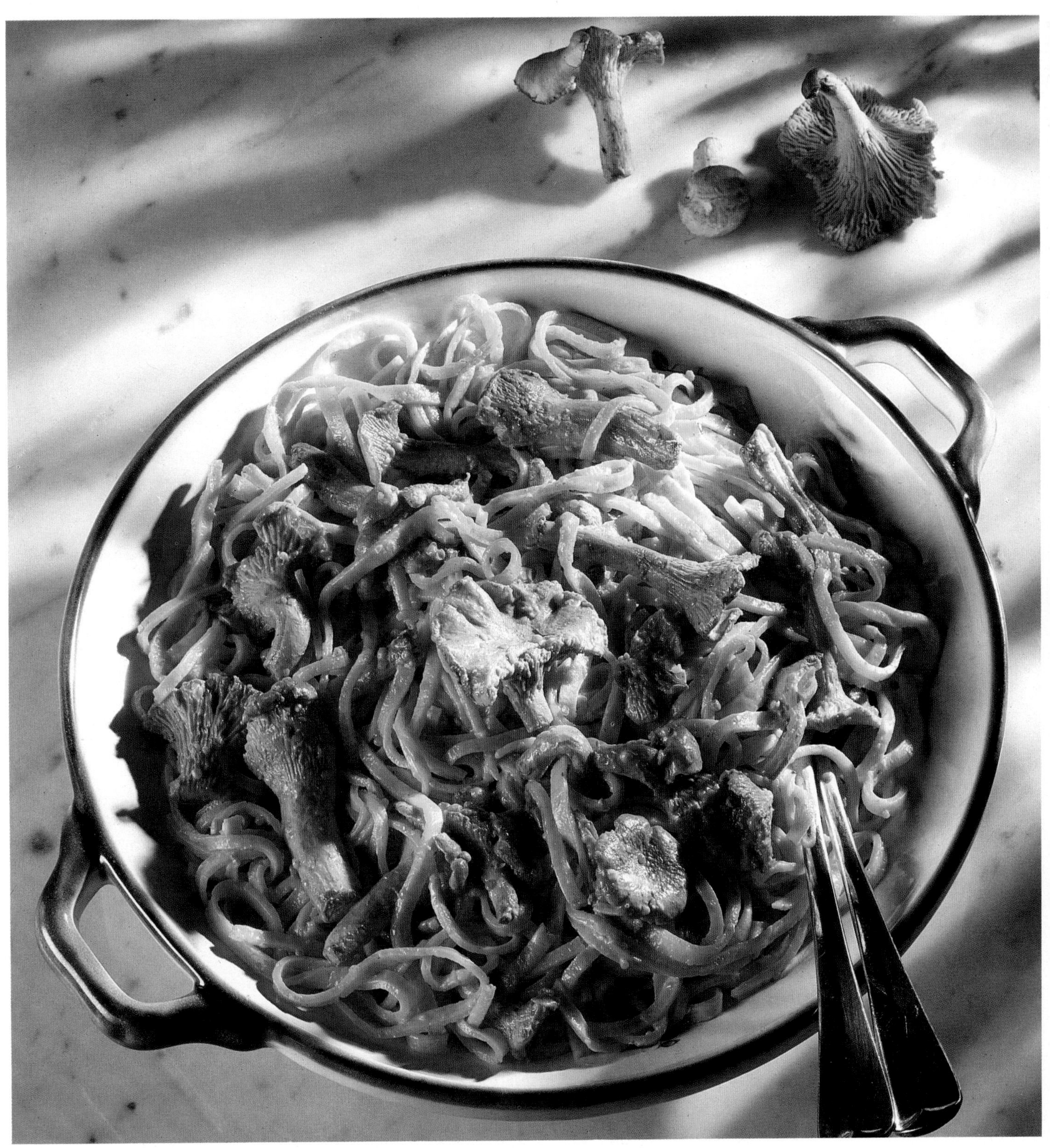

Hors-d'Oeuvre in the Microwave

In the creation of hors-d'oeuvre, the microwave oven is an invaluable ally to the busy cook seeking first-rate results. Not every dish is improved by microwaving: food that needs fast boiling, recipes with many steps and gratins requiring intense heat to form a crust are better cooked conventionally. But others lend themselves particularly well to this new way of cooking. Vegetables display hidden depths of subtlety and savour. Fish and shellfish retain a delicacy and juiciness often lost when treated in more orthodox ways. Fresh herbs do not fade or blacken. Spices such as yellow mustard seeds remain bright and vibrant.

Capitalizing on these advantages of the microwave, the collection of recipes that follows emphasizes simplicity: rich sauces and calorie-laden garnishes become superfluous when foods look appealing and taste so deliciously of themselves.

Things happen faster in a microwave, and many of these recipes are cooked in moments. The bacon-stuffed mushrooms on page 137, for example, need only about 5 minutes to cook, and the artichokes on page 134 only 16 to 20 minutes — less than half the time they would take if boiled on top of the stove.

But to a cook in the throes of dinner party preparations, the most alluring of the microwave's advantages may be its efficiency. With the first course under way in the microwave, the stove is completely free for the rest of the menu. And at the end of the evening comes a final blessing: less washing up. The dish in which the food is assembled and microwaved is often the same one in which it comes to the table.

Some of the recipes in this chapter call for food to be covered with plastic film: make sure that you use only film labelled microwave-safe. If covering a dish containing liquid, leave a corner of the film open, or slit the film with a knife, in order to prevent a dangerous build-up of steam.

The recipes have been tested in 650-watt and 700-watt ovens; the term "high" is used to indicate full power. Remember that food continues to cook after removal from the microwave; be sure to let it stand for a few minutes before you test it for doneness.

Golden Pasta with Chanterelles

Serves 6
Working time: about 45 minutes
Total time: about 2 hours

Calories **185**
Protein **6g**
Cholesterol **45mg**
Total fat **6g**
Saturated fat **2g**
Sodium **60mg**

175 g	*strong plain flour*	*6 oz*
30 g	*coarsely ground semolina*	*1 oz*
1	*egg*	*1*
¼ tsp	*saffron threads, pounded to a powder with a pinch of coarse salt in a mortar and dissolved in 2 tbsp of hot water*	*¼ tsp*
2 tsp	*yellow mustard seeds*	*2 tsp*
175 g	*chanterelle mushrooms*	*6 oz*
	Saffron dressing	
	small pinch saffron	
⅛ tsp	*coarse salt*	*⅛ tsp*
3 tbsp	*crème fraîche or thick soured cream*	*3 tbsp*
5 tbsp	*fromage frais*	*5 tbsp*

To prepare the dough in a food processor, sift the flour and semolina into the bowl, add the egg and process the mixture until it forms fine crumbs — about 30 seconds. With the processor switched on, pour in the saffron water a little at a time and process the dough until it forms a ball. To make the pasta dough by hand, sift the flour and semolina into a bowl, make a well in the centre, and add the egg and saffron water. Slowly incorporate the flour mixture into the liquid with a fork. If the dough is sticky, add a teaspoon more flour; if crumbly, add a few drops of water. Knead the dough on a floured surface until it is very smooth and elastic — about 10 minutes.

Let the dough rest for about 30 minutes —'or for 1 hour if you have prepared it by hand.

To cut the pasta, divide the dough into four pieces, and roll them out thinly on a floured work surface. Dust each rolled-out piece lightly with flour, pile up the pieces in a single neat stack, and cut the dough into very thin strips with a sharp knife or pastry cutter. Alternatively, roll out the dough and cut it into ribbons with a pasta machine. Hang the pasta over a rolling pin or a broom handle to dry for about 30 minutes.

Place the mustard seeds in a small bowl, and microwave them on high for about 2 minutes to release their aromatic oil. Remove the seeds from the microwave and crush them with a pestle. ▶

Bring 1.25 litres (2 pints) of water to the boil in a large saucepan. Meanwhile, place the chanterelle mushrooms in a dish greased with safflower oil. Cover them with plastic film left slightly open at one side and microwave on high for 2 minutes, turning the dish half way through cooking.

To make the dressing, pound the saffron in a mortar with the salt, mix it with the *crème fraîche* and *fromage frais*, and place in the microwave on high until it is warmed through — about 30 seconds.

Put the pasta in the boiling water and cook it until it is *al dente* — about 2 minutes. Drain thoroughly in a colander, rinse with hot water to remove all excess starch, and then drain thoroughly a second time.

Place the pasta in a large, warmed bowl. Toss it quickly with the saffron dressing, the crushed mustard seeds and the mushrooms, and serve hot.

EDITOR'S NOTE: *Tiny golden oyster mushrooms may be used instead of chanterelles. To cook them, place the mushrooms in a single layer in a round dish lined with kitchen paper, cover with plastic film left slightly open at one side and microwave on high for 1 minute, turning the dish after 30 seconds. Remove the mushrooms from the microwave and leave them to rest, still on the kitchen paper, for another minute.*

Baby Beetroots in Orange and Walnut Dressing

Serves 4
Working time: about 30 minutes
Total time: about 45 minutes

Calories **105**
Protein **2g**
Cholesterol **0mg**
Total fat **9g**
Saturated fat **1g**
Sodium **40mg**

6	*small beetroots (about 350g/12 oz), carefully scrubbed clean but unpeeled*	6
1 tbsp	*walnut oil*	1 tbsp
1 tbsp	*safflower oil*	1 tbsp
2 tbsp	*fresh orange juice*	2 tbsp
1 tsp	*grated orange rind*	1 tsp
15g	*shelled walnuts, finely chopped*	½ oz
	freshly ground black pepper	
90g	*curly endive*	3 oz
1	*onion, sliced into thin rings*	1

Put the beetroots into a casserole and add hot water to reach half way up the beetroots. Cover the casserole and microwave on high for 10 minutes. Using a spoon, turn the beetroots over, then replace the lid and continue microwaving until the beetroots are just tender — about 7 minutes more.

Remove the beetroots from the casserole with a slotted spoon and leave them to cool while you make the dressing. In a small bowl, beat together the walnut oil, safflower oil, orange juice, grated orange rind, chopped walnuts and some pepper.

When the beetroots are cool enough to handle, peel them with a sharp knife. Divide the curly endive among four plates. Cut the beetroots into thin rounds and arrange them, together with the onion rings, on top of the beds of curly endive leaves.

Stir the dressing rapidly with a fork and pour it over the beetroot slices and onions, making sure that the walnuts are evenly distributed.

Scorzonera with Walnuts and Chervil

BLACK-SKINNED SCORZONERA AND ITS PALER RELATIVE, SALSIFY, HAVE A DELICATE FLAVOUR SAID BY SOME TO RESEMBLE THAT OF THE OYSTER. INDEED, SALSIFY IS SOMETIMES KNOWN AS OYSTER-PLANT.

Serves 4
Working time: about 35 minutes
Total time: about 2 hours (includes chilling)

Calories **140**
Protein **2g**
Cholesterol **0mg**
Total fat **12g**
Saturated fat **2g**
Sodium **130mg**

3 tbsp	*fresh lemon juice*	*3 tbsp*
½ tsp	*salt*	*½ tsp*
500 g	*scorzonera or salsify, scrubbed well and cut into 5 cm (2 inch) lengths*	*1 lb*
2 tbsp	*safflower oil*	*2 tbsp*
1 tsp	*finely chopped parsley*	*1 tsp*
2 tbsp	*torn fresh chervil*	*2 tbsp*
	freshly ground black pepper	
2 tbsp	*shelled walnuts, chopped*	*2 tbsp*

In a deep bowl, combine 1 tablespoon of the lemon juice and ¼ tsp of the salt with 45 cl (¾ pint) of water. Add the scorzonera, cover the bowl with plastic film, leaving a corner open, and microwave on high until the scorzonera is just fork tender — about 10 minutes.

Drain the scorzonera in a colander, cover the colander with plastic film and let the vegetable rest for 5 minutes to finish cooking in its own steam. Remove the plastic film and set the scorzonera aside to cool.

Meanwhile, prepare the dressing. In a small bowl, mix the oil with the remaining lemon juice, the parsley and the chervil, stirring well until they are thoroughly combined. Season this mixture with the remaining salt and a some freshly ground pepper.

When the scorzonera is cool enough to handle, peel the dark skin from each piece with a sharp knife and place the peeled segments in a deep serving dish. Pour half of the lemon dressing over the scorzonera and set the rest aside.

Let the scorzonera cool to room temperature, cover it with plastic film and place it in the refrigerator to chill for about 1 hour. Just before serving, mix the chopped walnuts into the reserved dressing and spoon it over the chilled scorzonera.

EDITOR'S NOTE: *The scorzonera can also be served warm. While the vegetable cooks, combine all the ingredients for the dressing and mix in the walnuts. As soon as the scorzonera is cool enough to handle, peel it quickly, place it in a deep serving dish, spoon over the walnut dressing and serve the vegetable immediately.*

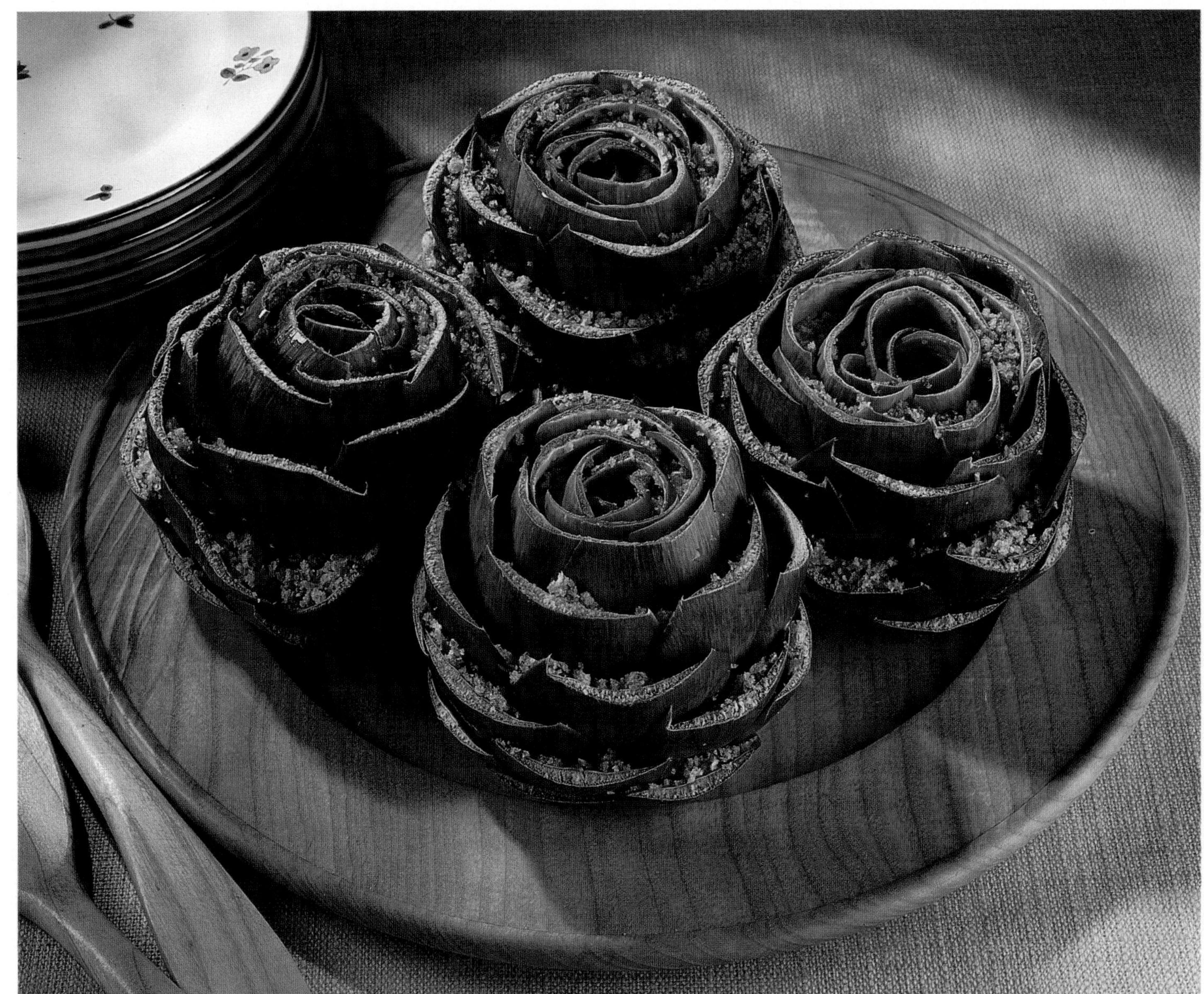

Stuffed Artichokes

BREADCRUMB-STUFFED ARTICHOKES APPEAR OFTEN IN SICILIAN AND SOUTHERN ITALIAN COOKERY. ARTICHOKES NOT ONLY COOK FASTER IN THE MICROWAVE BUT ALSO RETAIN A FRESHER, GREENER COLOUR THAN WHEN STEAMED ON THE STOVE.

Serves 4
Working time: about 40 minutes
Total time: about 1 hour

Calories **210**
Protein **10g**
Cholesterol **15mg**
Total fat **12g**
Saturated fat **4g**
Sodium **295mg**

125 g	*fresh wholemeal breadcrumbs*	*4oz*
4	*artichokes*	*4*
1½ tbsp	*fresh lemon juice*	*1½ tbsp*
4 tbsp	*finely grated Parmesan cheese*	*4 tbsp*
2 tbsp	*virgin olive oil*	*2 tbsp*
2	*cloves garlic, crushed*	*2*
2 tbsp	*finely chopped parsley*	*2 tbsp*
	freshly ground black pepper	

Spread the breadcrumbs for the stuffing in a shallow layer on a plate and microwave, uncovered, on high until they start to crisp — 3 to 4 minutes. Set the crumbs aside while you prepare the artichokes.

Discard the artichoke stalks, cutting them level with the base so that the artichokes stand upright. With a small, sharp knife, trim away about 1 cm (½ inch) from the tips of all the pointed leaves, and slice off about 2.5 cm (1 inch) from the top of each artichoke. Once cut, artichokes quickly lose their colour when exposed to the air; keep them green by dipping each one in water acidulated with 1 tablespoon of the lemon juice.

To cook the artichokes, measure 30 cl (½ pint) water and the remaining lemon juice into a dish that will be large enough to hold the artichokes compactly. Microwave the liquid, uncovered, on high until it boils — about 4 minutes. Arrange the drained artichokes, stalk ends up, in the hot liquid. Cover with plastic film, leaving a corner open, and microwave on high for 12 minutes. Remove the dish from the microwave and turn each artichoke upside down. Cover again with plastic film and microwave until the leaves can be pulled away easily and the base of each artichoke is readily pierced with a fork — 4 to 8 minutes, depending on their size.

Meanwhile, prepare the stuffing. In a small mixing bowl, combine the breadcrumbs with the cheese. Make a well in the centre and pour the oil into this hollow. With a fork, mix the crushed garlic and the parsley into the oil, grind in some black pepper and stir until all the ingredients are thoroughly blended.

Drain the cooked artichokes in a colander and stand them upright on a board. With your fingers, draw open the centre of each artichoke and pull out and discard a few of the central leaves. Using a teaspoon, scoop out and discard the hairy choke *(page 26, Step 2)*.

Gently draw the leaves away from the body of each artichoke to form pockets, and pack the openings loosely with the breadcrumb mixture. Sprinkle the remaining crumbs over the top of the artichokes.

Arrange the stuffed artichokes on a serving dish. Cover them with plastic film, leaving one corner open, and microwave on high until the artichokes are heated through — 6 to 8 minutes. Serve the artichokes hot.

Tomatoes with a Spinach and Tofu Stuffing

Serves 4
Working (and total) time: about 35 minutes

Calories **150**
Protein **9g**
Cholesterol **5mg**
Total fat **8g**
Saturated fat **2g**
Sodium **280mg**

1 tbsp	*flaked almonds*	*1 tbsp*
350 g	*spinach, stalks removed, leaves washed and finely shredded*	*12 oz*
2	*beef tomatoes (about 500 g/1 lb)*	*2*
60 g	*smoked tofu*	*2 oz*
1 tbsp	*grated Parmesan cheese*	*1 tbsp*
2 tbsp	*fresh wholemeal breadcrumbs*	*2 tbsp*
2 tsp	*finely shredded fresh basil, or ½ tsp dried basil*	*2 tsp*
	freshly ground black pepper	
⅛ tsp	*salt*	*⅛ tsp*
1 tbsp	*virgin olive oil*	*1 tbsp*

In a heavy frying pan, toss the almonds over high heat until they are golden-brown — about 1 minute.

Put the shredded spinach leaves in a bowl, cover them loosely with plastic film or with a lid, and microwave them on high for 3 minutes. Transfer the cooked spinach to a colander to drain thoroughly. Press the leaves gently to remove as much water as possible.

While the spinach drains, halve the tomatoes horizontally, scoop out their seeds with a spoon and discard the seeds. Using a sharp knife, cut out and reserve the tomato pulp. Chop 1 tablespoon of the pulp and set it aside; reserve the rest for another use.

To prepare the stuffing, finely chop the tofu and mix it with the spinach, chopped tomato pulp, Parmesan cheese, breadcrumbs, basil and some freshly ground pepper. Season the hollowed-out tomatoes with the salt and more pepper, then press the mixture into them with a spoon. Sprinkle a little of the olive oil over the top of each tomato.

Place the stuffed tomatoes on a serving dish and microwave them, uncovered, on medium low for 5 minutes. Give each tomato a half turn, then microwave them on low until the tomato shells are tender — 3 to 5 minutes more.

Garnish the top of each stuffed tomato with the toasted almond flakes and serve hot.

SUGGESTED ACCOMPANIMENT: *crusty bread.*

EDITOR'S NOTE: *Stuffed beef tomatoes make a substantial starter; for a lighter hors-d'oeuvre, you can substitute a smaller variety of firm-fleshed tomato and halve the quantity of stuffing. Smoked tofu (bean curd) is available from Oriental and health food shops; if it is unobtainable, however, plair tofu may be substituted.*

Aubergines Stuffed with Lamb and Buckwheat

WHEN AUBERGINES ARE TO BE COOKED BY CONVENTIONAL METHODS THEY ARE OFTEN SALTED AND RINSED FIRST TO DRAW OUT THEIR BITTER JUICES. COOKS HAVE FOUND THAT THIS STEP IS UNNECESSARY WHEN AUBERGINES ARE MICROWAVED.

Serves 4
Working (and total) time: about 40 minutes

Calories **200**
Protein **13g**
Cholesterol **30mg**
Total fat **11g**
Saturated fat **2g**
Sodium **140mg**

30 g	*roasted buckwheat groats (kasha)*	*1 oz*
2	*aubergines (about 200 g/7 oz each), stalks left on, skins pierced two or three times with a skewer*	*2*
1	*small onion, finely chopped*	*1*
1 tbsp	*safflower oil*	*1 tbsp*
30 g	*pine-nuts, finely chopped*	*1 oz*
150 g	*leftover cooked lean lamb, minced*	*5 oz*
3 tsp	*chopped fresh oregano, or ½ tsp dried oregano*	*3 tsp*
2 tsp	*sweet paprika*	*2 tsp*
¼ tsp	*salt*	*¼ tsp*
4	*medium tomatoes, puréed in a blender, sieved, skins and seeds discarded*	*4*
1 tbsp	*chopped parsley*	*1 tbsp*
	freshly ground black pepper	

Place the buckwheat groats in a small bowl and microwave on high for 30 seconds. Add 12.5 cl (4 fl oz) of hot water and microwave on high until the water is nearly absorbed — about 4 minutes more. Cover the buckwheat with plastic film and set it aside.

Arrange the aubergines in a deep baking dish and add 4 tablespoons of water. Cover with plastic film, leaving a corner open. Microwave on high until they are soft and their colour fades — about 10 minutes.

Meanwhile, prepare the stuffing. Put the onion in a glass bowl with the oil and microwave on high until soft — about 3 to 4 minutes. Stir in the pine-nuts and microwave on high for 1 minute; stir again and microwave on high until the nuts begin to brown — about 30 seconds. Stir in the lamb, oregano, buckwheat, paprika, salt and 2 tablespoons of the puréed tomato.

Halve the aubergines lengthwise. With a spoon,

scoop out most of the flesh from each aubergine half, leaving a shell about 5 cm (¼ inch) thick. Chop the flesh, stir it into the lamb and buckwheat, and pile this stuffing into the aubergine shells. Arrange the shells on a serving platter, leaving a space in the centre for a small bowl. Cover the aubergines with non-stick parchment paper and microwave on high until hot — about 4 minutes. Sprinkle with the parsley.

Meanwhile, season the remaining puréed tomato with plenty of pepper. Put the purée in a serving bowl and microwave on high for 1 minute. Place the bowl of purée in the centre of the aubergines and serve.

EDITOR'S NOTE: *This dish may also be prepared with 125 g (5 oz) very lean raw minced lamb. Crumble the lamb on to a glass plate, cover the plate with a paper towel and microwave it on high for a total of 90 seconds, stirring after 45 seconds.*

Bacon-Stuffed Mushrooms

Serves 4
Working (and total) time: about 20 minutes

Calories **100**
Protein **7g**
Cholesterol **15mg**
Total fat **6g**
Saturated fat **2g**
Sodium **500mg**

4	*large field mushrooms (about 300 g/10 oz), rinsed, dried, stalks removed*	*4*
1 tbsp	*dry vermouth*	*1 tbsp*
4 tbsp	*coarsely chopped parsley*	*4 tbsp*
100 g	*lean unsmoked bacon rashers, trimmed of rind and all fat*	*3½ oz*
1	*garlic clove, crushed*	*1*
1 tbsp	*virgin olive oil*	*1 tbsp*
15 g	*fresh wholemeal breadcrumbs*	*½ oz*
	freshly ground black pepper	

Arrange the mushroom caps upside down in a single layer in a shallow dish, and sprinkle them with the dry vermouth and parsley. Cover the mushroom caps loosely with plastic film.

To make the stuffing, cut the bacon into small strips. Put the bacon and the crushed garlic in a bowl, stir in the olive oil, and microwave on high until the bacon begins to release its juices — about 1 minute. Stir the breadcrumbs and some pepper into the bacon mixture. Microwave the mixture on high until it is crisp — about 1 minute. Cover the stuffing with plastic film and keep it warm while you cook the mushrooms.

Leaving the mushrooms loosely covered, microwave them on high for 3 minutes, until they are just tender. Remove the plastic film, spread the bacon stuffing on top of the mushroom caps, and microwave on high until they are hot — about 30 seconds. Serve the stuffed mushrooms immediately.

Scallops Anise

Serves 4
Working time: about 25 minutes
Total time: about 1 hour (includes marinating)

Calories **115**
Protein **3g**
Cholesterol **40mg**
Total fat **2g**
Saturated fat **1g**
Sodium **100mg**

500 g	*shelled scallops, bright white connective tissue removed, rinsed under cold water and patted dry*	*1 lb*
½	*fresh lime, juice and finely grated rind only*	*½*
350 g	*tomatoes, skinned, seeded (page 10) and finely chopped*	*12 oz*
7 g	*unsalted butter, softened*	*¼ oz*
1 tsp	*anise-flavoured liqueur*	*1 tsp*
1	*small bunch fresh chervil, large stems removed*	*1*
¼ tsp	*salt*	*¼ tsp*
	freshly ground black pepper	

Separate the fleshy part of the scallops from their corals. Pierce each coral once to keep it from bursting during cooking. If you are using large scallops, slice each one into two pieces horizontally; if you are using the smaller queen scallops, leave the scallops whole but pierce each one with the point of a sharp knife. Marinate the scallops and corals in the lime juice and rind for 45 minutes. Meanwhile, place the chopped tomato in a fine sieve and let it drain for 30 minutes.

In a small mixing bowl, cream the butter and the liqueur with a wooden spoon; set the mixture aside to allow the flavours to blend.

Spread the chervil on a 30 cm (12 inch) dish and arrange the drained scallops and corals in a single layer on top. Cover the dish with plastic film, leaving a slight opening. Microwave on high for 1 minute, giving the dish a quarter turn after 30 seconds. Let the scallops rest in a warm place while you prepare their sauce.

Place the anise-flavoured butter in a bowl and microwave on high until the butter sizzles — 20 to 30 seconds. Add the tomato to the butter and microwave again on high until the mixture is just heated through — about 30 seconds.

Season the scallops with half of the salt; sprinkle the tomatoes with the remaining salt and some pepper. Divide the tomato mixture among four plates, piling it to one side. Arrange the scallops and some chervil next to the tomatoes, and serve immediately.

Plaice with Lemon and Parsley

MICROWAVING FISH FILLETS ON A BED OF HERBS AND AROMATIC VEGETABLES RETAINS THE MOISTURE AND ENHANCES THE FLAVOUR.

Serves 8
Working (and total) time: about 30 minutes

Calories **65**
Protein **11g**
Cholesterol **35mg**
Total fat **2g**
Saturated fat **0g**
Sodium **125mg**

8	*plaice fillets (about 125g/4 oz each), skinned*	8
⅛ tsp	*salt*	⅛ tsp
	freshly ground black pepper	
1	*small onion, very finely chopped*	1
2 tbsp	*finely chopped parsley*	2 tbsp
3 tbsp	*fresh lemon juice*	3 tbsp
4 tbsp	*white wine*	4 tbsp
8	*thin lemon slices*	8

Lay the fillets flat on a work surface, skinned side up. Season them with the salt and some pepper.

In the base of a shallow serving dish, spread out the onion and parsley, and sprinkle with the lemon juice and white wine. Double over each fillet, with the skinned side in, and arrange the fillets on top of the onion and parsley in two overlapping rows. Tuck the lemon slices between the fillets.

Cover the dish loosely with plastic film, then microwave on high until the fish is opaque — 3 to 4 minutes. Rotate the dish once during the cooking time.

Let the fish stand, still covered with plastic film, for 3 minutes. Then remove the film and serve the plaice straight from the dish, spooning a little of the cooking liquid over each fillet.

EDITOR'S NOTE: *The fish and its cooking liquid may also be served cold, garnished with a salad of radicchio leaves.*

Glossary

Acidulated water: a dilute solution of lemon juice in water, used to keep certain vegetables from discolouring after they are peeled.
Al dente: an Italian term meaning "to the tooth". It is used to describe the texture and taste of perfectly cooked pasta: chewy but with no flavour of flour.
Almond oil: a highly fragrant oil used in small amounts to flavour salads. Its traditional role is as a flavouring agent in confectionery.
Balsamic vinegar: a mild, intensely fragrant wine-based vinegar made in northern Italy; traditionally it is aged in wooden casks.
Basil: a leafy herb with a strong, spicy aroma when fresh, often used in Italian cooking. Covered with olive oil and refrigerated in a tightly sealed container, fresh basil leaves may be kept for up to six months.
Batavian endive (also called escarole): a broad-leaved green with a pleasantly bitter flavour, best used in combination with sweeter greens.
Blanch: to partially cook food by immersing it briefly in boiling water.
Brochette: the French name for a skewer; also refers to skewered and grilled meat, fish or vegetables.
Buckwheat groats (also called kasha): the nutty-tasting seeds of the buckwheat plant, hulled, steamed, dried, and sometimes ground; often also toasted to intensify flavour.
Buckwheat flour: a strongly flavoured flour made from roasted buckwheat seeds.
Burghul (also called bulgur): a type of cracked wheat, where the kernels are steamed and dried before being crushed.
Calorie (or kilocalorie): a precise measure of the energy food supplies when it is broken down for use in the body.
Cayenne pepper: a fiery powder ground from the seeds and pods of red peppers. Used in small amounts to heighten other flavours.
Celeriac (also called celery root): the knobby, tuberous root of a plant in the celery family.
Ceps (also called porcini): wild mushrooms with a pungent, earthy flavour that survives drying or long cooking. Dried ceps should be soaked in hot water before they are used.
Chanterelle mushroom (also called girolle): a variety of wild mushroom that is trumpet-shaped and yellow-orange in colour. Chanterelles are available fresh or dried; dried chanterelles should be soaked in hot water before use.
Chervil: a lacy, slightly anise-flavoured herb often used as a companion to other herbs, such as tarragon and chives. Because long cooking may kill its flavour, chervil should be added at the last minute.
Chestnut mushroom: a cultivated mushroom with a dark skin and firm flesh. Its taste is stronger than that of button mushrooms.
Chicory: a small, cigar-shaped vegetable, composed of many tightly wrapped white to pale-yellow leaves. Can be cooked, or eaten raw in salads.
Chiffonade: a leafy vegetable sliced into thin shreds.
Chili powder: a peppery red powder made from dried ground chili peppers. It is available in various strengths from mild to hot.
Chinese five-spice powder: see Five-spice powder.
Cholesterol: a wax-like substance manufactured in the human body and also found in foods of animal origin. Although a certain amount of cholesterol is necessary for proper body functioning, an excess can accumulate in the arteries, contributing to heart disease. See also Monounsaturated fats; Polyunsaturated fats; Saturated fats.
Concasse: a sauce of a crushed or chopped vegetable, usually tomato; from the French word for crush or chop.
Concentrated butter: butter from which most of the water has been removed; suitable for stir-frying and pastry-making.
Coriander (also called cilantro): the pungent, peppery leaves of the coriander plant or its earthy tasting dried seeds. It is a common seasoning in Middle-Eastern, Oriental and Latin-American cookery.
Cornmeal: finely ground dried maize, usually used in combination with wheat flour.
Corn salad: see Lamb's lettuce.
Cottage cheese: a low-fat soft cheese with a mild flavour and a non-uniform texture. It is made from skimmed milk but the cottage cheese used in this book has added cream to give it a fat content of 4 per cent.
Coulis: a sieved vegetable or fruit purée.
Court-bouillon: a flavoured liquid used for poaching fish or shellfish. It may contain aromatic vegetables, herbs, wine or milk.
Crème fraîche: a slightly ripened, sharp-tasting French double cream containing about 35 per cent fat.
Curd cheese: any soft cheese made from separated milk curds. The medium-fat curd cheese used in this book contains 12 per cent fat.
Curly endive: a curly leafed green with a bitter taste similar to chicory. The lighter leaves are sweeter and more tender than the dark green ones.
Debeard: to remove the fibrous threads from a mussel. These threads, called the beard, are produced by the mussel to attach itself to stationary objects.
Devein: to remove the intestinal vein that runs along the outer curve of a prawn. To devein a prawn, peel it first then make a shallow cut along the line of the vein and scrape out the vein with the tip of the knife.
Dried prawns: small prawns that have been salted and dried. They are sold in Oriental grocery shops and must be soaked for about 20 minutes before use.
Fennel: a herb (also called wild fennel) whose feathery leaves and dried seeds have a mild anise flavour and are much used for flavouring. Its vegetable relative, the bulb — or Florence — fennel (also called finocchio) can be cooked, or eaten raw in salads.
Five-spice powder: a pungent blend of ground Sichuan pepper, star anise, cassia, cloves and fennel seeds; available in Asian food shops.
Fromage frais: a soft cheese made from skimmed milk. The *fromage frais* used in this book includes a small proportion of added cream and has an 8 per cent fat content.
Ginger: the spicy, buff-coloured rhizome, or rootlike stem, of the ginger plant, used as a seasoning either fresh or dried and powdered. Dried ginger makes a poor substitute for fresh ginger root.
Goat cheese: a pungent soft cheese made with goat's milk.
Groundnut oil: an oil extracted from peanuts with a slightly nutty taste. It can be used in salads or for frying.
Julienne: the French term for vegetables or other food cut into strips.
Lamb's lettuce (also called corn salad, mâche): soft tongue-shaped leaves with a nutlike sweetness and underlying astringency. It complements dressings made with nut oils.
Lemon grass (citronella): a long, woody, lemon-flavoured stalk that is shaped like a spring onion. Lemon grass is available in Asian shops. To store it, refrigerate in plastic film for up to two weeks; lemon grass may also be frozen for storage.
Macerate: to soften a food by soaking instead of cooking, usually in an aromatic or spiced liquid.
Mange-tout: flat green pea pods eaten whole, with only stems and strings removed.
Marinade: a mixture of aromatic ingredients in which meat or vegetables are allowed to stand before cooking to enrich their flavour. Some marinades will tenderize meat, but they do not penetrate deeply.
Marjoram: sweet marjoram and its heartier relative pot marjoram are aromatic herbs related to oregano, but milder in flavour.
Miso: a fermented soya bean paste often used in Japanese cuisine.
Monounsaturated fats: one of the three types of fats found in foods. Monounsaturated fats are believed not to raise the level of cholesterol in the blood.
Non-reactive pan: a cooking vessel whose surface does not chemically react with food. Materials used include stainless steel, enamel, glass and some alloys. Untreated cast iron and aluminium may react with acids, producing discoloration or a peculiar taste.
Nori: paper-like dark green or black sheets of dried seaweed, often used in Japanese cuisine as flavouring or as wrappers for rice and vegetables.
Oakleaf lettuce: a delicate red-leafed lettuce.
Okra: the green pods of a plant indigenous to Africa where it is called gumbo.
Olive oil: any of various grades of oil extracted from olives. Extra virgin olive oil has a full, fruity flavour and very low acidity. Virgin olive oil is lighter in flavour and slightly higher in acidity. Pure olive oil, a processed blend of olive oils, has the lightest taste and highest acidity. For salad dressings, virgin and extra virgin olive oils are preferred. Store in a cool, dark place.
Oyster mushroom: a variety of wild mushroom, now cultivated. They are stronger tasting than button mushrooms and are usually pale brown.
Paprika: a slightly sweet, spicy, bright-red powder produced by grinding dried red peppers. The best type of paprika is Hungarian.
Peppercorns: the berries of the pepper vine picked at various stages of ripeness and then dried. Black, white, pink and green peppercorns are available.
Phyllo pastry: a paper-thin flour-and-water pastry popular in Greece and the Middle East. It can be bought fresh or frozen from delicatessens and shops specializing in Middle-Eastern food.
Pine-nuts: seeds from the cone of the stone pine, a tree native to the Mediterranean. Pine-nuts are used in pesto and other sauces; their buttery flavour can be heightened by light toasting.
Poach: to cook gently in simmering liquid. The

temperature of the poaching liquid should be approximately 94°C (200°F), and its surface should merely tremble.
Polyunsaturated fats: one of the three types of fats found in foods. They exist in abundance in such vegetable oils as safflower, sunflower, corn and soya bean. Polyunsaturated fats lower the level of cholesterol in the blood.
Prosciutto: an uncooked, dry-cured and slightly salt Italian ham, sliced paper-thin.
Purslane: a small, leafy, succulent herb with a mild, slightly tart flavour.
Quark: a type of soft cheese with a mild, clean, slightly acid flavour; usually very low in fat, but smoother varieties have added cream.
Quenelle: a purée of meat or fish, bound with egg whites and *fromage frais* or yogurt, shaped into ovals and poached.
Radicchio: a purplish-red Italian chicory with a chewy texture and slightly bitter taste.
Ramekin: a small, round, straight-sided glass or porcelain mould, used to bake a single serving of food.
Recommended Daily Amount (RDA): the average daily amount of an essential nutrient as recommended for groups of healthy people by the U.K. Department of Health and Social Security.
Red lollo lettuce: a red-tinged, frilly lettuce.
Reduce: to boil down a liquid in order to concentrate its flavour and thicken its consistency.
Refresh: to rinse a briefly cooked vegetable under cold water to arrest its cooking and set its colour.
Rice vinegar: a mild, fragrant vinegar that is less assertive than cider vinegar or distilled white vinegar. It is available in dark, light, seasoned and sweetened varieties; Japanese rice vinegar generally is milder than the Chinese version.
Ricotta: soft, mild, white Italian cheese, made from cow's or sheep's milk. Full-fat ricotta has a fat content of 20 to 30 per cent, but the low-fat ricotta used in this book has a fat content of only about 8 per cent.
Rocket: (also called arugula): a peppery-flavoured salad plant with long, leafy stems, popular in Italy.
Roe: refers primarily to fish eggs, but edible roe is also found in scallops, crabs and lobsters.
Safflower oil: a vegetable oil that contains a high proportion of polyunsaturated fats.
Saffron: the dried, yellowish-red stigmas (or threads) of the saffron crocus, which yield a powerful yellow colour as well as a pungent flavour. Powdered saffron may be substituted for threads but has less flavour.
Salad burnet: a delicate cucumber-flavoured salad herb.
Salsify: a slender, tapering root, about twice the length of a carrot, with a white or yellowish skin and a faint oysterish flavour. See also Scorzonera.
Saturated fats: one of the three types of fats found in foods. They exist in abundance in animal products and coconut and palm oils; they raise the level of cholesterol in the blood. Because high blood-cholesterol levels may cause heart disease, saturated fat consumption should be restricted to less than 15 per cent of the calories provided by the daily diet.
Sauté: to cook a food quickly in a small amount of oil or butter over high heat.
Scorzonera: a thin, long, cylindrical root with brown or blackish skin, very similar in shape and taste to salsify (see above).
Sesame seeds: small, nutty-tasting seeds used frequently, either raw or roasted, in Middle-Eastern and Indian cookery. They are also used to make an oil with a nutty, smoky aroma.
Shiitake mushroom: a variety of mushroom, originally grown only in Japan, sold fresh or dried. The dried form should be soaked and stemmed before use.
Sichuan pepper (also called Chinese pepper, Japanese pepper or anise pepper): a dried shrub berry with a tart, aromatic flavour that is less piquant than black pepper.
Simmer: to cook a liquid or sauce just below its boiling point so that the liquid's surface barely ripples.
Skimmed milk: milk from which almost all the fat has been removed.
Sodium: a nutrient essential to maintaining the proper balance of fluids in the blood. In most diets, a major source of the element is table salt, made up of 40 per cent sodium. Excess sodium may contribute to high blood pressure, which increases the risk of heart disease. One teaspoon (5.5 g) of salt, with 2,132 milligrams of sodium, contains just over the maximum daily amount recommended by the World Health Organization.
Soured cream: cream that has been thickened by the addition of acid-producing bacteria which give it a tart taste. It has a 21 per cent fat content.
Soy sauce: a savoury, salty brown liquid made from fermented soya beans and available in both light and dark versions. One teaspoon of ordinary soy sauce contains 1,030 milligrams of sodium; lower-sodium variations, such as naturally fermented shoyu, may contain half that amount.
Spaghetti squash: a yellow-skinned squash whose cooked flesh resembles strands of spaghetti.
Squab: a young pigeon, weighing from 300 to 500 g (10 oz to 1 lb) when sold. Domestic pigeons reared for the table have paler flesh and a more mellow taste than wild pigeons.
Steam: to cover food and cook it in the steam created by a boiling liquid. Steaming vegetables preserves the vitamins and flavours that are ordinarily lost in boiling.
Stir-fry: to cook thin slices of vegetables, fish or meat over high heat in a small amount of oil, stirring constantly to ensure even cooking in a short time. The traditional cooking vessel is a Chinese wok; a heavy-bottomed frying pan may also be used.
Strong flour: a white flour milled from strains of wheat with a high protein content. The high proportion of protein, which combines with water to form gluten, produces breads with an even texture.
Tabasco sauce: a hot, unsweetened chili sauce.
Tahini (also called sesame paste): a nutty-tasting paste made from ground sesame seeds that are usually roasted.
Tarragon: a strong herb with a sweet anise taste. Because heat intensifies tarragon's flavour, cooked dishes require smaller amounts.
Thyme: a versatile herb with a zesty, slighty fruity flavour and a strong aroma.
Tofu (also called bean curd): a dense soya bean product with a mild flavour. Tofu is rich in protein, relatively low in calories and free of cholesterol. It is highly perishable and should be kept refrigerated, submerged in water; if the water is changed daily, the tofu may be stored for up to a week.
Tomato paste: concentrated tomato purée, available in cans and tubes, used in sauces and soups.
Total fat: an individual's daily intake of polyunsaturated, monounsaturated and saturated fats. Nutritionists recommend that fats constitute no more than 35 per cent of a person's total calorie intake. The term as used in the nutrient analyses in this book refers to all the sources of fat in a recipe.
Turmeric: a yellow spice from a plant related to ginger, used as a colouring agent and occasionally as a substitute for saffron. Turmeric has a musty odour and a slightly bitter flavour.
Vine leaves: the tender, lightly flavoured leaves of the grapevine, used in many ethnic cuisines as wrappers for savoury mixtures. Because the leaves are usually packed in brine, they should be rinsed before use.
Virgin olive oil: see Olive oil.
Walnut oil: an oil extracted from pressed walnuts. Its distinctive flavour adds balance to such bitter greens as curly endive. It should be purchased in small quantities; once opened, it can turn rancid within just a few weeks.
Wholemeal flour: wheat flour which contains the whole of the wheat grain with nothing added or taken away. It is nutritionally valuable as a source of dietary fibre and is higher in B vitamins than white flour.
Yogurt: a smooth-textured, semi-solid cultured milk product made with varying percentages of fat. Yogurt can be substituted for soured cream in cooking or be combined with soured cream to produce a sauce or topping that is lower in fat and calories than soured cream alone. An alternative is to use thick Greek-style strained yogurt. This contains 10 per cent fat, as compared to 18 per cent in soured cream.

Index

Picture Credits

Cover: Martin Brigdale. 4: top, John Elliott; middle, Chris Knaggs; bottom, Chris Knaggs. 5: top, Jan Baldwin; middle, Chris Knaggs; bottom, Grant Symon. 6: Chris Knaggs. 10-11: John Elliott. 12-13: Chris Knaggs. 14-17: Martin Brigdale. 18: Jan Baldwin. 19: Philip Modica. 20: Chris Knaggs. 21-22: Grant Symon. 23: Philip Modica. 24: Graham Kirk. 25: Chris Knaggs. 26: top, John Elliott; bottom, James Murphy. 27: top, John Elliott; bottom, Martin Brigdale. 28: Chris Knaggs. 29: Tom Belshaw. 30: Philip Modica. 31: Tom Belshaw. 33: John Elliott. 34-35: Tom Belshaw. 36: Chris Knaggs. 37: James Murphy. 38: Tom Belshaw. 39: John Elliott. 40: James Murphy. 41: John Elliott. 42: Martin Brigdale. 43: top, John Elliott; bottom, Chris Knaggs. 44: James Murphy. 45: Graham Kirk. 46: Jan Baldwin. 47-49: Chris Knaggs. 50: Martin Brigdale. 51: Tom Belshaw. 52: Chris Knaggs. 53: Jan Baldwin. 54: Grant Symon. 55: Graham Kirk. 56: James Murphy. 57: Tom Belshaw. 58-59: Martin Brigdale. 60: John Elliott. 61: Martin Brigdale. 62: James Murphy. 63: Grant Symon. 64-65: Chris Knaggs. 66: James Murphy. 67: John Elliott. 68-69: Chris Knaggs. 70-71: John Elliott. 72-73: Chris Knaggs. 74-76: John Elliott. 77: Martin Brigdale. 78: Philip Modica. 79: Grant Symon. 80: Philip Modica. 81: Tom Belshaw. 82: Chris Knaggs. 83: Jan Baldwin. 84: John Elliott. 85: Philip Modica. 86: Chris Knaggs. 87: James Murphy. 88: Chris Knaggs. 89: Tom Belshaw. 90: Chris Knaggs. 91: Tom Belshaw. 92: Chris Knaggs. 93: John Elliott. 94: Tom Belshaw. 95: top, John Elliott; bottom, Martin Brigdale. 96: John Elliott. 97: Chris Knaggs. 98: Jan Baldwin. 99: John Elliott. 100: Grant Symon. 101: James Murphy. 102: Tom Belshaw. 103: Philip Modica. 104: John Elliott. 105: Graham Kirk. 106-108: John Elliott. 109: Tom Belshaw. 110: Chris Knaggs. 111: Martin Brigdale. 112: Chris Knaggs. 113: Jan Baldwin. 114: James Murphy. 115: John Elliott. 116: Martin Brigdale. 117: Chris Knaggs. 118: John Elliott. 119: Martin Brigdale. 120-122: John Elliott. 123: Jan Baldwin. 124: John Elliott. 125: Tom Belshaw. 127: John Elliott. 128: Chris Knaggs. 129: John Elliott. 130: James Murphy. 132-139: Chris Knaggs.

Props: the editors wish to thank the following outlets and manufacturers; all are based in London unless otherwise stated. 12, 13: napkins, Ewart Liddell. 14: marble, W.E. Grant & Co. (Marble) Ltd.; bowl *(centre, back)*, Birgit Blitz, Gruiten, Germany. 17: plate *(right)*, Andrew McGarva, The Craftsmen Potters Shop. 19: small bowl and plate, Winchcombe Pottery, The Craftsmen Potters Shop; large bowl, Tony Gant, The Craftsmen Potters Shop. 21: Formica, Newcastle, Tyne and Wear. 25: marble, W.E. Grant & Co. (Marble) Ltd. 26: plate, Royal Worcester, Worcester. 30: under plate, Villeroy & Boch. 37: plate, Royal Worcester, Worcester. 39: platter, Thomas (London) Ltd. 41: plates, Rosenthal (London) Ltd. 42: platter, Thomas (London) Ltd.; 43: cutlery, Mappin & Webb Silversmiths. 46: plates, Inshop. 47: napkin, Kilkenny. 48: plate, Line of Scandinavia. 58, 59: plates, Villeroy & Boch; cutlery, Mappin & Webb Silversmiths; flower holder, Rosenthal (London) Ltd. 61: plate, Rosenthal (London) Ltd. 64: small bowl, Winchcombe Pottery, The Craftsmen Potters Shop; plate, Tony Gant, The Craftsmen Potters Shop. 65: plates, Chinacraft (Bond St.). 66: bowl, Winchcombe Pottery, The Craftsmen Potters Shop. 68: Formica, Newcastle, Tyne and Wear. 70: bowl, plate and platter, Villeroy & Boch; cutlery, Mappin & Webb Silversmiths. 71: plate, Inshop; place mat, Ewart Liddell. 78: cutlery, Mappin & Webb Silversmiths. 81: cutlery, Next Interior. 82: plates, Hutschenreuther (U.K.) Ltd.; cloth and napkin, Next Interior. 83: lace cloth, Laura Ashley. 89: Formica, Newcastle. 91: plate, Thomas (London) Ltd. 93: plates, David Mellor. 97: cutlery, Mappin & Webb Silversmiths. 98: pink cloth, Next Interior. 99: under plate, Fortnum & Mason; plates, Royal Worcester, Worcester. 100: plates, Villeroy & Boch; cutlery, Mappin & Webb Silversmiths. 102: plate, Villeroy & Boch. 103: plate and bowl, Kilkenny; napkin, Ewart Liddell. 104: tablecloth, Kilkenny. 105: plate, Rosenthal (London) Ltd. 106: plate, Royal Worcester, Worcester. 107: cloth and napkins, Next Interior; cutlery, Mappin & Webb Silversmiths. 110: plates, Rosenthal (London) Ltd.; forks, Mappin & Webb Silversmiths; napkins, Next Interior. 111: plates, Villeroy & Boch. 112: Formica, Newcastle. 115: place mat, Ewart Liddell; fork, Next Interior; plates, Thomas (London) Ltd. 116: cloth, Liberty & Co. 122: plate, Royal Worcester, Worcester; napkin and cloth, Kilkenny; small bowl, Rosenthal (London) Ltd. 128, 131: marble, W.E. Grant & Co (Marble) Ltd. 137: plate, Winchcombe Pottery, The Craftsmen Potters Shop; marble, W.E. Grant & Co. (Marble) Ltd.; place mat, Ewart Liddell. 139: fish servers, Mappin & Webb Silversmiths; napkin and cloth, Ewart Liddell.

Acknowledgements

The index for this book was prepared by Myra Clark, London. The editors also wish to thank: Rachel Andrew, London; David Barrett, London; René Bloom, London ; Andrew Cameron, London; Nora Carey, Paris; Sean Davis, London; Clare Ferguson, London; Rod Howe, London; Isabella Kranshaw, London; Brian Leonard, London; Paul Moon, London; Christine Noble, London; Oneida, London; Philomena O'Neill, London; Osborne & Little, London; Katherine Reeve, London; Sharp Electronics (UK) Ltd, London; Jane Stevenson, London; Toshiba (UK) Ltd, London; Paul van Biene, London.

Colour Separations by Fotolitomec, S.N.C., Milan, Italy
Typesetting by G. Beard & Son Ltd., Brighton, Sussex, England
Printed and bound by Brepols S.A., Turnhout, Belgium

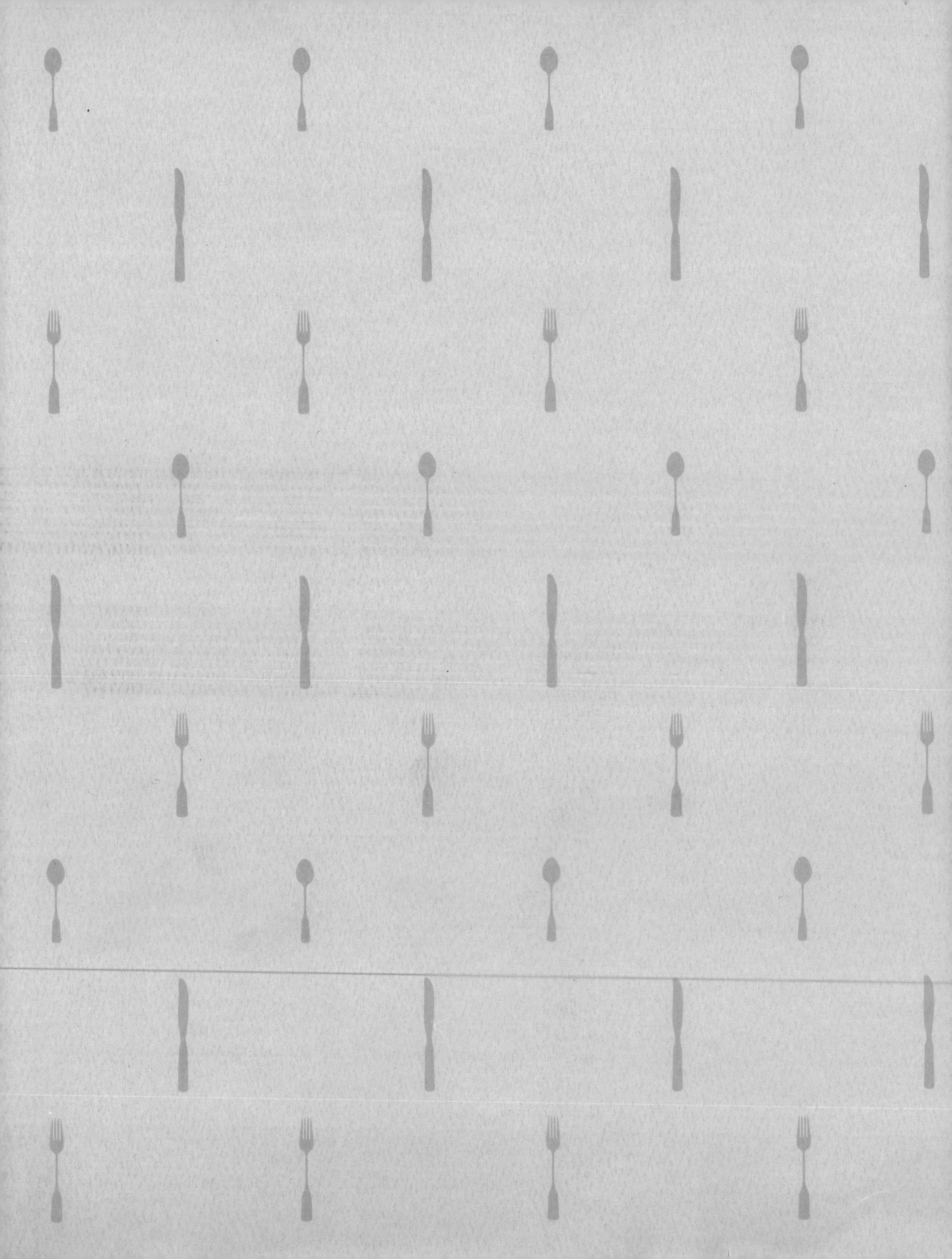